GOD, *Please* FIX ME!

A Breakthrough in Self-Esteem, Relationship Understanding and Personal Healing for Women

To Denise

NANCY NICHOLS

Couldn't have done it without you!
Nancy Nichols

EPIPHANY IMPRINT

XOXO

8-1-2015

EPIPHANY IMPRINT
Email: info@epiphanyimprint.com
www.knowitallnancy.com

Names, locations and identifying characters of people in the book have been changed to protect the privacy of individuals.

ISBN: 978-0-9795791-2-7

Library of Congress Control Number: 2015909237
Printed in the United States of America

This book is available for quantity discounts for bulk purchases.
For information, please email info@epiphanyimprint.com.

Editor, Denise Nall
Interior Design, Susan Leonard

To my husband, Leon, you are my rock,
my best friend, and my one and only true love.

To my creative, vibrant daughter, Krissy.
Our personalities are one in the same.

To my son, Roger, who supported and encouraged
me through my difficult writing journey.

To my brothers, Harry and Todd,
the bright stars in my eyes.

To my counselor, Stan Hays, who helped me
remove my blinders and begin life anew.

Contents

PART THREE
FIND YOUR AUTHENTIC SELF

PART FOUR
SUPERNATURAL SOBRIETY

Introduction

I have spent a lifetime seeking the answers to my personal problems. As far back as I can remember, I fell in love with, committed to, and even married men who were destined to maltreat me. My existence seemed to be a constant state of adversity, turmoil, heartbreak and regret. I always wanted to have a loving, supportive, stable man in my life—but I couldn't seem to get one. I've always wanted to share my love and affection with a wonderful man—but I continually wasted my efforts on men who were emotionally unavailable, dysfunctional, and often abusive.

The older I got, dating became more confusing and disheartening. I mistrusted my judgments about men. I questioned my understanding of a difficult relationship situation. I doubted my self-worth.

When I dated a man, I was afraid I would say or do the wrong thing and he would reject me. In a relationship, I was afraid to ask for the things I wanted and needed because I might anger him. I was afraid to confront a man for his hurtful or questionable behavior, because he might abandon me. I was sick of being the underdog in life.

It was my relationship failures, divorce and heartbreak that caused me to seek the answers to my problematic, dysfunctional life—all of which lead me to write self-help books for women, who, like me, struggle to find unconditional love, genuine acceptance and unwavering security within a relationship. After years of counseling, self-discovery, and even writing a dating and relationship book, I thought I was mentally armed to fall in love with the right man. And then life blindsided me with a consummate, life-shattering, life-altering relationship lesson that inspired my *God, Please Fix Me!* Trilogy.

The most hurtful, destructive, dysfunctional relationship I have ever experienced was with the man I called my "soul-mate."

David (not his real name) was a charming, talented, successful doctor, and although he was not the most handsome man in the world, his playful boyish spirit and affectionate nature instantly captured my heart.

When David and I met we fell quickly and deeply in love. We believed fate had somehow magically thrown us together. The first six months of our relationship was a state of romantic ecstasy, and then, as if overnight, a complicated, even disturbing side of David (aka Dr. Dirtbag) began to emerge. His once carefree social cocktails became nightly drinking episodes that seemed to trigger his cynical and irrational behavior. He was secretive, hyper-critical and unpredictable. Eight months into our relationship I recognized him to be the most controlling, manipulative and verbally abusive man that had ever crossed my path.

How did this happen? I asked myself. How did I, the expert and author of a successful dating and relationship book screw up so horrifically by falling in love with an arrogant, schizophrenic, noxious con-artist—a man who lacked all sense of compassion, moral values and social conscience?

I beat myself up trying to understand—WHY?

- *Why* did I discount the obvious signs of a man's bad behavior?
- *Why* did I give my heart to a man I suspected to be highly dysfunctional?
- *Why* did I stay with a man who demeaned and verbally abused me?
- *Why* did I allow another human being to rob me of my confidence, security and self-esteem?
- And *why*, after we broke up, did I cling to the memory of a love that never existed?

It took three dates for me to fall in love with David. It took a year for Dr. Dirtbag's abusive nature to maim my spirit. It took two years to break the crippling love addiction I had for him, undo his covert brainwashing, and ultimately regain my personal power.

What's Wrong With Me?

I cried out to God, *What's wrong with me?*

I'm tired of being with men who reject me and leave me feeling empty inside. I'm tired of misreading a man's intentions, giving my heart away prematurely, and then having a man dump me. I'm tired of dating a man and running him off with my stupid, inebriated behavior. I'm weary of men who want to manipulate, control and demean me. I'm tired of second-guessing myself and kowtowing to a man's demands and anger. I'm beat down by the roller-coaster ride of romantic ecstasy, breakups and relationship failures. I'm drained by the setbacks and the recovery process of divorce. I'm damaged from leaving bits and pieces of my mind, body and soul with men who mistreat me.

I fell to my knees in despair, extended my open hands towards heaven, and I wailed... *I'm tired. I'm tired. I'm tired. Please, Dear God... fix me!*

God, please heal my broken heart.

God, please fix my low self-esteem issues and lack of confidence.

God, please fill the gnawing void in my soul.

God, please correct my negative, self-defeating attitudes.

God, please cure my need for a man's validation and acceptance.

God, please increase my relationship know-how.

God, please fix my needy, co-dependent mentality.

God, please clean up my destructive, harmful addictions.

God, please erase my shame and guilt.

God, please heal my fears and insecurities.

Most of all, Dear Lord—*please help me to fall in love with a good man!*

My life has been a journey of personal growth. My books are a culmination of the knowledge and insight I acquired from a lifetime of hurtful experiences. *Secrets of the Ultimate Husband Hunter* is how I discovered the power of positive thought. *Never Date a Dead Animal* is the wisdom I gained, or I should say—I earned from dating and falling in love with highly dysfunctional men. *God, Please Fix Me!* is the final healing of my shame and guilt; my needy, fearful, co-dependent behavior; my impulsive, addictive personality; and ultimately, my low self-esteem issues.

I share with you the insight I have gained from a lifetime of seeking truth, understanding and relationship wisdom.

Part One

The Awakening

"You never know how strong you are, until being strong is the only choice you have left."

—Krissy

1 Above All Things—Seek Wisdom

Wisdom is supreme; therefore get wisdom. Though it cost all you have, get understanding.

—Proverbs 4:7

It was a beautiful, summer Sunday morning. I was in church service. People were sitting all around me in the church pews, but I felt horribly alone and downhearted. I watched Pastor Craig walk to and fro on stage, his mouth was moving, but his voice was white noise. I was ruminating the past two years of recovering from a hurtful, destructive relationship. I struggled to overcome the bitterness and rage I felt for Dr. Dirtbag. I wondered if I would ever find true love as a single mature woman. I labored to finish my two sequel books so I could get on with life. My life felt barren and melancholy. God was tight-lipped; he no longer fed me His encouragement and inspiration. I imagined that He had turned His back on me because of my impetuous nature and frequent flub-ups.

"If any of you lacks wisdom, he should ask God, who gives generously to all without finding fault, and it will be given to him."

My mind snapped to attention. Suddenly Pastor Craig's voice resonated and this familiar Bible verse held new meaning for me.

Hearing Pastor Craig's words, I realized that I had been asking for wisdom all of my life, not just in prayer, but in my desires, daydreams and actions. Every time I read a self-improvement book, I was seeking insight. Every time I cried on a girlfriend's shoulder, I was asking for guidance. Every time I visited a psychologist, I was looking for discernment. Every time I went to church or I watched a Sunday morning service on television, I was praying for divine understanding. God had not abandoned me; in fact, He declares that He is close to the brokenhearted, and He saves those who are crushed in spirit. He promises to give us wisdom, willingly and freely, without criticism or reproach—all we have to do—*is ask.*

When we try to do the right thing—
God imparts His wisdom.

It was an epiphany moment that morning in church. I've always known that God hears our prayers, listens to our hearts and observes our actions. But Pastor Craig's words rocked my universe. I realized that in my times of need and despair, God was not silent, He was, instead, hovering in the background, feeding me morsels of His wisdom. When I searched the bookstore aisles, He led me to self-help books that explained my fearful, self-protecting behavior, exposed my judgmental, hyper-critical attitudes and made me accountable for my irresponsible, foolhardy actions. God was moved by my heartbreak and genuine tears. He granted me girlfriends, who offered me not only compassion, but the brutal truth about my self-defeating, man-repellant behavior. God applauded my quest for personal growth and emotional healing. He gave me a wise spiritual counselor who helped me blaze my true path. But there were times when my personal growth seemed to come to a standstill, when my mind was influenced by worldly distractions, when my emotions were distraught and irrational, when my short-sightedness blinded me to God's supernatural assistance. Nevertheless, I tried to do the right things, and God, measuring my heart, intent and actions, rewarded me with timely, bite-size doses of insight into my personal problems—and he quietly pointed me in the right direction. Decades later, on a sunny, Sunday morning in church, I realized my relationship wisdom had manifested and my personal power had blossomed.

The wisdom God imparts to us is not always easily recognizable, and regrettably, it is often earned through life's most hurtful and difficult experiences. During those times of adversity, strive to do the right things and God will set your feet on the right path.

2 Dear Lord, My Filter is Broken!

Oh, how women love the bad boys!

What is the erroneous appeal which causes women to love an arrogant, self-serving, and sometimes, morally corrupt man?

Why do women pine for a man who is evasive, aloof, uncommunicative and unpredictable?

Why do women gravitate to men who are non-committal and emotionally withholding?

Why is it so hard for a woman to leave a man who lies, cheats and maltreats her?

Women will sacrifice their friends, finances and mental health to hold onto a deceitful, boasting, abusive, skirt-chasing man—and they snub a wonderful man who would love, honor and care for them till death do they part.

I ask you, *Are these women Lizzie Borden, nutty coo-coo crazy?*

We all view the world through individual filters, says Dr. Phil McGraw. Some filters may be healthy and constructive, while others may be distorted and destructive. Those filters—our personalities, attitudes, points of view, our "styles"—powerfully influence the interpretations that we give to the events in our lives: those interpretations, in turn, determine how we will respond, and therefore how we will ultimately be responded to.

Emotional filters are at the core of our relationship decisions. It's why we choose to be with some people—and not others. If our filters are unhealthy and distorted, that is, we view our world through fear, anxiety, anger, greed, resentment, sadness, hatred, jealously and envy, our perception of a potential mate will also be distorted and flawed. We will push away a man who would value, uphold, and respect us—and instead, we bond to a man whose dysfunctional behavior supports and agrees with our defective mindset. To illustrate: If I have low self-esteem issues, I will condone a man's maltreatment. If I drink in excess, I will be comfortable with a man who is a high-functioning alcoholic.

Penny and Ronnie viewed their lives through a cocktail glass.

Penny and Ronnie both had poor relationship skills, and they were both big drinkers. Their relationship was built on the commonality of drinking. They enjoyed frequent happy hours. They drank at home, at cook-outs, while boating, at football games, and at parties. Drinking lubricated their conversations, enhanced their fun, lowered their inhibitions and prompted their early sexual activity.

Drinking blinded Penny and Ronnie to one another's undesirable behavior. Wine masked Penny's low self-esteem issues, induced her unladylike behavior, and incited her needy, codependent mindset. Vodka momentarily drew Ronnie out of his moody, non-communicating shell. But lust doesn't last when a relationship is held together with vodka, vermouth and olives.

The intoxicating aphrodisiac that brought Penny and Ronnie together, began to erode their glass house. Drinking caused Penny to overreact to Ronnie's aloof, closed-mouth personality. Ronnie became defensive, blaming and withdrawn. Alcohol diminished their sex life: booze numbed Penny's sexual nerve endings, blocking her orgasms, and Ronnie couldn't get an erection. After a night of drinking, they would crawl under the covers, Ronnie's penis stood at half-mast, and Penny just wanted to be left alone so she could go to sleep. Eventually Penny quit wanting to have sex, and Ronnie disappeared into his dark cave. In the beginning, alcohol triggered their romantic connection. In the end, it destroyed a weak, pseudo relationship.

Faulty filters warp our reality and induce our bad behavior.

Faulty filters cause us to misinterpret a person's intentions, overreact to our partner's behavior, act out our unhappiness and discontent, all of which sabotage the trust and intimacy of a relationship.

Marilee, an attractive, intelligent, professional woman, was 42 when she married Ryan. Ryan, a handsome, financially secure, 55-year-old man, who divorced his wife of 26 years, was looking for a younger, attractive woman to wear on his arm. Marilee had spent her whole life searching for the love, acceptance and financial support of a man. They seemed the perfect match. Ryan married his trophy wife, and Marilee found her father figure.

Ryan was innately reserved and tight-lipped, and although he was dependable and considerate, his reticent behavior triggered Marilee's co-dependent issues. When they were dating, he called Marilee consistently, but irregularly. When she didn't hear from him for a couple of days, she worried that she did something to run him off, causing her to have anxiety attacks. She coped with her distress by overeating to the point of making herself physically ill, and then she countered the excess calories with obsessive exercise. She was able to conceal her insecurities and dysfunctional behavior while they were dating and living separately. After they married, Ryan dropped his attentive courtship behavior, and he reverted back to his naturally withdrawn self. His lukewarm, detached demeanor provoked Marilee's

Your emotions are the slaves to your thoughts, and you are the slave to your emotions.

—Elizabeth Gilbert

insecurities, causing her to erupt into tearful tantrums, followed by days of emotionally shutting down and sleeping in the guest bedroom at night.

Marilee tried to gain Ryan's attention by making him jealous. When a strange man flirted with her at a party, she told Ryan, "That man told me I'm beautiful."

Ryan frowned harshly, disapprovingly at Marilee and said, "Are you trying to make me jealous?" His words stung Marilee. She withdrew for days to cope with Ryan's rejection, she punished him with her silence, and Ryan slid deeper into his non-communicating vacuum.

Ryan's aloof relationship style was bad karma for an insecure woman like Marilee. True, he was a faithful, reliable, caring husband. True, he loved Marilee dearly, but it was difficult for him to articulate his love to Marilee. He demonstrated his devotion to her with his services. He painted the inside of his house in Marilee's favorite colors, and he gave her money to buy new furniture. He gave her his new SUV to drive. He paid for her golf lessons. He surprised her with an espresso cappuccino maker, and he splurged on an expensive leather coat for her Christmas present. Marilee never had to worry about where Ryan was, or what he was doing, because he had the loyalty of a Labrador retriever. But Marilee's filter was cracked. Her constant craving for Ryan's verbal affirmations of his love and affection blinded her to his acts of devotion and generosity. His aloof personality caused her to doubt the depth of his love and commitment.

Eventually Marilee's constant drama wore Ryan out. A year after they married he announced, "I think we've made a mistake. I want a divorce."

Faulty filters cause us to blame ourselves for our partner's hurtful behavior.

Stella, a stunning 31-year-old runway model, was recovering from a bitter divorce when she met Richard, a successful Latino businessman and diplomat. Richard had a penchant for beautiful women. Stella was attracted to Richard's good looks, wealth, status and power.

Richard wooed Stella in extravagant, high-style, and within a year, they married. Stella took up permanent residency in Richard's home in Mexico—and Don Juan Ricardo immediately began to unmask.

Richard started cheating on Stella in the first year of marriage. In the beginning he concealed his revolving door of girlfriends. He would disappear for days, sometimes for a week or more, and then he would return home without explanation. If Stella questioned him, he would explode, punch her with his fists, and verbally berate her, telling her if she weren't such a "piece-of-shit wife" he would want to come home. After his outburst he would act as if nothing happened, and he expected Stella to do the same.

Stella walked around her Spanish mansion in a foggy stupor. She took anti-depressants and handfuls of Tylenol to get through the day, and she swallowed over-the-counter sleeping aids and Ambien to sleep at night. Her hair fell out in clumps. She had intense thoughts of suicide.

Stella punished herself; thinking she did something to trigger Richard's violent temper she tried harder to please him. Even though she was a gorgeous professional model, she thought if she were prettier or smarter he would stop cheating on her and return to the way he was before they married.

After 10 years of brutal abuse, Richard divorced Stella to marry her best and only girlfriend in Mexico.

Faulty filters create illogical fear and desperation inside us.

My phobia in life was that I believed I couldn't take care of myself. This flawed belief perpetuated my innermost need in life—security. It's why I married the wrong men and divorced three times. I thought if I was married, I would have emotional and financial security. From the get-go, I saw Dr. Dirtbag through a faulty filtering system—I believed him to be my soul-mate. He sensed my core relationship needs—everything he said and did spelled—S-E-C-U-R-I-T-Y! He boasted of wealth, position and privileges. He showered me with expensive clothing, jewelry and gifts. "I'll always take care of you," he told me. His presentation was the "golden carrot" for a security-driven woman, making it easy for me to rationalize and shut my eyes to his questionable, hurtful behavior.

I had three faulty filters which influenced my beliefs.

Faulty Filter No. 1: I was supposed to be married.

I grew up in an era of domestic brainwashing. I thought my job was to find a husband, have children, and live blissfully ever after with my human security blanket. Whereas, my two brothers pursued higher education, I choose marriage over a career. I got married a year after I graduated from high school. A year later I was divorced with a small child, working for minimum wage as a secretary. I spent the next ten years looking for my next husband.

Lacking a college degree created my second defective filter.

Faulty Filter No. 2: I was afraid I couldn't take care of myself financially.

Without a college degree one can only hope to scratch out a living. With a small child, there were many times I worked two jobs to make ends meet. When I was 30, I was separated from my second husband with two small children. I worked full time as an advertising salesperson; every day I snuck away from that job at noon to work as a waitress on the lunch shift. Driving to the restaurant my first day at work, I was broke, my gas tank needle was on empty, and I desperately needed money for gas. I was terrified my car would croak on the side of the road, I would be late for my first day at work, and I would lose my waitress job. I placed a small piece of paper on the dashboard to hide the gas needle (out of sight, out of mind, so to speak), and I prayed, *"Please, Dear God, let my car travel on fumes."* Fifteen miles later I pulled into the restaurant parking lot. I earned enough tip money to buy gasoline and I drove myself back to my sales job.

Faulty Filter No. 3: I was afraid of being alone and lonely.

I was in my 50s when Dr. Dirtbag and I broke up. My mature age intensified my fear filter. I was afraid of being alone. I was afraid men would no longer find me attractive. I was afraid if I got sick, there would be no one to take care of me. I was afraid I would never find another relationship with such intense emotional and physical connection.

Security was the underlying, driving force in my life, and even though Dr. Dirtbag was a lying, abusive, controlling tyrant, I clung to him as if my life depended on it—because my faulty, distorted mindset believed he would take care of me for the rest of my life.

If you continue to view the world through a filter created by past events, then you are allowing your past to control and dictate both your present and your future.

—Dr. Phil McGraw

I believe that we can alter our destiny in any given moment by changing our thoughts.

I realized I couldn't change my filter—my lifelong need for security—but I could change my belief that I couldn't take care of myself.

Logic helped me to understand that my lifelong thoughts of needing a man's financial support were delusive and incorrect. I told myself, "You're an intelligent, capable, mature woman. You've taken care of yourself all your life. You have always had a job, sometimes you've worked two jobs to make rent—but you've always made it. You have your own good credit, a home (sometimes with a roommate), a houseful of furniture that you purchased over the years. Your car is paid for (you did that too!).

Whatever you worry most about in life, will filter the way you view your life

WHY did I ever believe that I couldn't take care of myself?

When I thought about the three things I needed most in a relationship: *trust, communication* and *security,* I realized none of these qualities ever existed with Dr. Dirtbag. He was an illusion, an elaborate façade of superficial charm, feigned emotions, sexual excitement and empty promises. The fallacy was—there was never true security with him. I never knew when he was going to walk through the door and bombast me with a cutting remark. I never knew when he was going to get drunk and embarrass me in public with his obnoxious behavior and mindless braggadocio. I never knew when he was going to bushwhack me with his hurtful comments while eating dinner in a restaurant. I never knew when he was going to lie about an investment or bank account. I never knew when he was going to blatantly, salaciously flirt with another woman, and then get angry at me for confronting him. I never knew when he was going to withdraw and punish me with his silence, or get mad at me, abandon me and abruptly go on a golf trip with his buddies.

Here's the joke: My security blanket was a boozing, delusional, deceiving, self-promoting dirtbag. The reality was: I would have been safer sleeping in the street under a micro-suede bedspread from Walmart.

Are your filters distorted and destructive? Ask yourself:

- Are you fearful, needy and codependent?
- Are you resentful?

- Do you have a chip on your shoulder?
- Are you overly critical and highly opinionated?
- Are you mistrusting?
- Are you self-serving?
- Are you naïve and blindly trusting?

"Yes" to any of these questions indicates an unhealthy, distorted filtering system.

My Homeless Woman Within falls asleep in her automobile, wrapped in a recycled Martha Stewart comforter, content, knowing that when the sun rises Dr. Dirtbag won't be there to verbally batter her.

3
It's Supposed to Hurt

The heart wants what the heart wants.

I just couldn't understand it. As horrible as Dr. Dirtbag was to me, why did I keep going back to him for more of the same abuse?

My relationship with Dr. Dirtbag was a vicious, injurious cycle of abuse, with varying stages of love and affection—arguments and verbal battering—rejection, withdrawal and separation—a cooling off period—band-aid apologies—make-ups and intervals of pseudo-peace. I knew in the pit of my soul that he was never going to change. He wasn't going to stop drinking and he wasn't going to stop lying and verbally abusing me. He seemed to be permanently broken and content to inflict pain on me. Either way, it seemed like a no brainer—*right?* Not so when our hearts are thinking for us.

> *It had been a year since Dr. Dirtbag and I were together, and yet, I continued to agonize over the loss of him throughout the day and night. I begged God for an understanding of WHY our dreamlike relationship had failed so miserably. I prayed to understand HOW I could still love an abusive, maiming monster, and I begged for release from the demonic hold he had on my heart. My answer came in the self-help book,* A New Earth, *by Eckard Tolle.*

According to Eckard Tolle, every person has within them an accumulation of old emotional pain that is "revived continuously" and becomes "part of our sense of self." Tolle coined this psychological state as a person's "pain-body." He says, we unknowingly seek the emotional pain from the past relationships of our childhood, adolescence, teen and young adult years, for that pain is familiar and oddly comfortable. Sometimes, when similar pain-bodies collide, men and women believe they have met their soul-mate. A woman, who was abused by her father, may feel a "magnetic pull" to a man who will give her more of the same pain. The emotional intensity of that pain is sometimes misinterpreted as "falling in love." A young girl, who witnessed her father verbally or physically abuse her mother, might not think it so bad when her boyfriend occasionally slugs her. His behavior is not foreign to her, and can even be within her comfort zone. Or a man who never received the mother's love that he needed as a child, may, as an adult, manifest hatred and a compulsion to "conquer and seduce" almost every woman he meets to gain the "female love and attention that his pain-body craves."

We are drawn to people who mirror our pain-bodies

The Victim Pain-Body

She dated men who supported her role as "the victim."

The victim mindset gravitates to people who are certain to maltreat her. She attracts and dates men who are arrogant, self-absorbed and uber-controlling. Her friends and family see through her boyfriend's calculating, charming facade, and they warn her to stop dating him. The victim ignores their pleas, and she becomes intimately involved him. He quickly drops his nice guy façade, and then she bawls to everyone about his deceit, infidelity, and verbal and physical abuse. She sucks you into her drama with her woe-is-me stories and feigned helplessness. Being a good friend, you try to save her from her stupidity, and seemingly, her inability to take care of herself, emotionally or financially. She rejects your advice. She faults everyone for her problems and unhappiness. She continues her relationship with a toxic, abusive personality. She wears you out with her see-saw emotions, her constant crying jags, and her unwillingness to take responsibility for her dilemma. And when her abuser dumps her (which they always do), she blames the demise of her relationship on his dysfunctional behavior.

The victim craves validation and acceptance.

Rita's last boyfriend, Vince, was a real work of art. Vince, age 62, tried desperately to be Brad Pitt. He teased and combed back his thin hair, holding it in place with cement spray. He wore a 2-day stubble on his Shar-Pei jaws and chin. His face was orangish-brown and splotchy from self-tanner. He dyed his sideburns, a dark brown thumbprint could be seen on the side of his face. He wore cowboy boots special made in Mexico; the lift inserts inside the boots helped him to stand almost 5-feet-7. His clothes were wrinkled, faded thrift store discards (Look at me! I don't have to dress nice because I'm beautiful!). Every Wednesday night Vince would sit at the local bar, wearing super-sized, extra-dark Raybans, believing all the women wanted him and the men were jealous of him, when in truth, everyone was snickering behind his back because he looked like a blind, broken-down bum.

Rita was impressed with Vince's pompous, wannabe charm. They began dating. He was boasting, condescending and self-interested. He had a false sense of entitlement, and he believed himself to possess superior intelligence. He fancied himself a studmuffin. He blatantly flirted with women in front of Rita. Vince was paranoid; he kept a loaded pistol beside him when he watched TV in his living room, on a night stand next to his bed, and on a patio table next to his chaise lounge when he reclined by the pool in his backyard. Vince bathed once a week (Rita said she could hardly stand to sleep next to him because of his bad breath and sour body order). He was cheap. He let his friends constantly pay for his drinks and dinner, but he never reciprocated by picking up a friend's tab. He gave Rita chintzy, costume jewelry for her birthday. He mooched off of Rita, eating her food and drinking her booze, and he borrowed money from her that he never intended to pay back.

Rita sucked it up, telling herself she needed to contribute to their relationship.

Vince immediately isolated Rita from her friends and family and he began to verbally and physically abuse her. He demeaned her appearance; he called her fat, stupid and ugly. He was explosive and physically threatening. Her slightest comment would detonate him; he would grab whatever was at his fingertips and hurl it across the room, barely missing Rita's head a plate or a bookend would crash into the wall. Rita blamed Vince's deplorable behavior on his childhood, claiming as a child, his mother was emotionally withdrawn and punishing.

After a night of drinking, Rita spent the night with Vince. When Vince couldn't get an erection he exploded in a fit of rage. He sat up in bed and he screamed at Rita, "What the fuck is wrong with you, you stupid bitch! This is your fault [that he couldn't get an erection]," and he violently and repeatedly slapped Rita across the face.

Rita laid in bed frozen, afraid to speak or cry, tears silently slid down her cheeks.

Rita should have bludgeoned Vince with his Mexican elevator boot, she instead cried to me about his heinous, abusive behavior. I gave her my honest advice.

"Get rid of this jerk," I implored her. "How can you date this monster? If you keep dating him, he'll destroy you."

Rita whipped out her feel-sorry-for-me victim card.

"I'm just not going to date anymore," she whined. "I'm not fit to date. I'm stupid. I'm ugly. I don't deserve to have a good man in my life."

I felt guilty for making Rita feel bad about herself, and I quickly back-peddled.

"Don't say that! That's not true! You are attractive, intelligent, caring and funny. Any man would be lucky to have you."

Rita continued to date her worn-out Brad Pitt—and I kept my mouth shut. Three months later Vince unexpectedly, and cruelly dumped Rita, fulfilling her role as the helpless, innocent, abused victim.

I picked up Tolle's book and I continued to read.

It is the pain of our past which contributes to the pain of our present.

Pain-bodies love intimate relationships, said Tolle, and it will attempt to "provoke" and "push the buttons" of his partner or close family member so it can "feed on the ensuing drama."

My relationship with Dr. Dirtbag was rapidly disintegrating before my eyes. Our arguments were frequent, explosive and damaging, both of us saying unforgivable things that were indelibly burned into our consciousness. I clung to the deep-seated hope that he would repent and cease his hurtful behavior. But he seemed to thrive off the emotional pain he inflicted on me. His behavior was erratic and turbulent. One moment he was calm and congenial, and the next moment he was agitated, disconnected and angry, and then, for absolutely no reason, he would verbally pulverize me.

I tried to swallow my hurt and anger and ignore his spiteful put-downs. But he seemed to know exactly what to do and say to break my resolve, crush my spirit and ignite my anger. If I tried to reason with him, he would wear me down with his double talk, denial and derision, sending me to bed in a state of depression. If I tried to ignore him, he would torment me with his accusing, cutting jabs until I erupted into a fit of rage and tears. When I demanded that he cease his ridicule and bullying, he would look at me in contempt, blame me for our relationship problems, and then punish me with his silence. As time went by he grew callous, hostile and indifferent towards me—while I sank deeper into despair and more desperate than ever to regain his love and commitment.

I continued to read Tolle's book:

"It's hard to resist another person's pain-body that is determined to draw you into a reaction," said Tolle. "It instinctively knows your weakest, most vulnerable points. If it doesn't succeed the first time it will try again and again. It is raw emotion looking for more emotion."

Omigosh! Finally I understood! That was the toxic, twisted, addictive relationship I had with Dr. Dirtbag. The crippling, aching, longing feeling that I thought was my love for him—it wasn't love—it was my pain-body reaching out for his pain-body. When we argued, my pain-body craved his acceptance and validation. When we separated, my loneliness, fear and desperation grieved for his adoration and affection. Regardless of Dr. Dirtbag's destructive, oppressive, abusive behavior, being with him was the only thing that would temporarily soothe my wounded soul.

Dr. Dirtbag and I were tied together at the "soul level" by kindred pain-bodies. My pain-body misconstrued his pain-body to be a sacred love. His pain-body saw my pain-body as his divine mate. But, alas, he was willing to let go of me because he had more resolve than I did—or he was emotionally dead inside—or he was sedating himself with alcohol and women. The only thing that would pacify my grieving soul was to reunite with him—and so I would contact him. My pain-body would trigger his pain-body's need for intimacy, and he would take me back for the umpteenth time. And with each reconciliation his pain-body became more enraged and abusive, our arguments worsened, his passion for me lessened, and my hopelessness increased.

Gradually I began to understand the insanity of my roller-coaster emotional pattern. Dr. Dirtbag would abuse me. I would become angry and retaliate and break up with him. Days, sometimes weeks, and even months later, I would miss him and I would minimize his abusive behavior. I would imagine he was repentant for his hurtful behavior and that he still loved me. I would succumb to my pain-body and I would go back to him to start the vicious cycle over again.

It became clear to me that the only way I would ever be free of Dr. Dirtbag was to purge him from my mind. I had to throw away his pictures and hide his gifts of clothing and jewelry. Delete his phone numbers and email address. Get rid of his past correspondence, block his incoming phone calls and emails, and defriend him on Facebook. I could have nothing around me that could accidentally remind me of him. I could have zero communication with him. It had become a matter of life and death.

Feed the Pain-Beast

It's difficult to give love, when you don't feel loved.

Angel's pain-body was so strong that it resulted in her death.

I met Angel in a singles Sunday school class. She had recently divorced and moved to Memphis with her two small children to start her life over. At age 35, Angel was tall and slender; she had long, curly black hair, creamy complexion and big, warm brown eyes. She was vivacious, friendly and caring. Everyone, men and women alike, immediately adored Angel.

Angel's divorce was a devastating blow to her. The daughter of a preacher, her life's purpose had been to be a loving wife, good mother and an exemplary Christian. She struggled as a single mom.

She worked long, exhausting hours as a manager of a mall jewelry store. She scrambled to find a trustworthy babysitter to keep her two pre-school children in the evenings and on weekends. She worked overtime during the Christmas season, leaving her little time for her children, a social life and her church activities. But mostly, Angel struggled with loneliness. At times her pain-body was so heavy it was palpable. Even her faith in God couldn't seem to fill the aching hole in her heart.

Angel survived a difficult Christmas that year, she took her children to stay with their Dad in Nashville, and she took a vacation to Cancun with her friends. There she met a handsome Latino hotel manager, and a relationship between them ignited. Five days later Angel's Mexican vacation ended, her budding romance was cut short, and she flew home to her stressful, despondent life.

Angel felt alive when she was with her Cancun man. She felt empty inside without him. They communicated by email and phone calls, but the demands of her daily existence intensified her loneliness and heartache. Four weeks later she took her children to stay with their dad and she returned to Cancun to reunite with her Latino boyfriend.

We were all concerned about Angel—we advised her against returning to a foreign country to be with a man she barely knew. Two days after Angel's arrival in Cancun, her fully-clothed body was discovered at daybreak, lying on the beach near the hotel. She had died of an overdose.

It felt like a bad dream. One day Angel was standing in front of us smiling and laughing. Two days later she was a lifeless, forsaken body lying on a sandy beach in a faraway country. We mourned the loss of Angel, and we grieved for her two small children who had lost their beautiful mother. The local authorities ruled out foul-play in Angel's death. Her body was brought back to the States for her funeral. Her family and friends could not accept the authorities' speculation that their sweet, spirited Angel committed suicide. We believed she died of a broken heart.

Little Girl Pain

She grew up with a broken heart.

Daughters and fathers have a special relationship; daughters are uniquely affected by their father's involvement, or his absence in her life. A loving, supportive father shapes his daughter's self-esteem, self-image, confidence and her opinions of men. Women choose men who are like their fathers. Women, who were neglected or mistreated by their fathers, will date and marry men who are emotionally unavailable, self-absorbed, non-committal and often abusive. A daughter who didn't receive the love and support of her father as a child, will spend a lifetime seeking a man's love and acceptance. The problem is: we can never fill the emotional void in our soul with another person—no matter how much they love us.

Caroline was conditioned at a very young age to believe that she didn't deserve to be loved. Her mother married at age 16 and had a baby girl. She divorced at age 19, remarried to a traveling salesmen, and she gave birth to Caroline and her older sister. Her mom and her stepdad were both chronic alcoholics. Caroline and her family traveled with her stepdad, moving from town to town, existing in shabby hotels, eating in greasy diners, while her stepdad peddled his chintzy jewelry and merchandise in mom-and-pop stores, on the sidewalk and at flea markets. Her stepdad squandered their rent money on liquor and prostitutes. Her family was evicted from their shanty house. Her mom stole money out of her stepdad's wallet, she packed Caroline and her two sisters' clothes in garbage bags, they fled from their home and they hopped on a bus to Chattanooga. Her mom got a job as a waitress at the Day's Inn restaurant and they lived rent-free in a tiny, dingy room at the Day's Inn motel. Caroline's sisters slept in the bed with her mom. Caroline slept on the filthy, cracked linoleum floor, crawling with cockroaches and mice.

Caroline's mom began drinking heavily and bringing strange men home. She told Caroline she was the strong one and she sent Caroline to live with her 18-year-old drug addict sister living in a two-bedroom duplex. At age 12, Caroline was curvaceous and attractive. Her sister's doped up guy friends made lewd, solicitous remarks to Caroline. At night, Caroline locked herself in the bedroom with her sister's cat, and she turned up the music on the radio to drown out the noise of her sister's cocaine party and the dopeheads beating on her door.

Caroline eventually moved back home to live with mother and her new boyfriend, Randy. Her mother worked long hours at the restaurant, leaving the house at four in the morning and not returning until 10 at night. Randy left for work at 7 a.m. to work at a building supply store. Caroline woke up in the early morning hours and found Randy on top of her, with her gown pulled up to her neck and his hand on her nude breast. He raped Caroline at gunpoint. Every morning, while Caroline's mom was at work, Randy crept into Caroline's bedroom. He laid his pistol on Caroline's nightstand, he made Caroline perform oral sex on him, and he raped her repeatedly until he had to get dressed and go to work. Randy told Caroline if she cried he would do worse things to her, and if she told her mother he would kill her and her mother. Every morning, when Randy finished molesting Caroline, she got out of bed, took a shower and she walked to school.

In high school Caroline felt dirty and ashamed. She slept with guys because she thought that was the only way to get a boyfriend. Her reputation for "putting out" fueled her morbid sense of feeling damaged and unlovable. As a young adult, Caroline gravitated to men who were controlling and abusive. She married and divorced two men who verbally and physically battered her. At age 40, Caroline's intense pain-body demanded relief; she needed a man to make her feel complete. She didn't care if a man had a girlfriend or a wife; she wanted to be the center of attention

Her pain-body told her she didn't deserve to be loved.

of every man. She used her sexuality to attract men. She flaunted her curves and large breasts; her long auburn hair and thick, dark lashes intensified her sad green eyes. When she walked into a bar, her sultry under-current gave men an erection, and the wives and girlfriends held onto their boyfriends and husbands. Caroline slept with a lot of men. She had flings with married men. She sparked the pursuit of her girlfriends' boyfriends, and she claimed they were just "friends," or it was business.

Caroline's relationships were turbulent and short-lived. Her best girlfriend and roommate, Ginger, advised Caroline to not date Pete, a moonlighting, married man. Caroline got mad and broke her lease agreement with Ginger, and Pete immediately moved Caroline into a small apartment. Caroline thought she had found her savior and benefactor. Eight months later, Caroline demanded that Pete leave his wife, and Pete gave Caroline the boot. In the beginning men were smitten by Caroline's allure and sexuality. In the end her insatiable emotional furnace created a man's disdain, rebuke and abuse.

Caroline eventually located her natural father and she called him. They talked for a few minutes, and then he told her, "I hope you are doing well, but I can't do this," and he hung up on her.

One wonders how much sorrow a pain-body can endure.

The Pain-Body Glutton

People with heavy pain-bodies will accept insufferable abusive treatment from their partners.

After Carrie, a 39-year-old mother of a 10-year-old boy, divorced her second husband, a verbal and physical batterer, she swore to never again be in a relationship with an abusive man—and then Shawn latched onto to her pain-body and nearly destroyed her.

The warning flags of Shawn's malign behavior were blood red. He lost his six-figure job because of a DUI, and he couldn't find a decent job. He drank excessively, and Carrie heard him verbally berate his 11-year-old son—and yet, she became intimately involved with him.

Carrie's relationship with Shawn was an addictive, volatile cycle of verbal abuse. Carrie repeatedly broke up with Shawn for his toxic behavior, and he repeatedly pulled her back into the relationship with his tearful pleas and the lure of sexual gratification. Then one night he did the unthinkable—he showed up unexpectedly at a nightclub, saw Carrie dancing with another man, and he cold-cocked her in the middle of the dance floor.

Shawn fled the nightclub and he made a beeline to Carrie's townhouse. Carrie's roommate, unaware of the assault, allowed Shawn into Carrie's townhouse. Inside their home, he stormed through the house, he ransacked Carrie's bedroom, he ripped her lingerie to shreds, stole the jewelry and trinkets he had given Carrie and he demolished the massive pots of summer flowers on her patio.

Pain-bodies innately attract noxious people, hurtful situations and misfortune.

The police arrested Shawn in the early morning hours cruising by Carrie's townhouse—he was drunk and no doubt still looking for revenge. He spent the night in jail. The next morning he posted bail and he called Carrie, pleading for a ride home. Unbelievably Carrie felt sorry for Shawn. She picked him up at the jailhouse and took him home. More unbelievable was, she apologized to him for dancing with another man. It was exactly what Shawn needed to hear for he knew there was no limit to the abuse she would accept from him.

She seemed to always love men who mistreated her.

Carrie resumed her tumultuous relationship with Shawn.

It was Sunday evening, Shawn didn't show up at Carrie's house as promised. Something didn't feel right to Carrie. She drove to Shawn's townhouse and she staked out his back door. An hour later the door to Shawn's townhouse opened, and Shawn walked out with a woman. It was obvious they had just crawled out of bed. His hair was disheveled, he was shirtless and barefoot, wearing only his boxer shorts. He walked the woman to her car, pushed her up against the side of the car, pressing her hard with his body, he kissed her aggressively. The woman got into her car and drove off, and Shawn stumbled back into his townhouse.

Carrie was outraged at Shawn's betrayal. She jumped out of her car, stomped onto Shawn's patio and banged on his sliding glass door. Shawn came to the door, half-naked and dazed. It was obvious, in addition to humping the hussy, he was drunk.

Carrie pushed past Shawn, stood in his kitchen and yelled, "How could you do this?"

Shawn shoved Carrie against the wall, clamped his hand over her mouth, and he screamed through gritted teeth, "Tell me the truth, WHAT THE FUCK did you see in that guy?"

Carrie was stunned. She flew out the sliding glass door and then half way to her car, she froze—she had left her expensive prescription eyeglasses on Shawn's kitchen counter. She couldn't see to drive without them. She walked back to Shawn's patio door and she tapped on the glass. Shawn shuffled up to the locked patio door and he glared at Carrie wordlessly, menacingly through the glass.

"I left my eyeglasses," Carrie beseeched.

"Tough shit!" Shawn growled through the plate glass. "Buy yourself another pair!"

Carrie's repressed rage erupted.

Shawn's patio was bedecked with clay pots overflowing with colossal blooming Impatiens. Carrie eyed his flourishing flowers. She thought how Shawn had decimated the beautiful flowers on her patio and her wrath exploded. She hurled the large clay pots onto the brick pavers, leaving a quake of broken terracotta and shredded flowers on Shawn's patio.

Shawn stormed onto the patio, grabbed Carrie's arm, jerked her upward and screamed, "You stupid bitch! You can forget about your fucking eyeglasses. Clean this mess up!" He went into his house, came back with a broom and a dustpan and thrust them at Carrie.

"Fix this mess or I'm calling the police."

Shawn had Carrie right where he wanted her. Powerless. Distraught. And terrified.

Carrie scooped up the loose dirt and flowers with her hands, stuffed it back into half-broken pots, and she swept the debris off his patio. Shawn handed her a bottle of Windex and paper towels, demanded that she clean the patio glass doors, and he went back into his townhouse, locking the patio door behind him. Carrie cleaned the glass doors and she meekly knocked on the patio door. Shawn came to the door, opened it, and he glared at her in contempt.

"It's clean," Carrie said, hating the words coming out of her mouth. Shawn handed Carrie her eyeglasses and she drove home a despondent, broken woman.

> **People with heavy pain-bodies usually have a better chance to awaken spiritually than those with a relative light one—they cannot live with their unhappiness any longer, and so their motivation to awaken becomes strong.**
>
> **—Eckard Tolle**

Nothing could alleviate the intense pain-body that now gripped Carrie's wounded soul. Her life spun out of control. She haunted happy hours and she drank excessively. She brought strange men home with her and she slept with them. The next day she felt dirty, worthless and despondent. She obsessed that Shawn might seek revenge on her, and she was overcome with depression. She isolated herself in her townhouse, hiding out in the daytime instead of making sales calls, sleeping long hours. Carrie hit rock bottom. Fearing for the outcome of her life she sought the therapy that she so desperately needed.

For a year and a half year Carrie dug into her personal issues that were causing her to self-destruct. Week after week, month after month, her counselor listened to her cry and blame her worthless husbands and abusive boyfriends for her problems and relationship failures. Eventually her counselor helped her to understand that she was answerable for her negative mindset and destructive behavior, and that she was accountable for her choices in life. Angry uncontrollable tears erupted as decades of Carrie's pain-body came rushing forth. She resurrected family members, failed relationships and the past hurtful events that hacked away at her self-worth. Carrie faced her deep-rooted feelings of self-loathing, hatred and rage. Gradually she dispelled the disparaging beliefs she had about herself: that she was inferior to others, that people judged and disliked her, and that she was unworthy of a man's respect.

Time passed and Carrie saw herself as a valuable human being worthy of respect and love. Her self-esteem and confidence increased, and she eventually found inner peace and a sense of rational happiness.

Today Carrie's pain-body is light, it visits her infrequently, but when her pain-body does surface unexpectedly, it's manageable. More importantly, Carrie is quick to recognize and avoid relationships, with men and women alike, which trigger her past emotional issues.

Pain-Bodies Die Hard

Dr. Dirtbag and I finally broke-up, permanently and irrevocably. Even so, it was not a cut-and-dry ending for me. I had irrational, lingering feelings for him. I called him several times, and I saw him once—but it wasn't the same. My mind knew we were finished. I was waiting for my heart to catch up. And then a miracle happened—I found out that Dr. Dirtbag had slept with another woman. He found a new pain-body to identify with, and he no longer needed to feed off mine. Dr. Dirtbag did for me what I couldn't do for myself. He completely severed our relationship to be with another woman.

A year later Dr. Dirtbag married his new pain-body, Bimbo. I called my dear friend Annie to share the news.

"Guess what," I said dejectedly, "Dr. Dirtbag married Bimbo."

"How do you feel," she asked, knowing that it was a milestone for me.

"I won't lie to you. It hurts and I still hate his guts."

"It's a good thing," Annie replied soothingly. "You grew from being with him. Now he's her problem, and you have a second chance and a second book."

"You're right," I replied "He was the gift that came in an ugly package."

💔

There comes a time we must realize that the pain of staying, hurts more than the pain of leaving.

4 I Would Let Go If He Would Let Me

Just when you begin to regain your dignity and mental health—he calls you.

Have you ever broken up with a man and you spent weeks, months, and even years, missing him and trying to get over him? Week after week you agonize, fantasize, and you hope that one day he will call you, say he misses you, he's never gotten over you, and he wants you back. You ache for him to apologize for his hurtful behavior and ask for your forgiveness. You pray that he has mended his evil ways and he will plead for a second chance. It's an obsessing, torturing fantasy that fogs your brain in the daytime, wrecks your sleep at night, and zaps your ability to enjoy life.

Time passes. Your life is quasi-normal. Your thoughts and longings for him have lessened. And then—when you least expect it—*he texts, emails or calls you.*

At first it's small talk. He'll ask in his buttered-up, pleading voice, *"How've you been?"* or *"How's work?"* You agree to have coffee with him—*you know,* just "to talk." Then you have dinner and drinks with him, and you go back to his place and you sleep with him. You tell yourself you can "handle it," and before you know it, you're back in the worst relationship of your life. But his passion for you has diminished. Your arguments worsen. And your codependency and hopelessness increases.

Girlfriend! Have you lost your ever-loving mind? Where is your sense of survival and good judgment? You struggled for months, even years to get this immoral, ground-crawling sleazebucket out of your life. You know the moment he tells you he loves you, your heart will melt, and you will forget every despicable thing he ever said and did to you. You know he's bad for you. You know he erodes your confidence, shreds your self-esteem, nukes your energy and throws you into dark depression. And regardless of what he promises, you know he will again betray you with his lying words and abusive behavior.

Wouldn't it be less painful to super-crush your breast in a mammogram machine?

> **Deep down you know it best for you, but you hate the thought of him being with someone else.**
>
> **—Anonymous**

Sometimes my defective brain seemed to think for me when it came to Dr. Dirtbag.

Dr. Dirtbag had moved on with his life with his new girlfriend, Bimbo—and yet, a year later I text messaged him on Valentine's Day. My message read:

> Happy Valentines Day! I still think of you. I hope she makes you happy.

I knew I never wanted to see his worthless sad-sack face again, but I wanted him to think about me, and I wanted to ruin his Valentine's Day. The problem was—my text message made me obsess about him, ruining my entire week.

> **If you choose the behavior of staying with a sick and destructive partner, then you choose the consequence of pain and suffering in your emotional life.**
>
> **—Dr. Phil**

You're a Survivor

Why is it so hard for women to stop loving the liars, womanizers, cheaters and abusers? It seems the worse they treat us, the deeper grows our love. The more outrageous lies they tell us, the more gullible we become. The more abusive they evolve, the more forgiving we are. The more non-communicating they become—the harder we work to figure them out.

In one year, Dr. Dirtbag had crushed my spirit and replaced it with a sense of despair and hopelessness—and yet, I continued to love him. I asked myself: Is it possible, that in a sick and twisted way, I enjoy the pain and suffering inflicted by a malfunctioning man?

> *I was horribly addicted to the crippling, roller coaster love-breakup-reconcile cycle of abuse with Dr. Dirtbag. I knew I was being slowly destroyed, and I tried a hundred times to sever my relationship with him. But he kept drawing me back into a relationship with him with his expressions of adoration, worthless excuses and pleas for my forgiveness. I believed him when he promised to stop drinking and verbally abusing me, and I would reconcile with him. He would straighten up for a week, and then he would sneak a drink, get smashed and blindside me with an angry jab. After his assault, a bandaid gift would magically show up on my doorstep. I was optimistic when he got meds for his mood swings and he consented to go to counseling. I wanted to believe that he loved me and that he would cease his intolerable behavior—but the longer I was with him, the more destructive he became.*

Millions of women can identify with me, that even though our boyfriend, fiancé or husband repeatedly wounds our spirit, we hold onto the hope that he will quit lying, cheating, drinking, drugging and abusing us. Despite the glaring evidence of his maiming conduct we make excuses and tolerate his irresponsible, deceptive, abusive behavior. We cling to false security and we endure the pain, anger and resentment of a toxic relationship.

The first step to healing from a toxic relationship is recognizing you are in one.

💔

If you have never been in an abusive relationship—*you may not know what you are dealing with.* You may not know that abusive language is "coded," the gestures are underhanded and the overall assault is scheming. Covert abuse is hidden aggression. The perpetrator communicates in ways that are sly, vague, underhanded and confusing. Its aim is to control and dominate you without you knowing. Your partner may pass his demeaning comments off as "constructive" criticisms or sarcasms disguised as "jokes." You may mistrust your instincts that your boyfriend or husband is lying to you, demeaning you, manipulating and controlling you. You may minimize his bad behavior; you may think: he's having a bad day, he didn't mean it, or alcohol makes him abusive. You may think you are over-reacting and crazy—as he claims you are—and you blame yourself and try harder to suppress your anger.

If you have never been in an abusive relationship, you may not understand the psychological dynamics of that relationship. You may not realize that the abuser's cruel and unpredictable behavior is designed to undermine, confuse and beat you down, while his intermittent deeds of affection and kindness are intended to draw you deeper into his cycle of abuse.

The abusive cycle is addictive and deadly. The abuser sets you up to punish and batter you. After the abusive episode he is often on his good behavior. He may say he's sorry (don't hold your breath) and ask for your forgiveness (it's feigned). You may experience the "honeymoon" phase when he is charming, adoring and generous—as he was during your courtship. He may take you to dinner and bring you flowers and make-up gifts. His renewed attention and affection give you renewed hope and a false sense of security. You are grateful for his change of heart and you experience a feeling of revived love for him. This cycle of abuse creates "traumatic bonding" in its victims.

You become dependent on and crave his acceptance and approval, while accepting more and more of his abuse, and you sink deeper and deeper into his cauldron of darkness.

Understanding the complicated, intense emotional dynamics which keep your heart perpetually tied to an abusive ex-boyfriend or ex-husband (or a current partner) can help you start the healing process.

A sexually addictive relationship will cause a woman to accept outrageous, hurtful behavior from a man.

Beneath his sex appeal, charm and flattery was the Craig's List killer.

Jackie, an attractive 45-year-old mother of two teenage boys, was no dummy. She had learned to be cautious about the men she dated. She stopped dating handsome, successful men who displayed questionable behavior. She ran background checks on several men. But she was overwhelmed by Kenny's striking good looks, charm and intense pursuit.

There was an instant and intense mental and physical attraction between Jackie and Kenny. Kenny portrayed himself as a good husband and father with his morally contrived questions: "Are you a good mom?" "Do you smoke?" "Are you a Christian?" He made Jackie believe he was selective about the women he would date. Kenny said and did all the right things. If Jackie said she liked a song, the next day it was playing in his car's CD player. He surprised her with a greeting card under the windshield of her car, and he deliberately took her to her favorite restaurants. He held her hand, stared at her rings and bracelet, and he asked her, "Do you prefer silver or gold jewelry?" He told Jackie he had never felt this kind of chemistry with another woman. Two weeks into dating Kenny, he told Jackie he was in love with her.

Sex with Kenny was erotic and habit-forming. Kenny was worldly and knowledgeable. He introduced Jackie to sex toys and oral sex with intense orgasms. He pushed her to have concealed sex in public places; in a park at night laying on a blanket under a tree, in a nightclub restroom and in a parking garage. Sitting at a table in a restaurant, Kenny would slip his hands under Jackie's skirt, touch her and arouse her. Sex with Kenny was naughty, intoxicating and addictive. The downside was: Kenny was extremely jealous, possessive and pathologically suspicious.

She said it was the best sex she ever had. And then she barked. Arf! Arf! Arf!

Kenny imagined that Jackie flirted with other men, or that she was conspiring to cheat with another man. He rummaged through her waste baskets and outdoor trash can, looking for evidence of her infidelity. He pieced together torn and crumpled restaurant receipts, and he demanded to know who she had lunch or dinner with. When she got home from work, or going out with her girlfriends, he would grab her by the arm, pull her into him and sniff her hair and clothes to see if he could smell a man's scent on her. He kept track of her menstrual cycles and birth control pills. When she shaved her legs and underarms, he accused her of primping to have sex with another man. He checked the mileage on her car and he drilled her about her whereabouts. He pried into her phone call history and he called the logged numbers to see if a man would answer. He destroyed or hid anything he thought was a gift from a man. When they broke up he stole her perfume, jewelry, clothes and shoes, so she couldn't wear them around another man.

Jackie repeatedly broke up with Kenny, but he repeatedly seduced her back into their turbulent relationship. She was hooked on the erotic sex of their relationship. The erotic sex numbed her emotional pain, fogged her brain, and caused her to believe she still loved Kenny, while warping the reality of his abuse.

Jackie finally broke up with Kenny and he went psycho. He stalked her, he threatened her physical harm, and he keyed her car outside her apartment. Jackie called the police. A female officer with the domestic violence squad ran a background check on Kenny. She discovered that Kenny had been arrested twice for a DUI, disorderly conduct and domestic assault. The officer told Jackie, "There was a similar incident like this last year in your neighborhood. A woman's boyfriend was verbally and physically abusive, she keep going back and forth with him, and then one night he got drunk and he slit her throat. You're guy is capable of doing the same thing."

❦

It's hard to go back to plain, old vanilla, when you've had Fifty Shades of spank-me, cuff-me, blindfold me, and don't you dare tie me to the bed post.

5 Mistakes After a Breakup

It'll take one bottle of wine
to get over this asshole. Bartender!

Mistake No. 1: Staying in Touch with Your Ex

You broke off with your boyfriend, or you left your husband, because he was withdrawn, neglectful and uncommunicative, or he cheated on you, or he was verbally or physically abusive. You're trying to get on with your life without him in it. You had a decent week. And then suddenly he calls you.

Why does a guy contact you weeks after a breakup?

Duh! To boost his ego and lessen his discomfort of feeling dejected and alone.

Why does a guy contact you months, and even years after he dumped you?

Because his new girlfriend broke up with him—or he hasn't found a suitable woman who will put up with his crap!

> *When Dr. Dirtbag and I were together, I loathed his obnoxious, hurtful behavior. I detested how he got drunk, made a boasting fool of himself in public, and humiliated me in front of our friends. I hated how he made me feel with his empty promises, vague explanations and sneering innuendos. But when we broke up, I couldn't stand the sick-to-my-stomach feeling of rejection, and so I weakened and I called him, and he was delighted to have his punching bag back.*

I couldn't stand to be with him, but I couldn't stand to be without him.

Sometimes Dr. Dirtbag would call me when we broke up. His favorite get-his-foot-back-in-the-door line was: "Hey—whatta you doing," he'd say in a forlorn voice, followed by, "I thought you woulda called me by now." It was the same contrived, pretentious, conciliatory performance every time. Dr. Dirtbag never called to apologize, and he acted as if nothing had ever happened. He knew if he could get me to talk to him, he could soften my heart and he could jump back in the saddle. I knew if I were ever to be free of the emotional hold he had on me, I had to bite the bullet, block all communication with him, eliminate him from my life, detox, and look forward to the time when he no longer permeated my brain cells.

If you truly don't want to talk to him—block his frikkin calls!

Ex-boyfriends, ex-husbands and ex-lovers know exactly what to say and do to woo you back into a relationship. They know your weak spots and they will play you like an acoustic guitar. If you *truly* want to get on with your life without him in it—don't answer his phone calls, don't return his texts or emails, and don't open your door to his surprise visits, giving him the opportunity to slither back into your life.

Mistake No. 2: Thinking You Failed

Breakups are a part of life. It's how we evaluate what we need and want in a relationship. It's how we determine the traits and qualities that are important to us in a mate. It's how we identify the character flaws and dysfunctional behavior that we positively refuse to accept in a partner. Learning from our breakups contributes to our wisdom, maturity and personal growth.

You can't get on with your life as a woman without at least one miserable man in your life. A hurtful breakup can open your eyes to your dysfunctional, bad behaviors. However, thinking you did something to cause your boyfriend's or husband's withdrawn and punishing demeanor, his betrayal and infidelity, or his explosive, disruptive, abusive behavior, is a slippery, self-destructive slope.

Controlling, narcissistic, abusive men don't apologize for their hurtful actions—*and genuinely mean it*. They don't admit to any wrong doing, and they don't take responsibility for their part in a failing relationship.

Robert's relationship motto was: blame, shift and deny.

Amy's fiancé Robert was a master at manipulation and conspiracy. He would deliberately start a fight with Amy, berate her unmercifully, and then divert the attention from his malign behavior by claiming he was the wounded one. He would grab Amy's hand and shove her 3-carat diamond engagement ring in her face, force her to look at it and bellow, "Look at this! Do you not understand how much I love you?" He cast cunning, blaming accusations to make her feel sorry for him, claiming, "The problem with us is, YOU don't understand me." And to make her feel bad about herself, he squawked, "Do you know how much money I've spent on you?"

For the record: Amy's 3-carat diamond engagement ring was appraised as a fake!

> *Dr. Dirtbag blamed me for our relationship problems. I punished myself thinking our relationship would improve if I could be a better person—if I wouldn't over-react to his cruel and insensitive remarks—if I could be more patient and understanding—if I could be the strong one—a biblical example of a caring, devoted, loving partner, he would see the bright light and forsake his evil ways. I tried to ignore his irrational behavior, dodge his accusations and jabs, and hold my tongue, but he kept taunting and persecuting me until I exploded in an uncontrollable fit of anger, and then I was, of course, the bad guy.*
>
> *The sad part of my approach—trying to be the "strong one"—was I used my strength against myself. I struggled to*

stay balanced and calm when Dr. Dirtbag verbally attacked me. I tried to endure his unpredictable outbursts and mental torment. I wore myself down trying to figure out what I was doing that caused him to be so angry and abusive. It seemed the harder I tried to appease him, the angrier he got; and the angrier he got, the more confused and despondent I became.

You can't change the spots of a cunning, stalking, meat-eating leopard, and you can't change the angry mindset of a pathological lying, narcissistic, sociopathic partner. Thinking you failed in an abusive relationship is suffering double-time.

Mistake No. 3: Thinking You're Unlovable, Unwanted or Undesirable

Thinking you somehow failed in a hurtful, dysfunctional relationship or marriage will undermine your confidence and self-esteem, cause you to withdraw from your friends and family, and create feelings of neediness, dejection and despair within you.

It took decades for me to overcome my low self-esteem issues. My overactive, hyper-critical inner voice would tell me I was unattractive, unintelligent and undesirable. I eventually conquered my disparaging mindset. When I met Dr. Dirtbag I was happy, confident and optimistic. It took Dr. Dirtbag only eight months to resurrect my self-doubting, insecure demons.

Like most abusive men, Dr. Dirtbag built himself up by tearing me down. He belittled my abilities. He made snide remarks about my body. He told me evasive, contradicting half-truths to confuse and frustrate me. One night he callously called me a "three time loser" (referring to the number of my divorces). I knew then we were in a slay-your-opponent war, because if he would say that to me, he would say and do anything to diminish me.

You had a decent week without him there to constantly tell you that you're overweight, old and stupid. And you want him back—WHY?

Before Liz married Mike she was cheerful, sassy and confident. A year after she married Mike, she was depressed, uncertain and distrustful of men.

Liz, a beautiful 40-year-old woman, dated Mike a year before marrying him. During their courtship he was considerate, doting, extremely affectionate and sexual. Two weeks after she married him, Liz adorned herself in a lacy, black nightie and positioned herself seductively at the doorway of his home office.

"Take that off! You look like a skank!" Mike screamed.

Liz was painfully dumbstruck. It was a side of her husband she had never seen. Before they were married, Mike would have thrown his computer out the window to make love to Liz. His demeaning, spiteful remark was an obvious attempt to devalue Liz as a woman.

You can never really know a man until you live with him.

The moment Mike married Liz he felt entitled to dominate and disparage her. He criticized everything she said, did or liked. He condemned her menu selection in a restaurant. He carped about her cooking, the way she kept house and the TV shows she wanted to watch. He bad-mouthed her friends. He especially ridiculed the way she dressed, saying she wore too much make-up and her hair was an ugly color. If she wore a low-cut blouse, at his request, he told her she looked like a slut. When she wore conservative clothing, he told her she looked frigid and frumpy. When Liz stood up to him for his hurtful comments, he said, "Geez, I can't say anything to you. I was just trying to help you be a better person. I'll just leave you alone."

Liz knew in her heart that she was an attractive woman, but Mike's constant put-downs pulverized her self-worth.

Liz divorced Mike after one year of marriage, and she began seeing a therapist. She told her therapist she felt unattractive and undesirable, and she thought no man would ever want her. Her therapist helped Liz to understand that Mike's demeaning behavior arose from his own self-loathing and insecurities—to feel good about himself, he tore Liz down.

Mistake No. 4: Staying Stuck in Anger and Grief

Every time I thought about Dr. Dirtbag the heartbreak of my past became the pain of my present. Every time I entertained an angry, resentful, vindictive thought about him, I zapped my energy, I poisoned my femininity, and I eroded my happiness. Every time I wished bad for him, I attracted the same for myself.

> **Consider how much more you often suffer from your anger and grief, than from those very things for which you are angry and grieved.**
>
> **—Marcus Antonius**

Reba spent a lifetime mistrusting, resenting and protecting herself from men. As a child, her dad would come home drunk, verbally batter and assault her mother, and terrorize Reba and her younger sister. After he passed out on the sofa, her mom would hurriedly pack their suitcases, sneak out the back door, and load Reba and her sister into their beat-up Rambler. Reba's mom was afraid to start the engine, for fear it would wake her husband. She put 8-year-old Reba behind the steering wheel and she put the car in neutral. Reba leaned up so she could see over the dashboard to guide the car, while her mom pushed the car to the end of the driveway, and then her mom would jump in beside Reba, crank the ignition and they fled to a neighboring city to find shelter. Reba's father seemed to always find them. He would show up drunk outside the shelter, ranting and raving until her mom consented to come home.

Reba married at age 19 to escape her unhappy home life. Reba's husband and his buddy got drunk one night in their home. Her husband passed out in the upstairs bedroom and his drunk buddy sexually assaulted Reba. Reba fought him off, ran upstairs and locked herself in a bedroom. The next morning she told her husband his buddy tried to rape her, showing him the cuts and bruises all over her body. Her husband blamed Reba, claiming she did "something" to cause his attack.

Reba shut down. She wouldn't allow herself to feel love and she vowed to never again trust or be hurt by a man. Her deep-seated contempt fueled her determination to never depend on a man for her happiness and security. She put herself through college, and she became a successful, six-figure attorney. She exercised compulsively; a vain and aggressive outlet for her suppressed anger. Standing 5-foot-11, beautiful, shapely and uber-confident, Reba felt a sense of power over men. She snubbed the average man. She had a history of tumultuous, sexual relationships with affluent men. She had a serious falling-out with her attorney-boss. While her repressed anger empowered her to be an independent woman and successful attorney, her ball-busting persona sabotaged her romantic relationships and held her back in the corporate world.

> *I was stuck in on a state of anger and resentment. I hated Dr. Dirtbag for everything he did to me. I hated Bimbo because in my mind's eye—she was the other woman. I was pissed because Bimbo ignored my warnings about Dr. Dirtbag and she married him. I was irked because she believed his claims that he was the misunderstood, mistreated one—and I was the raging she-beast. I resented her thinking that she was the better woman for landing Dr. Dirtbag. No matter, as long as I kept reviving and reliving my sick and twisted memories of Dr. Dirtbag—I remained the loser.*

Mistake No. 5: Trying to Fast-Track Your Recovery

Trying to mask the pain of a relationship breakup by: (1) immediately looking for the next relationship; (2) throwing yourself into work, or (3) avoiding dating altogether, only delays the recovery process.

What you can feel, you can heal. Take time to heal from your emotional wounds and correct your harmful relationship behavior; otherwise, you will recycle it into your next relationship.

Dr. Dirtbag and I broke up and I immediately signed up on Match.com. I couldn't bear the thought of not having a man in my life. I thought a man would be lucky to have me. I was attractive, intelligent, fun-loving, and I was an author for Pete's sake! In truth, I was a walking-wounded corpse, desperately looking for a relationship to fill the hole in my soul.

Rebound dating increased my feelings of loneliness and anxiety. Men instantly recognized my aura of needy desperation and sprinted to the hills. I had lost my sense of purpose and direction. My recovery plan was: good in, garbage out. I forced myself to do things that would promote positive energy and personal growth. I exercised regularly. I ate healthy foods and I increased my vitamins. I read books that inspired and uplifted me. I planted flowers and I tried out new recipes. I lit soothing, fragrant candles, and I bought fresh flowers for my home. I played lively musical CD's. I spent time with my new granddaughter. I went to new restaurants, and I attended social events. I began writing my third book. I even started my own women's social and business networking group. Gradually my woebegone feelings were replaced with hope, faith and contentment.

A year later My Woman Within said, *Dr. Who?*

TIP: If you can't find a women's social or business networking group to attend, you can start your own group on the nationwide platform, www.meetup.com. All you need is a social agenda, a smile and wine—and they will come!

6 How Long Will I Mourn?

I missed him so much I thought I would die.

At one time or another, almost everyone carries in them some degree of emotional pain spawned from a hurtful divorce, failed relationship or the death of a loved one. Anger, disbelief and sorrow live within us, and can linger for months, for years and even a lifetime.

Dr. Dirtbag and I broke up permanently and I moved to another city 600 miles away. A year passed—and, in spite of his horrific lying and verbal abuse, I still grieved for him. There was not a day, not even an hour, not even a minute that I didn't think of him. I thought about him the moment I woke up and the last second before I fell asleep. I longed for how he would cup my face in his hands, gaze into my eyes and call me his "blonde baby." I missed our fun times together; our road trips when we would spontaneously stop at a hamburger dive; or driving down the road, the two of us singing loudly to an old tune blasting from the CD player; and going to antique auctions, I would marvel at his extensive knowledge of period furniture and fine crystal. I missed how we cuddled on the sofa to watch TV, and every night in bed, just before falling asleep, we would hug, kiss and tell one another, "I love you." And, yes, I missed the stability of his financial support.

I tried to focus on my work and get on with my life but I couldn't quit obsessing over him. My mind kept reverting back to the hurtful events of our relationship. I used an egg timer to try to control my compulsive thoughts of him. I told myself,

"Work from nine to noon. At noon you can have fifteen minutes to cry, scream and anguish over that bogus, lowlife douchebag." At noon my egg timer would buzz and I let loose with a neurotic, bawling seizure. Afterwards I dried my tears and I reset my timer for a 5 o'clock tantrum. Cocktail hour would finally roll around, my egg timer would sound and I indulged in thirty gratifying minutes of wailing and trashing Dr. Dirtbag.

Losing weight because of a bad boyfriend can be a definite perk —I'm just saying!

Those were tough days for me. I moped around the house in my pajamas in a state of apathy and hopelessness. I was extremely fatigued and I had insomnia. I couldn't concentrate. I suffered frequent meltdowns and I cried at the drop of a pin. My appetite was decimated, my weight dropped drastically, and I contracted shingles. I took Wellbutrin in the day to function. I ran at night so the passersby couldn't see the tears streaming down my face. I downed Tylenol PM and Ambien at bedtime so I could finally fall sleep.

> **I used to think I was tied to a heartache; that was the heartbreak.**
>
> **—"Even the Nights Are Better," Air Supply**

I was in a state of shock, denial and disbelief after Dr. Dirtbag and I broke up. And then I was so angry at him I wanted to beat his head in with my high heel—and then the sickening, tidal-wave grieving process began. I was overwhelmed by varying, intense emotions. I was restless, agitated and angry. I felt helpless, betrayed and hollow. I experienced severe bouts of fear, guilt, regret, rage, sorrow and despair. I had suffocating anxiety attacks. My heart pounded wildly, recklessly in my chest. I thought I was having a heart attack and I threw myself across my bed to calm my throbbing pulse. In the afternoons I would succumb to the weight of my depression. I shut my bedroom door, I closed the blinds and I crawled into my dark bed. The next morning I would arise, momentarily refreshed. Dr. Dirtbag would invade my thoughts. I would miss him. I would minimize the horrible things he said and did to me. I would forgive him and I would fantasize that he still loved me and missed me. He, instead, married Bimbo—and I threw myself into an angry, despondent state of mourning.

> **To give up the final hope may be the most difficult of all.**
>
> —***How to Survive the Loss of a Love***

Part of my grieving process was to pray for Dr. Dirtbag's healing as well.

> *Without a doubt Dr. Dirtbag was rotten to the core. I just knew he was headed to hell in his Maserati, but I still loved him and I wanted to see him in heaven when I departed this earth. I cried and prayed for my pain and suffering—and then I cried and begged God for the redemption of his dark, wicked soul. Sub-consciously I hoped that a bolt of lightning would strike him, causing him to stop lying, drinking and abusing—and then he would beg for my forgiveness and come crawling back to me.*
>
> *Why did I keep deluding and punishing myself? I knew I'd done everything humanly possible to make our relationship work. I lowered my expectations of him. I compromised my values. I minimized and excused his hurtful behavior. I forgave him over and over for his despicable, shameful deeds. I dragged him to three counselors and church, hoping for his supernatural healing. I threatened to leave him, and when that didn't work, I left him—all the while, praying that he would wake up, smell reality, and act like a decent human being.*
>
> *The sad fact was: the core of our relationship was permanently broken. I knew Dr. Dirtbag didn't want to lose me, but his narcissist, angry nature controlled him. Our trust*

was replaced with suspicion. Our meaningful conversations became sessions of blame and condemnation. The understanding and affection we once enjoyed was displaced with indifference and rejection. Most nights I slept on the far side of our bed with my back turned to him, my body comatose, my heart aching, and my thoughts racked with confusion. But I kept clutching to the illusion that he still loved me.

In my heart I knew the truth: Dr. Dirtbag was hopelessly impaired and our relationship was doomed. Why then was it so hard for me to move beyond him? Because I kept hoping he would have a change of heart and revert back to the man he represented himself to be in the beginning of our relationship—a man who was caring, patient and considerate. A man who wanted altruistic love and commitment. A man with whom I could trust my life, as he once had me believe.

It was the loss of a dream-come-true, which kept my heart hopelessly tied to Dr. Dirtbag.

I think about you. But I don't say it anymore.

—Marguerite Duras, Hiroshima mon amour

For me, acceptance was the hardest part of grieving—accepting the fact that I would never again have Dr. Dirtbag in my life. Subconsciously, I was afraid to stop hating and mourning for him, because if I still hated him, I could mentally hold on to him. If I continued to grieve for him, I could maintain a fantasy relationship with him. But if I quit hating him or grieving for him, I would have to accept the excruciating reality that I would never again see, feel or touch Dr. Dirtbag, and I would be totally, utterly, painfully and fearfully without him—*forever.*

I wondered: Is the grieving process more difficult, more intense, more long-lasting if we lose a boyfriend, fiancé or husband to death, rather than a breakup or divorce? I mean, if Dr. Dirtbag had accidentally drowned in his vodka, or my BMW unintentionally ran over him, would my pain be greater than if we had just broken up? The logic being: if he were alive and I missed him, I could at least pick up the phone, call him and listen to him demean and reject me again. But if he died, and I could never, ever again talk to him, could that prolong the grieving process—indefinitely?

Betsy's husband, a 44-year-old Army demolition expert, was killed in a vehicle rollover while deployed in Afghanistan. When I met Betsy, her husband had been deceased for several years, but her present-day grief was visibly intense and painful. I lost track of Betsy. Four years later I saw her at church and social events. Her core identity was: she was a "widow." When she spoke of her deceased husband, tears welled up in her eyes. It was as if his funeral were yesterday.

Her mourning was a shroud of morose sadness.

Betsy belonged to a singles group, and yet she never dated. I invited her to parties and events, but she always shut me down. I offered to help her post an online dating profile, but she was offended by my offer. She attended my *God, Please Fix Me!* Seminar and she weep through the entire presentation. I wondered: will she ever move beyond her crippling, never-ending mourning?

Betsy clung to her husband's death because if she let go of her grieving, she would have to get on with her life, and in her mind, she would betray the memory of her deceased husband.

Janice was stuck in a state of perpetual mourning for her 11-year-old grandson, Mark. Mark drowned in his backyard swimming pool. It was a heartbreaking tragedy. Janice's family and friends supported her during her intense mourning. Two years passed, and Janice continued to openly grieve about her grandson's passing. Her Facebook page served as a memorial to Mark. Her profile picture was a photo of Mark in his football uniform, and she regularly posted snapshots of him playing baseball, him and his dog, and him at family holiday get-togethers. She celebrated his birthday on Facebook, posting comments like, "The love of my life is in heaven" and "I miss you so much."

"He's all she talks about," her younger sister said. "We all loved Mark, and we all grieve privately for him. I had to stop having dinner with her because she insists on dwelling on his death."

Recognize the pain. Be with your pain. Give yourself time to heal—but heal, we must.

Healing for me was a daily process of clinging to uplifting thoughts from self-help books and my Bible. In the daytime, when anxiety gripped my soul, I would look at a small gold frame sitting on my desk and find strength in the scripture:

> **Fear not, for I am with you; do not look around you in terror and be dismayed, for I am your God.**
>
> **—Isaiah 41:10**

I scribbled scriptures on small pieces of paper. When I was overwhelmed with fear and despair, I read my stack of scriptures and I claimed God's promises to protect me from my psychotic, abusive enemy. Bedtime was the worst part of my daily survival. I laid in my bed at night, alone and despondent, pleading to fall asleep, but instead tossing and turning, while my digital bedside clock ticked away the hours. I was terrified of what was going to happen to me. I curled up under my sheet and blanket, I clutched my NIV Bible next to my heart, and I prayed to escape my excruciating heartache in slumber.

One night I sought comfort in Joel Osteen's book, *Your Best Life Now.*

Joel wrote, "If we continue to dwell on our past disappointments we will block God's blessings in our lives today." To illustrate he told the familiar biblical story of God's beloved prophet Samuel. I will share my abridged version.

> *The prophet Samuel had been the one to anoint Saul as the first king over Israel. But it wasn't long after Saul became king that he disobeyed the Lord. In fact, his behavior was so displeasing to God, that God disowned Saul. Samuel was devastated over Saul's moral failure, as well as his failure as a spiritual leader. Samuel went into seclusion for years to grieve. God observed Samuel's extended grief. He came to Samuel and He said, "How long will you mourn for Saul?"*

My mind jolted and my heart jumped and in that supernatural moment, I grasped God's power and wisdom. How long, indeed, I thought. How long will I mourn for a man whose daily life's pleasure was to demean, ridicule and berate me?

"If we will quit mourning and get going," wrote Osteen, "God will show us a new, better beginning. And it is better than we can imagine."

That's right! I exclaimed. I gave Dr. Dirtbag over three years of my life. I endured a year in relationship hell with him. I suffered two years in mourning and healing from the abuse trauma he inflicted on me.

Enough! demanded My Woman Within.

My Woman Within shook her fist and screamed at me, Get up and get moving! God has a better plan for you! God has a fabulous writing and speaking career for you. He has new friendships, travel, business connections and social events waiting for you. He has a new home in Nashville prepared for you, with new faces, intellectual stimulation, and personal growth. He may even have a wonderful man who is waiting to share his life with you. But you will never experience any of this if you continue to dwell on the "what could've beens" and the "should've happeneds" of your past relationship. You will never experience God's divine plan if you continue to grieve over the illusion of a man that never existed.

"Your best days are not behind you. They're in front of you," said Osteen.

And just like that, as Samuel had done before me—I picked myself up—I wiped the tears from my eyes—and I embraced God's miraculous healing power. There was but one thing left for me to do to receive God's blessings—I had to forgive my oppressor.

5 Stages of Grief

> **The process of healing and growth is not the smooth progression many people assume. It's more a "lightning bolt full of ups and downs, progressions and regressions, dramatic leaps and depressing backslides." Knowing this can help you realize, the healing process is under way.**
>
> ***—How to Survive the Loss of a Love***

Denial: "It's a bad dream. This can't be happening to me."

Divorce, the loss of a lover, or the death of a loved one leaves us feeling devastated, dazed, frightened and numb. You're in shock at what has happened to you. Your heart rejects the truth. "This can't be real," you cry. You are unable to accept your loss. You cling to the hope that you will eventually reconcile with your partner; that your boyfriend or husband will show up on your doorstep full of remorse. You somehow expect your deceased partner to magically appear, because you can't grasp the finality of his death. Denying the finality of your relationship delays the inevitable; meanwhile, you are stuck in a state of denial and unhappiness.

Anger: "Why is this happening? I don't deserve this."

The numbing effects of denial begin to thaw, and your pain emerges. But you are not ready to accept the reality of the loss. Your intense emotions are deflected, redirected and expressed as anger. You are angry at your husband or boyfriend for their betrayal. You're angry at God, the doctors and your deceased partner for leaving you. You need to blame someone for the injustice that was done to you, and you project your resentment and anger onto anyone who crosses your path. Anger is a sign of underlying emotional issues. You must feel the pain to diffuse your pent up and misdirected anger.

Bargaining: "Please stop the pain. I'm sorry. I promise to do better."

You plead with God, you bargain with yourself, and you beg your ex to take you back to avoid the painful reality of your loss. You may irrationally blame yourself; you think, "If only I had said or done something differently." You offer up prayers to your Higher Power, hoping that He will somehow intercede your circumstances. You fantasize that things will go back to the way they were. You hope to run into your ex at the store, gym, coffee shop or a party. You invent an emergency to get his attention, or you find an excuse to go to his home, hoping that when he sees you his passion for you will rekindle. If you are dealing with an abusive or emotionally unresponsive partner, you may lower your standards, convince yourself to accept less in the relationship, be less demanding, and even turn a blind eye to his hurtful behavior—if only he would come back to you. But your partner continues to lie, rebuke and reject you, your attempts to change things are futile, and you sink deeper into depression.

Depression: "I've lost interest in everything. All I want to do is sleep."

Extreme sadness, guilt, fear and regret are part of the grieving process. You have feelings of despair, emptiness, yearning and intense loneliness. You cry a lot and uncontrollably. You may have weight loss, weight gain, panic or anxiety attacks, insomnia, or acute fatigue. You may drink in excess. Your mind is foggy and your body feels sluggish causing you to crave sleep and isolation. You are unable to function at work, home or school, or perform normal daily activities. You shut out your friends and family. You feel guilty about your failed relationship or divorce, thinking you could have done something to prevent it. You may feel guilty for feeling relief when a partner dies after a long and difficult illness. The loss of a partner can trigger your fears. You worry about your future without your boyfriend or husband. You feel worthless, helpless and hopeless. You may feel you have nothing to live for, and you may have thoughts of suicide. If this happens, you need to seek professional help.

Acceptance: "It still hurts, but I know I'll be okay."

You come to terms with the loss of your relationship: the loss of his love, security and companionship, and your future together. You finally realize you are blessed to be free of your lying, abusive boyfriend. You accept the fact that your good-for-nothing husband ran off with a 29-year-old waitress. And although your heart aches daily, you surrender to the death of your partner. You may still have feelings of guilt and anger, but you accept the reality of your situation. You acknowledge that your relationship is over, your partner is no longer a part of your life, and you begin living life as an independent individual.

There is no "right way" to grieve; but resisting the grieving process prolongs the process of healing. Give yourself permission to have a bad day, to momentarily withdraw from the world to cry and feel anger. Maintain relationships with your friends and family; embrace their help and goodwill. Express your heartbreak, loneliness and fear to a trusted friend. Seek counseling, group therapy and medical services. Read spiritual, inspirational and grief recovery books. Go to church. Journal your feelings to express your inner conflict. Get out of the house regularly; meet a friend for coffee, dinner or a movie. Exercise, enroll in a new Pilates class, jog in a new neighborhood, take a walk in the sunshine. Surround yourself with things that are alive: a new plant, a puppy, a kitten or a guppy, and fresh flowers. Stop playing the love tunes and play uplifting music. Postpone dating until you are emotionally stable.

7 Forgiveness: The Final Emotion

When we hang on to anger, resentment and hate—we are the loser.

Eckard Tolle defines grievance as the "baggage of old thought and emotion."

After a while it wasn't the grieving which hopelessly tied me to the hurtful memory of Dr. Dirtbag. It was the resentment, rage and bitterness I harbored towards him that kept me emotionally crippled. I was angry at his deception and cruel abuse. I was angry at him for dumping me for Bimbo. I hated Bimbo for being the new woman in his life. I hated both of them because they had each other, and I had no one.

I drove myself crazy thinking about Dr. Dirtbag and Bimbo. During the day my mind obsessed, imagining them together, him doting over her, him lying next to her in bed and having sex with her. I knew their honeymoon existence wouldn't last. I envisioned their dream-like bliss deteriorating into mistrust, anger and brutal quarrels—just as it had for Dr. Dirtbag and me. At night, when I finally fell asleep, my obsessive thoughts manifested in disturbing, neurotic nightmares in which Dr. Dirtbag cold-heartedly trashed me to be with Bimbo—*night after night after night after night.*

Let's face it—women think about vengeful acts against the men who have wronged them. My girlfriend drilled holes in her cheating boyfriend's truck tires and filled his truck door locks with super glue. Another woman I knew lied about her estranged husband, telling everyone she divorced him because she found him in bed with another woman.

I enjoyed fantasizing of ways to get my revenge on Dr. Dirtbag. I considered sending him a phony Facebook friend request so I could keep tabs on his activities. I knew the password to his email account. I went into his emails and I discovered a receipt for the moissanite engagement ring he purchased for Bimbo. No doubt he told her it was worth a fortune. I considered sending Bimbo the receipt for her gaudy-large counterfeit stone. It would have certainly been amusing to post Dr. Dirtbag's social security number on the internet as a public commodity. I restrained myself from emailing Bimbo and posting Dr. Dirtbag's social security number. Lucky for him, I had a squirrel-size conscience.

It took a lot of time, effort and negative energy for me to fantasize, obsess and hate Dr. Dirtbag and Bimbo. I'm certain that's why I lost 10 pounds. I was stuck in a constant state of anger, denial, grief and panic attacks because of my inability—*no*, because of my unwillingness to forgive Dr. Dirtbag.

> **Forgiving the person who hurt you is a choice, an act of obedience to God . . . The longer you hold on to that abuse, betrayal, rejection, or injustice, the farther you'll be from your destiny.**
>
> **—Joyce Meyer**

The question was not should I forgive Dr. Dirtbag—but would I make the choice to forgive him?

And so I began to recite in prayer, *"I forgive him. I forgive him. I forgive him. I forgive Dr. Dirtbag for lying to me, unmercifully abusing me and trashing me for another woman. I don't feel it in my heart, but out of obedience to You, Lord, I forgive this worthless good-for-nothing douchebag. Amen."*

The Poison of Unforgiveness

If you love me you'll give me gifts and money.

Forty-year-old Nicole viewed her world through a cloud of insecurity, animosity and a fear of abandonment. Her adult relationship with her mother was: Give me money and I will forgive you for my hurtful upbringing. Deny me, and I will hate you and punish you.

Nicole never knew her biological father. Born outside of marriage, her father disappeared when she was a month old. Her 22-year-old mother Eva raised her single-handedly. When Nicole was 7, her mother began dating Carl. Carl presented himself as a decent husband and a good father. He attended Nicole's spelling bees and her sporting events. He took her to school and he picked her up in the afternoons. Eva was lonely and financially strapped. She wanted a husband and she wanted Nicole to have a father, and so she married Carl. Carl verbally and physically assaulted Eva and he squandered his paychecks in bars. He had a hair-trigger temper. He would get mad at Nicole and lunge at her with his closed fist. Eva threw herself in front her husband to shield her young daughter from his assault. Eva knew Carl's behavior towards Nicole was severe and unacceptable, but her own father walloped her upside the head when she misbehaved as a child. She believed Carl's behavior was typical of an angry father.

At age 7, blue-eyed, blonde Nicole was bubbly, energetic and inquisitive. A year after her mother married Carl, Nicole's personality changed. She was timid, hypersensitive and withdrawn. She demanded her mother's attention and she threw wailing temper tantrums.

In high school Nicole was unmanageable and defiant; her anger was combustible and uncontrollable. She isolated herself in her bedroom and she repeatedly ran away from home to her grandmother's house. Eva took Nicole to counseling. Her stepdad Carl never missed a session. Eva thought he was a caring father. The counselor advised

Eva that her daughter was on drugs. Eva put Nicole in a 6-month rehabilitation program and she rode out Nicole's teen years in an armored truck.

Nicole went to live with her grandmother in her high school senior year. Eva divorced Carl after 10 years of an abusive marriage. Nicole turned 20; her single life was chaotic and unstable. She worked nights and weekends as a waitress, she existed on her tips, she partied late hours and she went through a series of toxic, romantic relationships. Nicole's relationship with her mother was estranged and explosive. Eva's conversations with Nicole were strained and volatile; if Eva said or did something Nicole didn't like, Nicole would erupt into an irrational, blaming tirade and banish her mother from her life for months, and even years. Eva eventually learned to keep her mouth shut.

As an adult, Nicole seemed to exist in a constant state of high alert, expecting someone to criticize her, mistreat her or reject her. Her aura was tense, her eyes were worried and her brow was permanently knitted. She seemed to be mad at the world. Nicole's life's equation was: money equals love, happiness and security.

At age 30, Nicole married a successful investment broker, had two beautiful children and she swore she would be a good mom to her son and daughter. She insisted on being a stay-at-home mom. She strived to create a home of warmth and comfort, while presenting an enviable lifestyle to the outside world. The truth was: Nicole spent money way beyond her husband's means. She spent $250,000.00 remodeling and decorating their $300,000.00 house. She insisted that her husband buy her expensive jewelry and her family wore nothing but high-end designer clothes. They ate out constantly, they drank top shelf booze, smoked pot and they threw frequent, elaborate soirees. They maxed out their credit cards, owning over $200,000.00. They had first and second mortgages on their home. They constantly paid bank overdraft fees. Nicole borrowed money from her mother to buy booze and food for her pool party.

And then, without warning, Nicole's facade crumbled. Her husband lost his job for insider trading.

Carl would never again work in the financial industry. His parents paid his $25,000.00 attorney fees, saving him from jail time. He eventually got a job as a car salesman, earning a driblet of his stock broker salary. They sold their over-priced home at a substantial loss, hocked their expensive jewelry, filed bankruptcy, and they moved into a modest 3-bedroom house. And even though they were desperate for money, Nicole insisted that she continue to be a stay-at-home mom. Nicole and her husband struggled to make ends meet. Nicole continued to mismanage Carl's paychecks with frivolous spending, and she and her husband drank, smoked dope and partied hearty.

> **Forgiveness is what you do for yourself, not for other people.**
>
> **–Dr. Phil McGraw**

Nicole's was in her 30s when she told her mother the source of her inner conflict. She said her stepdad Carl had secretly abused her as a child. When Eva wasn't looking, he would flash menacing looks at Nicole. He told Nicole she was fat and ugly and no one wanted her. When Eva was at work, or away from the home, he would belittle, ridicule and bully Nicole. At night he would open her bedroom door, evade her space and threaten to whip her with his belt if she didn't turn out her light and go the bed. He would drive Nicole to school and when this precious little girl slid out of his truck, he told her, "Everybody hates you. Have a good day."

Eva was stunned. Tears welled up in her eyes. She looked at her grown daughter and I said, "I didn't know. Why didn't you tell me?"

"I was afraid to tell you," Nicole said. "He threatened me. He told me if I caused problems between you and him, he would make my life miserable and you would send me to grandmother's to live."

Eva suffered extreme guilt for Nicole never having a father, and she grieved the fact that she was blind to her ex-husband's clandestine abuse of Nicole as a child. Nicole hated her mother for never knowing her biological father, and she harbored deep-seeded angry toward her mother for not protecting her from her abusive stepfather.

Nicole adamantly blamed her mother for all her problems. She used her hurtful childhood and her down-and-out circumstances to extort money from her mother. There was always a tragic story of why she needed money: Her electricity was turned off. She didn't have money to buy groceries. She only had $17.00 in her checking account and her husband didn't get paid until next week. Her 12-year-old son had holes in his soccer shoes. Her 9-year-old daughter had to have a $200.00 American doll for her birthday. The brakes on her car were scraping. IRS was going to garnish her husband's paycheck. Nicole cried to her mother, "I don't have anyone to help me. I feel so isolated. I sleep all the time because I'm depressed. I've had thoughts of suicide."

Nicole used her two children as a tool of manipulation and punishment against her mother. If her mother bought into her sob stories and wired her money, she would allow Eva to talk to her grandchildren on the telephone and visit them in their home several states away at Christmas and holidays. If Eva refused to give Nicole money, Nicole would verbally assault her mother and deny her the right to talk to her grandchildren or participate in their lives.

Eva was not a rich woman; at age 62, she lived off of her social security and a moderate retirement account. Through the years Eva gave her daughter over $25,000.00 to bail her and her husband out of debt. No matter how much money Eva sent Nicole, it was never enough.

Eva finally denied Nicole a sizable so-called loan. Nicole angrily hung up the phone on her mother, and then she texted Eva, saying, "I hate you, you fucking self-absorbed bitch, you only care about yourself. I hope you get cancer and die a painful death and you rot in hell. I don't want my children to have anything to do with you. Don't bother to text back, I am blocking your phone and emails."

Eva erected a wall to protect her heart.

No amount of apologies, atonement or money could heal Eva's relationship with her daughter. Nicole's unwillingness to forgive her mother poisoned her children, damaged her relationship with her husband, and robbed her of the three things she wanted and needed most in life: love, happiness and security.

Until Nicole embraces her hurtful past, goes through the grieving and healing process, forgives her mother and takes responsibility for her own life, she will continue to blame everyone and everything for her sad station in life.

Resentment and anger harm you more than it ever harms the person that hurt you.

My best friend forever, Mona (not her real name), trashed me for a married man. When I cautioned her about dating him, she erupted in a histrionic fit of tears. She told me her married man made her feel beautiful and I didn't understand. Mona excommunicated me from her life to be with her cheating dirtbag. I was heartbroken. Mona was the sister I never had. She was my fun friend, my best friend and my sole confidante. Mona was my female soulmate.

A year later, Mona's married guy dumped her (as adulterous married men often do). I was secretly avenged at her predictable, distraught situation. Several months later I ran into Mona at one our hangouts. We talked. She confided in me that her married man broke her heart. I felt sorry for her and I consoled her. I forgave her for trashing me.

We resumed our close relationship—and a month later, Mona again knifed me in the back by going to a movie and dinner with a man I was quasi-dating. I confronted her. She told me they were just friends. I loved her. I minimized her hurtful behavior, and I again forgave her.

Months passed and Mona again betrayed me by entertaining the amorous advances of my newest ex-boyfriend, who I was openly trying to win back his heart.

That was the last straw. I hardened my heart to Mona. I privately discredited her to several of my friends. I grieved the loss of a friend I loved dearly.

Mona moved out of state and I lost contact with her. When I thought about her, I oozed bitterness and resentment. A year later Mona texted me a half-apology. I rebuffed her apology, filed my anger away and I went on with my life.

Four years passed. Mona and I stumbled on to each other on Facebook and we friended one another. I had mixed feelings. Part of me didn't trust her. Part of me still resented her. And the larger part of me still loved her and wanted to forgive her for hurting me.

I thought about my past life. When I was emotionally stunted and self-absorbed with my problems. Mona and I were the same. She struggled with low self-worth issues. She believed she needed a man to survive and she committed to men who were self-serving and abusive. The difference between us was: I was 13 years older than Mona and I had somewhat completed my personal work. Mona had just begun to heal her wounded inner child.

Mona and I kept in touch with each other on Facebook, and months later I found myself visiting her city on business. She texted me asking to see me and we met for lunch. I realized that Mona's betrayal was not intentional. She did what she thought she had to do at the time, to make her world work.

I forgave Mona. The animosity and mistrust I felt toward her for four years dissipated. And I renewed my friendship with my kindred spirit.

How Could I Forgive Someone Who Hurt Me So Deeply?

Sometimes the only way to get closure is to be validated by the "other woman."

Grasping the reality of a destructive, abusive relationship can be extremely difficult. It is beyond our understanding that a man, who claims to love you more than life, would intentionally harm you. If your boyfriend or husband constantly tells you that you are the problem and the instigator of all your arguments, you may need affirmation that he is, in fact, the "bad guy" to help you sever the bond you feel for your abuser.

I struggled for a year with the caustic thoughts I had for Dr. Dirtbag and Bimbo. I wanted their relationship to crumble into a heap of futile, bitter ashes, just as my relationship with him had. I warned Bimbo about Dr. Dirtbag's deceptive, malign behavior. Against my warning, she married him. I was certain his lethal behavior would eventually alienate and destroy her. Call me sick and twisted, but it soothed my heartbreak to write the fantasy demise of their relationship.

Bimbo Finally Calls Me

I am sure one day I'll hear from Bimbo—after Dr. Dirtbag has stripped her of her joy, hope and security, she'll call or email me in search of answers. She'll want to know why her once dream-like relationship with him transformed into a hellish, abusive nightmare—seemingly overnight. By then his verbal battering will have taken its toll on her. Her thinking will be foggy and her ability to reason will be clouded. She'll ask me, "Am I over-reacting to David's covert punishing remarks? Am I the one who is at fault for all of our relationship problems—like he says I am? I don't know any more," she'll say. "My life with him is a distorted, horrible dream."

I will listen to Bimbo whine and cry and complain about Dr. Dirtbag's calculated, pernicious treatment of her, and then I'll tell her, "I warned you about David. I told you he was a lying, abusive bastard, but you wanted him to be real. You wanted to marry a doctor who would dote over you, spend money on you, and take care of you. You ignored my warning, you closed your eyes to his obvious deceptive, boasting, drunken, berating behavior, and you allowed him into your life—just as I did years ago."

I will peer into Bimbo's woeful eyes and I will see her skepticism and her last shred of hope. I will say to her, "What? Did you think you were more special than me? Did you think you were a better woman than me? Did you truly believe he loved you more than me? I was his blonde baby—the love of his life. And yet he lied to me, abused me, and cheated on me with you. What he did to me—he will certainly do worse to you."

And then I will laugh and say, "Oh, I get it... you believed the lies he told you about me, as I believed the lies he told me about his ex-wife. You believed him when he claimed I was a nut case. I was severely depressed. I had a major hormonal imbalance, and like his ex-wife, I was in therapy and heavily medicated. And did he also tell you, as he told me about his ex-wife, that I was hateful and demanding, and that I spent his money as if it grew on trees? And that I started every fight, and he could never do anything to please me—no matter how hard he tried?

"Yes, it's true, his ex-wife stayed in bed with severe depression for the last three years of their marriage—and now I know why—he battered her into submission. And it's true, I did throw a wine glass at Dr. Dirtbag one evening when he kept berating me, on and on and on, for over an hour he maliciously pushed me to the edge until I exploded in a fit of anger and hurled my glass at him, cutting his arm."

Bimbo's sad, hollow eyes will tell me she knows I'm telling the truth—but I'm not finished turning the knife.

"Oh, Bimbo, I understand why you stayed with Dr. Dirtbag after each abusive event, and how he sucked you back into his caustic relationship with his token gifts and worthless promises to stop lying, drinking and verbally abusing you. And how, with pitiful, pleading crocodile tears streaming down his hangdog face, he would declare his undying love and devotion for you, beg you for another chance, so he could regain control of your mind, body and soul.

"Yes, Dr. Dirtbag was an extraordinary liar. He was logical, compelling and exceedingly convincing. Rarely, if ever, can you disprove his devious, distorted reality. And no matter how horrible his offense was, he would somehow elicit our forgiveness, while we sank deeper into a relationship that was gradually destroying us."

Tears will trickle down Bimbo's cheeks and I'll look at her, part in self-gratification because she got what she deserved for coming between Dr. Dirtbag and me, and part in compassion, knowing the pain she's suffered at his hands. And I'll tell her, "Now, Bimbo, you are like me and his ex-wife; you're distraught, you're demoralized, and your heart is full of rage for the abuse he has so cruelly heaped upon you. But the ultimate betrayal will be when he is finally finished with you, he will dump you for another woman, and he will blame you and lie about you to his family and friends. I know—because I also endured his cruelty."

And then I will hand her my book, Never Date a Dead Animal, *smile sweetly and say, "Here, Bimbo, read this, you're gonna need it."*

Finally—my heart was clear.

Warning: When an ex-girlfriend or ex-wife tells you that her ex-man is a lying, controlling, cheating, abusive sociopath, the odds are—*she's telling the truth!*

Fake It Till You Make It

I can't say that I ever forgave Dr. Dirtbag for his treacherous behavior against me. I prayed that I would forgive him. And I had moments when I felt leniency and compassion for him, but I just couldn't seem to shake the animosity I felt for him.

A year passed and I thought less and less about Dr. Dirtbag. My anger subsided. The pain and resentment I felt towards him began to fade. I no longer wished ill-will toward Bimbo. My emotional wounds began to heal. I moved on with my life, and Dr. Dirtbag seemed a distant, unpleasant memory. And then one day, I realized I was again full of joy, hope, love and vibrancy.

Maybe that's what forgiveness feels like. I don't hate him. I don't love him. I don't like or dislike him. There's no feeling—because I just didn't care anymore.

Part Two

Power Up

For I know the plans I have for you, declares the Lord, plans to prosper you and not to harm you, plans to give you hope and a future.

—Jeremiah 29:11 NIV

8 Our Power Within

What was meant to be a stumbling block turned into a victory.

Logic, Intuition and Positive Attitude are a woman's three most powerful, personal resources.

- Logic is the foundation of a woman's wisdom.
- Intuition is her supernatural knowing.
- A Positive Attitude is her aura of influence.

The problem is, girlfriends, our emotions dilute our ability to reason, we mistrust our gut instincts, and our negative attitudes work against us.

As women I believe we know in our guts the right things to say and do when it comes to men, dating and relationships. Most of it is common sense. *Right?*

Single women—we know we're not supposed to chase a man, talk negatively about our ex-boyfriend-husband, blab our personal problems, drink too much, or sleep with a man on the first (or second) date. *Right?*

Why then do we do it?

I contend that, as single women, we do recognize the warning signs of a man's unreliable, discourteous and deceitful behavior, and we suspect him to be a potentially undesirable partner.

Why then do we suddenly become deaf, blind and stupid to a man's obvious, disrespectful behavior, continue to date him, fall in love with and commit to him when our internal voice screams,

"Run! Run! For pity's sake! Grab your Chanel Boy Bag and run for your life!"

Married and committed women, I believe we sense when a man is distorting the facts, denying the truth, twisting our words (it's called crazy-making), and he unjustly blames us, or he discounts our worth as a human being. We're not stupid! We know the truth!

> *WHY* then are we unable to stand up to a man's wounding behavior?
>
> *WHY* are we unable to challenge his vague explanations and cock-and-bull stories?
>
> *WHY* are we unable to accept the reality of his hurtful behavior?
>
> *WHY* is it so hard for us to leave an emotionally dead, lying, cheating, abusive man?

Time to Separate the Women From the Wimpy, Whiny Girls

For thirty years I sought an understanding of men, dating and relationships. The answer I found was this: **Logic**, **Intuition** and a **Positive Attitude** are the quintessence of a woman's personal power. Working in cohesion, these three attributes will alter the way you interpret information. It will change the way you evaluate people and situations. It will shift the way you interact and express yourself to others.

- When I learned to base my decisions on facts and reality, instead of my unpredictable, irrational emotions, my understanding of relationships exploded.
- When I began to trust and act upon my intuitive instincts, instead of being influenced by what someone told me, my wisdom blossomed.

- When I said or did what was in my best interest, not in the interest of holding on to a man or to avoid his criticism and condemnation, my confidence soared.
- When I replaced my narrow-minded, judgmental attitudes with an accepting, affirming, open-mindset, my personal power magnified.

My Woman Within had another argument with her lizard boyfriend. She confronted him for flirting with the buxom, lipo-lip blonde at the Super Bowl party. He got mad at My Woman Within; he told her she was over-reacting and that she was always trying to start a fight and he punished her by not calling her the following day.

My Woman Within is drained from dodging her boyfriend's demeaning accusations, and she's tired of kowtowing to his angry outbursts. She's sick of feeling confused and distraught. She's tired of questioning the truth about his hurtful behavior. She's weary of doubting her self-worth. She's tired of feeling oppressed, exploited and helpless in life.

I asked My Woman Within:

Are you applying logic to the situation?

Are you trusting your gut instincts?

Are you thinking with a positive mindset?

Logic, **Intuition** and a **Positive Attitude**—therein lies your wisdom, personal power and relationship understanding.

9 Logic: The Cornerstone of Sound Judgment

"Choose your life's mate carefully. From this one decision will come 90% of all your happiness or misery."

—H. Jackson Brown, Jr.

Life is a series of decisions. Some decisions are simple and inconsequential: Which designer shoes will you wear to the party tonight? Where will you go on vacation? What will you eat for dinner? What color will you dye your hair? These everyday choices have fleeting effects on our lives. If your Jessica Simpson peep-toe high heels wore blisters on your feet at the party, you won't wear them again. If you didn't have a good time in Aruba, you won't go back. If you didn't enjoy your sushi, next time you'll order a steak well done. If you don't like orange hair, you'll go to a different hair stylist. No harm. No foul. These routine decisions gone amiss have uncomplicated remedies. Other important decisions, however, can have permanent, long-suffering effects on our lives.

Bad relationship decisions occur when a woman's emotions rule her life.

If there is one thing I learned from being with Dr. Dirtbag, it was to pay attention to the warning signs of a man's dysfunctional, harmful behavior, and consider the consequences of an impulsive relationship with him.

When I dated Dr. Dirtbag I wanted to be in love, and I wanted to marry a doctor who would whisk me away and give me a happily-ever-after life. I ignored rational reasoning that his behavior was odd and iffy. I slept with him early in the relationship. I made excuses for his pretentious, ambiguous behavior. I chose to stay with him after he gave me ample reason to doubt his stability and moral character. I paid dearly for ignoring my gut instinct that Dr. Dirtbag was bad news.

Logic Backs Up What Our Intuition Suspects

Logic is the study of facts, probability and reasoning. It's what helps us to distinguish correct reasoning from poor reasoning. Deductive reasoning is using what we know to ascertain that which we don't know.

For example: All bachelors are single. Robert is single. Hence, Robert is a bachelor.

Let's look at that in dating and relationship terms:

> If a man is discourteous or impolite to those around him, he will also be rude and inconsiderate to you.
>
> If a man is quick-tempered and insulting to others, he will demean and disrespect you.
>
> If a man is evasive, his facts don't match up or he exaggerates the truth to his friends or family, he will lie and deceive you.
>
> If a man is unpredictable and he does not follow through on his spoken word, he will be irresponsible, unreliable and untrustworthy in a relationship with you.
>
> If a man is selfish and tight-fisted with his children and family, he will be a tightwad with you and resent your spending.

If the man you are dating shows great interest in his hobbies and interests, but he hedges on your requests to dine out, go to the theatre or go on a vacation, he will be insensitive and indifferent to your wants and needs in a relationship.

If a man bad-mouths his ex-wife or ex-girlfriend, and he denies all responsibility in his failed relationships, he will unfairly blame, criticize and condemn you.

If a man is non-communicating while dating him, he will be withdrawn, tight-lipped and withholding in your relationship.

If a man is jealous and controlling in the beginning of a relationship, he will be super-controlling and abusive when you commit to or marry him.

Girlfriends, what part of this do we not understand? Facts don't lie—dysfunctional men do.

Lesson in Logic: If he cheats on his wife with you, when the stars line up just right, he will also cheat on you.

Diane was the epitome of a needy, co-dependent woman desperately looking for love. A divorced, 42-year-old mother of a 7-year-old daughter, she earned a mediocre salary and her deadbeat ex-husband gave her no support. She was emotionally exhausted from the demands of her career and being a single mom. Her lonely, desperate aura scared off the decent men she dated.

Diane was introduced to Nate, a tall, rugged construction worker, who had recently started a home building business. Nate bought a high-dollar crew-cab pickup truck, he leased a commercial office building, and he boasted of the wealth he expected to earn in the coming years. Diane fell fast and hard for Nate, they had sex—and the lies and turmoil began.

Nate told Diane his ex-wife was a belligerent, crazed bitch whose meddling, rich parents destroyed his marriage. His ex-wife got custody of his 4-year-old son, she moved back home with her mommy and daddy and Nate remained in the family home.

Diane felt sorry for Nate and she took to "mothering" him. She made sure his favorite beer was always in her refrigerator. She cooked dinner for him most every night. They had spontaneous, combustible sex. She took him shopping for clothes (even though she couldn't afford it) because he never seemed to wear a decent shirt or jeans—and she, of course, laundered his new duds.

Nate practically lived at Diane's modest two-bedroom apartment. He met her friends and family. He went grocery shopping with her, and he drove her 7-year-old daughter to school. He brought his young son to Diane's apartment to play with her daughter. At bedtime he took his son home to his ex-wife.

From the beginning Nate was habitually and horribly late arriving at Diane's apartment. When he took his son home to his ex-wife (only fifteen miles away), he told Diane he would be back in 30 minutes, and then he would disappear for hours; sometimes he didn't return to Diane's apartment until daybreak. He didn't call to explain, and he wouldn't answer his phone. Diane laid awake all night, tossing and turning, worrying, imagining he was in a fatal car crash, or robbed and stabbed, or worse yet, the ex-wife-bitch had drugged him and buried him alive in his new designer threads. When Nate did reappear, Diane's stomach was a mangled, knotted mess.

Nate told a different story every time he went MIA. He told Diane he got in a knock-down-drag-out fight with his ex-wife-bitch and he went home to "cool off." He took his son home, tucked him into bed, and while reading him a bedtime story, he fell asleep. His brother was taken to the emergency room. His mom fell and hurt herself. The burglar alarm went off at his office building. He ran out of gas. He had a brain seizure. Despite Nate's outrageous, untrustworthy behavior, Diane bought his excuses and she believed his stories that his ex-wife was the culprit.

Months passed. Diane and Nate became engaged, his vanishing acts and flimsy excuses continued—until one morning the irate ex-wife-bitch showed up banging on Diane's apartment door.

Turns out Dodge-Ram Nate was not divorced. He talked like a divorced man. He ran around like a divorced man. But he was categorically married. True, he and his wife fought like guerilla Pit Bulls. True, he wanted a divorce, but he couldn't afford to get one. Nevertheless, he lived at home with his wife and son, while simultaneously shacking up with Diane.

Her "need-a-man" cravings overpowered her intuition and common sense.

Nate weaseled his way back into Diane's desperate life, and for the next three years he claimed he was getting a divorce. For three years Diane wore herself out screaming, threatening and spying on Nate. So upsetting was his behavior she was hospitalized for an acute spastic colon.

Diane waited for Nate to get his divorce, and then she married him and had a baby. A year later his construction business went belly-up and his hot-shot Ram truck was repossessed.

Nate verbally and physically abused Diane. He quit paying their bills and their house went into foreclosure. And then one morning, in the wee hours, Diane awoke to find Nate strangely missing.

Don't be a ninny! Most married men who cheat don't intend to leave their wives. They may talk as if they want to, but in reality—*they don't.* Cheating husbands fear financial ruin—they're afraid if they ask for a divorce their wife will clean their clock and their bank account. Some wives are oblivious to their husband's infidelity—or they turn a blind eye to his cheating because they don't want a divorce. Either way, the wife is keeping the night light burning, and he knows if he loses you, he has her to go home to.

If a man repeatedly lies to you and you continue to date him, you can blame no one but yourself for your constipated, convulsing, inflamed, ulcerative intestines. *Can you say, Colectomy?*

Lesson in Logic: If he gets knee-walking drunk on the first date, he may not be able to drive you home.

I met Jeff on Match.com. He was the embodiment of a tall, blonde, blue-eyed, successful Carolina gentleman. His conversation was gracious. His Polo attire was yummy. The fine lines around his eyes and mouth and light grey flecks gracing his temple added extra appeal. He was obviously from wealth and breeding.

I met Jeff for lunch on our first date at a small boutique restaurant. He laughed at my stories, his smile was warm and his blue eyes twinkled. I was mildly intimated by his refined aura. I thought, this might be my man. He called me immediately after our lunch date and invited me to dine the following week.

I was nervous about meeting Jeff for dinner at a 4-star French restaurant. It took me two hours to perfect my hair and clothes. I felt first-class in my sleeveless, silver-trimmed black tunic top, tight black leggings, open-toe pumps and a pink silk pashmina draped over my shoulders. I studied myself in the full-length mirror and I smirked, *Bring it!*

Jeff was seated at a round white-linen table when I arrived at the restaurant, his forearm was resting on the table top, caressing a glass of red wine, his trousered legs stretched out casually in front of him. The bottle of merlot on the table was half empty. He stood, greeted me warmly, seated me with gentlemanly air, and poured me a glass of wine.

At lunch Jeff was stingy about the details of his personal life. At dinner, he repeatedly refilled his wine glass and he blabbed the sordid aspects of his life. He said his ex-wife gouged him financially, and that one of their fierce arguments landed them both in jail for disorderly conduct. He bad-mouthed his 28-year-old daughter, saying he booted her out of his house because she was a greedy, irresponsible alcoholic.

Jeff and I quickly finished our bottle of wine. He ordered a second and he continued to babble about his life and he expressed a sincere interest in me. We finished Merlot no. 2, and Jeff ordered a third bottle of wine with dessert. He was glassy-eyed and thick-tongued. And then—*whoosh*—out of the blue yonder, for no rational reason, he insulted me.

"You know, I would never date you seriously," he slurred. "You will never be a part of my life."

My Woman Within snapped to attention, *What the shut the front door is he talking about!*

I was stunned. Appalled. Dumbfounded. I jolted erect in my chair and I stared at him wide-eyed, wondering what the heck he was he talking about. I tossed my cloth napkin on the table, picked up my Brahmin clutch purse, threw my pashmina over my bare shoulder, bared my teeth and snarled, "Don't ever call me again!" and I stormed out of the restaurant, flashing my waiter an angry, indignant glance.

I left the restaurant that evening feeling bewildered and dejected. Jeff had wounded me, deeply. He made me feel like I was damaged and undesirable. Logically I knew different—but he triggered my past self-esteem demons. My logic told me, screw him!—but inside my heart was weeping.

Jeff phoned me two days later; I ignored his call and he didn't leave a message. The following day he sent me an email apologizing profusely, claiming his behavior was totally out of character. He blamed his unconscionable conduct on drinking too much wine, and he asked me for a chance to recompense his wrong. I ignored his email. Several days later he emailed me, again asking me to forgive him, pleading that I go out with him "one more time" to prove his integrity. I ignored that email—and then Jeff vanished into his wine cellar.

I rationalized Jeff's erratic behavior: I ascertained that he was a chronic, functioning alcoholic, suffering from a Jekyll and Hyde personality disorder. In the daytime, when he was sober, Jeff put on his Ralph Lauren seersucker suit and he presented himself to the universe as a charming, competent businessman running a successful company. But when the sun set, he uncorked a bottle of Chateau Cheval Blanc, and with a crystal goblet perched in his hand, he morphed into an angry, belligerent tyrant.

But why did Jeff verbally assault me at dinner when he obviously was enjoying my company?

Jeff jabbered endlessly about the skeletons in his closet. I laughed politely at his shenanigans, but inwardly I was shaking my head. When he realized that he had tarnished his chivalrous façade with his dirty laundry and obnoxious drinking behavior, he tried to regain his dignity by tearing me down.

Jeff's pleading emails told me that my abrupt and scathing departure was a serious blow to his image. His goal was not to recapture my interest so he could pursue a relationship with me—contraire! His underlying, self-serving motive was to get me to accept his apology to repair his injured, sagging ego. I felt it was important that Jeff experience the discomfort of his narcissistic, alcoholic behavior—and I ignored his pleas for clemency.

Left-Brain Girl VS. Right-Brain Girl

Scientific research shows that the two different sides, or hemispheres, of the brain are responsible for different manners of thinking. The left hemisphere of the brain controls the analytical, linear and verbal processes; while the right hemisphere governs the intuitive, nonlinear and nonverbal thought.

Let's apply this known scientific fact to women:

The left-brain girl is interested in logical, analytical thinking and accuracy. She is practical, perceptive, and she typically plays it safe. In her world, facts rule. She is "reality based."

The right-brain girl embraces aesthetics, feeling, creativity and random thinking. She can be impetuous and risk-taking. In her universe, imagination affects her sensibilities. She is "fantasy based."

How can two women see the world so differently? Let's take a look at their relationships.

The right brain girl is subjective. She looks at things as a whole. She's influenced by her feelings. Her thinking is modified by her emotionally biased belief system. She thinks and says:

> *I just love Benjamin. He's supportive, considerate and affectionate. He listens to my problems. He calls me before he comes over to see if I need him to bring wine or food. He surprises me with flowers. He's the best sex I've ever had. He is the most loving, sweetest man I've ever known—that is—when he's not drunk and berating me. But overall [as a whole] he's a great guy.*

The right-brain girl subconsciously (or knowingly) disregards the warning signs of a man's hurtful behavior. She dwells on his good traits, and she ignores and justifies the harmful aspects of his personality. She operates in denial, and she continues to date and impulsively falls in love with a man who is destined to maltreat her.

On the other hand, the left-brain girl separates the intellectual process into parts. She thinks and says:

> *I really do care for Gerald. He's intelligent and generous. He likes to travel. He maintains a nice home and he shares my love of antique shopping. He's attentive and romantic. He surprises me with thought-out gifts and he prepares candlelit dinners for us. The problem is, he loses his temper over small things. He flirts with other women and he talks derogatorily about his ex-girlfriend. I am concerned that he will be a relationship risk.*

Now, the left-brain girl is goo-goo ga-ga about her guy. The difference is: the left-brain girl is objective. She keeps her emotions and sexual desires in check. She considers the different facets of Gerald's conduct and personality. She weighs the pluses and minuses of a relationship with him. And then she makes a logical decision whether to continue dating him or cut bait and run. Her decisions are grounded in sound judgment.

As an adult, my emotionally-charged right brain always got me into trouble. My attraction to men was based on looks, feelings and impulse. I thought that was what love was all about; if the chemistry was there and a man seemed to fulfill my basic needs, I thought I was supposed to fall in love and hopefully get married. It never occurred to me to put a lid on my passion and consider the facts of a man's compatibility and overall character in the interest of relationship stability.

10 Logic, Men and Sex

Men are genetically wired to get a woman to say "yes."

In the early stages of dating a woman must keep a "clear head" to accurately read the undesirable traits in a man. That's not going to happen once she sleeps with him. Sex can overpower a woman's ability to make rational and wise decisions about a man. Sex can cause a woman to sugar-coat and deny the worst of character flaws in a man. Sex can cause a woman to emotionally bond with a man who has proven himself to be unworthy of her love and commitment.

When it comes to men, women can be downright foolish. We swoon for a man's twinkling electric-blue eyes, naughty smile and rippling biceps. We trip over ourselves trying to get the attention of the handsome man in the Armani suit. We are duped by the smooth-talk of the romance artist. We fall prey to the boasting, self-absorbed narcissist. Even sadder is, we turn our noses up at a man who is thoughtful, predictable and stable, while remaining loyal to a manipulating, controlling scumbag.

Prematurely sleeping with a man can cause a woman to lose her ability to reason.

The fast track to finding the right man is to avoid sexual involvement with the wrong man.

Sex is a heavy-duty, mind-altering drug. It changes the focus of a new relationship. It distorts the interpretation of a developing relationship. It skews the reality of an unhealthy relationship. Sex can hold a woman captive in a destructive, abusive relationship.

Arlo was a hot-blooded, 59-year-old Italian and successful casino businessman. His job as the Vice President of player development in casinos in Atlantic City, New Jersey and Chicago was the exciting life of the rich and famous. He relocated to St. Louis to manage a prestigious casino. There he saw Gina, an attractive 54-year-old blonde, dining with her girlfriends. Arlo sent word to Gina that he wanted to meet her. Gina was, of course, extremely flattered to be pursued by such a worldly man.

Gina met Arlo for a drink and he set out to wine and dine her in high style. Everyone in St. Louis seemed to know and revere Arlo. In the bars, bartenders and customers greeted him by name. When dining, the restaurant owners came to his table to pay homage and pick up his tab.

Arlo made Gina feel special and beautiful. He fed her constant compliments and he spoke of their future together. He sent his workers to her townhouse to help her move furniture. "Whatever you need, babydoll," he told Gina. "I'm here to help." He did and said all the right things to get past her bedroom door and underneath her sheets.

Gina was smitten by Arlo's attention and she was impressed with his notoriety. He treated her like a princess. She knew life with him would be a fairytale. She suspected that sex with him would be a rock-her-world experience. She struggled to keep her feet on the ground, but the sexual tension between them was overwhelming. Three weeks into dating Arlo she gave into to his seduction.

The "desire for sex" befuddles a woman's brain, making an insincere man look like a dream man.

Two days later they had a date to go motorcycle riding. When Gina arrived at his house, instead of his usual passionate, attentive behavior, he seemed distant and preoccupied. After the cycle ride, Arlo announced he couldn't be involved with her because he was relocating to Miami. This was no surprise to Gina; he had mentioned his intention to move to Florida, telling her he would fly her out to visit him. The shock was—his sudden apathetic, withdrawn behavior two days after she slept with him.

Logic check!

From the beginning Gina felt in her heart that Arlo wasn't the right guy for her. He boasted of wealth and possessions. He had a roving eye for women. He ran in fast circles and he was moving to Florida. He had a longstanding affair with a casino cocktail waitress while he was married. The truth was, Gina thought Arlo was odd-looking; he was short, his schnoz was sizable, and he smoked like a chimney. But, oh my goodness, he walked, talked and dressed like a Jersey Gambino boss, dripping in expensive jewelry, carrying a fat wallet and driving a black Mercedes SL convertible.

Gina was impressed by Arlo's extravagant lifestyle. She was hypnotized by his sweet talk. She was drugged by the "desire for sex." She slept with Arlo, and then staying true to his playboy form, he dumped Gina to chase a new skirt.

Gina got her heart broken and she was angry at herself for succumbing to a man she knew logically and intuitively was an unsuitable match.

A woman needs time to evaluate the man she is dating.

Desire and passion are extremely important to fully embrace the intimate aspects of a relationship—but when a woman surrenders to her sexual urges before she fully knows and trusts a man, she can waste years coping with the emotional issues from committing to the wrong man.

Women succumb to a man's seduction to fill their own emotional void, of wanting and needing a man's approval, validation and financial security, or they seek the love and acceptance from a father figure. Women have sex with a man believing sex will pull him into a committed relationship. But when she has sex with him, and the relationship does not move forward (or it ends abruptly), she feels deceived and devalued. Self-doubt sets in and she asks herself: *Did I do the wrong thing? Does he still respect me? Will I ever hear from him again?*

Like it or not, it's a woman's job to put-on-the-brakes when a man is moving too fast sexually. It is a woman's responsibility to stay in control of her conduct while curtailing his advances. It tells a man that she respects herself, she values her body, and if he wants the relationship to continue, it will require his attention, respect and commitment.

When a woman repeatedly accepts a dysfunctional man into her life, **the man is not the problem**, *regardless* of his shortcomings. The problem lies within her low self-esteem issues, her wishy-washy standards, and her unwillingness to hold out for the right man.

When logic and intuition come together, you will experience power and control in your life.

11 Can You Hold Your Ground With a Man?

"Here's all you have to know about men and women: women are crazy, men are stupid. And the main reason women are crazy is that men are stupid."

—George Carlin

Maybe you are in a relationship with a man who is blaming, controlling and unsympathetic. You can't reason with him because he's uncompromising and illogical. You can't win an argument with him because he twists your words and denies the truth. You can't expose his lies because he's a crafty, delusional narcissist who operates by his own improvised rules.

Women who reject logic, and rely solely on emotions, are left in the weak position of having to argue with their feelings.

Your most intelligent decisions are formed when logic and intuition work in agreement. In other words: Temper your right-brain urges with left-brain logic.

Dr. Dirtbag was a master at manipulating the conversation to make me look like I didn't know what I was talking about. God does answer prayers, for one day I nailed him for a bald-faced lie.

Dr. Dirtbag promised me the world if I would come back to him. One evening he was exceptionally creative in his manipulating trickery. He called me on my cell phone, exclaiming he had just gotten off the phone with his overseas banker and he had great financial news.

"What," I asked, skeptical, but curious. This was the first time he had spoken of an "overseas" bank account.

"I can't tell you over the phone," he claimed. "Someone may be listening, and it could undo what I'm trying to accomplish."

Paranoia was another one of Dr. Dirtbag's fabulous features.

Dr. Dirtbag was stonewalling me. I threatened to hang up on him if he didn't cease his charade. Reluctantly he told me his most preposterous story to date. He said he had a substantial Bahamian bank account that had been sequestered several years ago by the authorities. He claimed his money had just been released and he instructed his overseas banker to transfer $30 million dollars to a secure Swiss account. "I hope you're happy," he exclaimed, accusingly. "This money was for us, and if the authorities have this line tapped, we stand to lose it all."

"What?!?!?" I screeched through the phone. "Do you think I'm an idiot? You can reveal the intimate details of your bank account on the telephone with your overseas banker, but you can't talk about it with me for fear someone is listening in?!?! Are you insane?" I screamed.

To which Dr. Dirtbag sheepishly replied, "Oh yeah, I see what you mean," meaning: Oops, he got caught.

There was no $30 million dollars and there was no overseas bank account. It was another one of his neurotic ploys to (a) antagonize, frustrate and control me, and (b) try to get me back with a monetary carrot.

Dr. Dirtbag never admitted to his falsehood, but he knew he had been outmaneuvered with logic.

When a woman's emotions influence her life—all the more reason to apply logic.

Naomi, a naïve and emotional 54-year-old woman, ignored the flagrant warning signs that Kent was a fly-by-night, abusive douchebag.

Naomi dated Kent, a successful 64-year-old CFO, and within two weeks she gave her heart, body and soul to him. Naomi swooned at Kent's full-press courtship. He texted her throughout the day. He called her every night. He sent flowers to her office and mushy cards in the mail. He insinuated a Pandora bracelet, an engagement ring and other monetary perks. He tantalized Naomi with his talk about their future together.

Four weeks after they started dating, Kent abruptly moved to Kansas City for a promotion. He immediately started talking about getting married and going on a honeymoon, and moving Naomi to Kansas City to live in his new house. He advised Naomi to sell her house and her furniture. He insisted that they prepare their prenuptials.

Kent insisted that he and Naomi meet each other's relatives and grown children right away. Naomi's family and friends were duly impressed with Kent. He was gentlemanly and good-natured. He clowned with her son and son-in-laws, he schmoozed her mom, father and daughters, he coddled her pooches, and he indulged her grandchildren.

Naomi quickly changed her lifestyle to accommodate Kent. She shortchanged her girlfriends to talk to Kent for hours on the phone at night. She stopped drinking white wine and she exclusively drank his favorite red wine. Kent liked to cook and swing dance; she secretly took cooking and dancing lessons. Kent wanted to lose weight; Naomi (a size 6) quit eating desserts around him, and she enrolled in an expensive workout program.

Kent returned every six weeks to visit Naomi, and he flew Naomi to Kansas City on occasion to visit him. Naomi began to see a drastic change in Kent's personality. He was moody, hotheaded, blaming and arrogant. He would jab Naomi with a cutting remark, and if she confronted him, he would confuse and frustrate her, saying, "You always over-analyze things!" "You're over-reacting. I can't say anything without you getting mad at me!" "I don't remember saying that. If you say I said it, I guess I did." He made it sound as if he were empathizing with Naomi—when in fact, he was denying her reality.

Kent constantly had friction with his new job. He bad-mouthed his boss, and he was always at odds with his co-workers. Naomi blamed Kent's ill-temper on his job. "He doesn't mean it," she claimed. "His work is demanding. It's his business personality; he forgets he's talking to me and not one of the guys at work."

Kent was a cheapskate. He steered Naomi to the low-priced entrées on the restaurant menu, and he quibbled about the cost of everything. He pried into Naomi's finances and he criticized the way she spent her money. Kent made a handsome income and he had substantial IRA accounts; and yet, he told Naomi she would have to work until she was 62, or longer, so they would have enough money to retire.

He strung her along like a super-charged yo-yo.

When Naomi tried to discuss getting married and moving to Kansas City, Kent stonewalled her. His language was calculating, wavering and controlling. He told her he had trust issues. He wanted to be certain they were compatible. He wanted to pay off his house, boat and car and save more money for their retirement before they got married. Naomi defended Kent's wishy-washy, flip flop behavior, claiming she didn't want to push him because he had commitment issues.

Months passed. Naomi's relationship with Kent became more and more conflicting.

In the beginning Kent called Naomi long distance every morning before going to work, he texted her incessantly throughout the day and he called her every night, talking for hours. Time passed and she heard from him infrequently during the day, and he began calling her while driving home from work, saying he had a nerve-wracking day, he was exhausted and he was going to bed early—and then she wouldn't hear from him until the next day.

Kent disappeared for an entire weekend. His excuse was, "I was playing golf. You told me you were baby-sitting your grandson all weekend. I didn't want to bother you." Other times he used the hard-to-refute excuses, "My [phone] battery died." "I dropped my phone in the toilet. I had to get a new phone." When they were together he kept his phone on vibrate and he took it everywhere with him, even to the bathroom. When he answered his phone, he would take it outside to talk in private. Naomi's heart wrenched, but she accepted Kent's asinine excuses.

Within a matter of months Naomi's personality changed drastically. Before she dated Kent she was quick-witted, fun-loving and secure in who she was. Two months after she started dating him, she walked around in a constant state of bewilderment, tears and uncertainty. Five months after she started dating him, she was angry, despondent and fearful about her future.

Naomi called me one night, boohooing about Kent's mercurial, pernicious behavior.

"It sounds like he is trying to break up with you," I said.

Naomi agreed, and yet, she continued to date Kent and she pulled away from me.

Kent continued to babble about them getting married. He talked Naomi into listing her home for sale and selling her furniture—and then she called me bawling her eyes out.

"What's wrong?" I exclaimed, knowing full well, Kent had again stabbed her in the heart.

"We were making love. I went down on him, and after he had an orgasm, he rolled over in bed and he said, 'I don't feel right. This is against my Christian beliefs. I don't want to have sex with you again until we're married.' "

My blood boiled.

"Are you ******* kidding me! He's setting it up so he can date other women!" I screeched. "Or he's already dating someone else."

Naomi was devastated. She wailed, "What should I do?"

"Don't ask me if you don't want to know," I said plainly.

"No, tell me. I can't do this anymore."

"You need to tell that asshole to take a permanent hike. You've been unhappy ever since you've known him. You're miserable and he's destroying you."

"You're right," Naomi moaned.

Naomi sent Kent a breakup email, and he immediately called her. He told her that she was over-analyzing and over-reacting, and that plenty of people stopped having sex prior to getting married. Naomi accepted Kent's terms of a no-sex relationship, and she continued to date him.

A month later Kent gave Naomi a Cracker Jack diamond engagement ring. She sold her house and most of her furniture and Kent dumped her to pursue other women, telling Naomi they could still be friends.

Naomi had to quickly buy a townhouse to have somewhere to live. She went into a tailspin. And I lost a special girlfriend because she couldn't deal with the truth.

The lesson in logic I learned was: Don't get between a girlfriend and her asshole.

Logic of a Controlling, Non-Committal, Abusive Personality

- He pushes you for quick involvement.
- He has a history of failed relationships.
- He doesn't take responsibility for his hurtful behavior.
- He doesn't follow through on his spoken word.
- He tries to control your financial security.
- He punishes you by withholding sex, emotional intimacy and communication.

Seriously! Really! A 64-year-old man with a healthy hard-on suddenly wants to stop having sex because he unexpectedly develops a moral conscience?

More Logic About Men

The most frequent, complaining question I hear from single women is, "Why does a man not call back?"

Here's the scenario. You go out with a man. You had a wonderful time and you're certain he did too. He laughed easily. He talked openly. He listened attentively. He reached across the restaurant table to hold your hand. At the evening's end, he walked you to your door, gave you a lingering kiss, and he said, "I'll call you next week... let's get together." And then—*Don Juan Playa never called back.*

Here's the logic:

If you're sure you did nothing wrong, meaning you didn't talk too much. You didn't bad mouth your ex's or talk negatively about others. You didn't talk about expensive clothes, houses, automobiles or money. You weren't rude to the waiter. You didn't try too hard or act overly confident and cocky. You didn't reveal too much personal information. You didn't snort when you laughed. You didn't drink too much, trip and fall off your 5-inch Prada heels. You were instead, smiling, cheerful and present in the moment. You carried on an intelligent conversation that included his interests, sprinkled with genuine compliments. You displayed good manners. You spoke kindly of your friends and associates. You walked out of the restaurant standing upright in your amazing stilettos. Then the reality is—he's just not interested in you.

Consider this: Maybe it was bad timing. Maybe he's consumed in his career, or he's coping with problems at work or financial difficulties. Maybe the chemistry was not reciprocal; it was there for you, but it wasn't there for him (not a good reason to beat yourself up). Maybe he's healing from a past relationship or recovering from a recent divorce. Maybe he's concealing a girlfriend or a wife. Maybe there's something wrong with him, and not you!

There should be a relationship mandate which requires a man (or woman), who is on the rebound, to wear a bright orange neon sign across their forehead, flashing:

I Just Broke Up With The Love of My Life!

I dated a man in Memphis. He was tall, nice-looking and a superb dancer. On our first date he showed up at my front door with a single long-stem red rose and a black silk blindfold. Grinning, he told me he was taking me on a fantasy date to a surprise restaurant. I accepted the rose and I declined the blindfold.

We had a spectacular time at a downtown restaurant. He was intelligent, talkative, charming and attentive. After dinner he took me home. I invited him in for a nightcap, and we shared a half an hour of smoldering kisses. I saw him again the following week at a party at the Madison Hotel rooftop overlooking the Mississippi River. We spent the evening together talking, laughing and dancing. He drove me home after the party, and again the chemistry was—smoking. And then, poof! Copperfield vanished, never to be seen or heard from again.

I was completely bumfuzzled and hurt by his unexplained disappearance.

I moved to Houston. Three years later, I visited Memphis and I ran into Mr. Copperfield sitting at the bar in a neighborhood restaurant. We greeted one another and I sat down beside him to talk.

My rejected heart flip flopped. I still had a "thing" for the slippery Mr. Copperfield.

Over drinks Mr. Copperfield finally shared the truth about his mysterious disappearance. He told me before we dated, his girlfriend of six months had recently broken up with him. He saw her at the rooftop party with another man, and after driving me home and sucking my lips numb, he went home and he bawled for an hour because he was still in love with her.

Are you kidding me! I fantasized and lamented over a sniveling milquetoast for over a year, thinking I did something to run him off—when in reality—he was lovesick over a woman who dumped him.

Looking back I could have saved myself a lot of grief by merely asking Copperfield, "What the crap happened?" I believe he would have told me the truth, I would have accepted it and chalked him up to another dating casualty.

Kinsey had a similar story, with a different logical ending.

She got drunk, and a man does what a man does best with a drunk woman—he took advantage of her.

Kinsey loved her cocktails. She enjoyed wine because it helped her to relax and have fun at social gatherings. Martinis took the edge off when dating a new man. Short, sweet and Sangria—Kinsey enjoyed the soothing buzz and the instant party she got from liquor. The problem was: drinking lowered Kinsey's inhibitions and her resistance to a man's sexual advances.

Kinsey visited her girlfriend in Louisville. They were sitting at the bar in a downtown restaurant when an adorable man strolled in—Kinsey's and his eyes locked, the chemistry ignited and he slid onto the bar stool next to Kinsey.

Kinsey and Derrick were adorable together. They were both petite, stylish, good-looking Scandinavian blondes. Kinsey looked fetching in her strappy sundress with her long flaxen hair brushing against her tan bare shoulders. Derrick was all smiles and perfect white teeth; his eyes danced and his conversation was animated and attentive—and he was successful and rich.

Derrick was clearly into Kinsey. He was the most handsome, enchanting man Kinsey had met in years. They were both exuberant drinkers. They sat at the bar for nearly two hours talking and gulping down cocktails. Neither of them wanted the night to end. Kinsey followed Derrick to his golf course mansion and they imbibed more wine by his pool. Kinsey reasoned that she was too intoxicated and it was too late for her to drive to her girlfriend's house. She intended to only smooch with Derrick on his big fluffy king bed. She instead, as she always did when she drank, had sex with him.

The next day Kinsey drove home to Indianapolis. She worried whether or not she would ever hear from Derrick. To her delight, Derrick texted and called her constantly for two weeks. He expressed sweet nothings and he made plans to visit Kinsey the upcoming weekend. Kinsey was ecstatic. She cleaned her house and she changed the sheets on her bed. She went to the grocery store, she bought fresh flowers and she stocked up on beer and liquor. She made arrangements for her 14-year-old son to stay with his dad for the weekend. Derrick called Kinsey late Friday afternoon, telling her he had a problem at work and he would leave Saturday afternoon to come see her—and then, just like her Chianti—Derrick disappeared. Kinsey believed that she had once again screwed up her chances of being with a really great guy.

Three months passed and Kinsey returned to Louisville to attend her girlfriend's wedding. Kinsey downed two glasses of celebratory champagne and she texted Derrick, "I'm in town at a wedding. Wanted to say hi."

Derrick texted Kinsey back, "I want to see you."

Kinsey met Derrick at a waterfront restaurant. Sitting at an isolated table overlooking the Ohio River, Derrick gazed at Kinsey tenderly and said, "You've cut your hair. I like it."

Kinsey melted.

The waitress came to their table. Cindy ordered a gin and tonic. Derrick ordered iced tea.

"I've quit drinking," Derrick said calmly. "It caught up with me. I've been going to AA meetings. I had to change my lifestyle."

That's right—even with your naughty, foolish behavior, it's not always about you! Derrick canceled his trip to see Cindy because he was a newbie recovering alcoholic and he knew their weekend together would revolve around cocktails and a good time.

A final story in logic:

My girlfriend Tammy exchanged emails for six months with a man she met on Facebook. He kept saying he wanted to meet her, but he had yet to ask her out. Tammy complained, "He texts me several times a day. He acts like he is really interested in me, but he never asks me out. What's the deal?"

My eyes rolled back into their sockets.

"Tammy! This guy is not serious about you. Until he invites you to meet him for coffee, or he asks you out for a date—he's playing you along."

A man who repeatedly text messages a woman, but never asks her out, is toying with her. It's a source of entertainment for a man, like listening to the radio while riding down the street.

My girlfriend Tanya says she can always tell when her Bubba is traveling on business because he starts texting her, *"Hey, beautiful, whatcha doing?" "Miss you."* He texts this boldly because he knows he's taking it nowhere. When the weekend rolls around, she quits hearing from him.

The evidence is: he texts but he doesn't ask you out. Logic reasons: he's playing games. The reality is: he's not interested in dating you.

Here's what you need to remember. If you went out with man and you don't hear back from him—forget about him! It's not worth your time, effort and loss of confidence to wonder *WHY* a man didn't call you back. Period.

Make a note in your iPhone:
Evidence + Reasoning = Reality.
Not just with men, but in all of life's situations.

12 Black and White Reality

"Trust but verify," said President Regan. Sounds like good relationship advice to me!

Men are programmed to tell women what they want to hear. When a man pursues a woman, his job is to win her heart and seal the deal, be it sleeping with you or marrying you. For a man, courtship is game-time. Everything that is important to you, becomes important to him. He tells you: "Of course I like your family and friends." "You look good in everything." "I don't mind watching *The Bachelor* with you."

As the relationship progresses, men are "experts of all explanations" for their bad behavior. He claims his ex-wife put him in a bad mood. His phone was in the other room on silent. He only had a couple of beers. The postal service misplaced your birthday present.

When you become a couple, or you marry him, his excuses become outright whoppers. He wants you to believe that: The booze made him abusive. He tried to call you. A virus was surfing porn on his computer. He wasn't flirting with the 38DD redheaded woman with a tight-ass. He had to work late (at his girlfriend's apartment.)

Men know that women are, for the most part, forgiving (and often gullible) creatures, and we will buy into their contrived sad stories and flimsy excuses

Note to reader: If you are a woman who has a strong sense of self, and you have no trouble standing up to a man's bull-crap, you can skip this chapter. But if you are a woman, as I once was, who is easily manipulated and hoodwinked by a man, or you are afraid to confront a man for his hurtful behavior, grab yourself a jumbo yellow highlighter and keep reading.

It's our job, as women, to see through a man's emotional manipulation and smoke screens.

With Facts Emerges the Truth

In the past, it was my impulsive, gullible, lovesick nature which got me into hurtful relationships. I would develop a crush on a man. He would say or do something unkind or inconsiderate. I was afraid to confront him, and so I downplayed his thoughtless behavior.

When I was in love with a man, I rationalized and minimized his hurtful behavior so I could continue my relationship with him. But I was tired of falling head over heels for a man I barely knew, and then coping with his upsetting, wounding behavior. I wanted to find a man who shared my values, my interests and my life's goals. But I didn't trust my heart, my gut or my judgment, and so I began keeping a diary about the men I dated. I wrote down what a man said and what a man did. If he was consistently reliable, thoughtful and caring, my notes confirmed his trustworthiness. But if my journal testified that he was misleading, inconsiderate, selfish, undependable or non-communicating, I knew it was in my best interest to stop dating him. I paid especially close attention to a man's follow-up, because if he didn't do what he said he would do, everything else was moot.

Single Women

When a single woman is smitten with a man, she is inclined to close her eyes to a man's bad behavior so she can rationalize a relationship with him.

Writing down a man's behavior can help you see through a man's intense romantic pursuit. It can help minimize your confusion and keep your emotions in check, so you can rationally assess a man's character, stability and compatibility.

Journaling can help YOU avoid sexual entanglement with the wrong man.

Married or Committed Women

If you are married, or you are in a committed relationship, journaling can help you debunk your husband's or boyfriend's confusing, yet extremely convincing catfish story. Keeping a diary of a man's hurtful behavior can help you see through his manipulation, control and deceit. Writing down the facts of a hurtful event (what *actually* happened and what was *actually* said—not a man's revised and contrived rendition) will validate your reality. Journaling will help you keep your knee-jerk "right-brain" emotions in check. Journaling can sharpen YOUR relationship skills.

Belief can be manipulated. Only knowledge is dangerous.

—Frank Herbert

Documenting the dynamics of a dysfunctional relationship exposes the fiction of a loving relationship. Recording the irrefutable evidence of a boyfriend's or husband's inconsiderate, deceptive or immoral behavior corroborates that you weren't dreaming, you're not crazy, and you weren't over-reacting. It's hard to deny a man's repeated bad behavior, as vague as it may seem, when it's staring you in the face in black ink.

If I had gone on all the cruises that men had proposed to me I would have traveled the world 100 times.

I dated Allen, a psychiatrist, for four weeks. Being a psyche major he knew how to have "touchy feely" conversations—a big relationship plus. He performed small romantic gestures: he showed up at my house with a single rose and a new garlic press to use for the dinner we were preparing together that night. He called me regularly and he invited me to go on a

Caribbean cruise. Allen seemed like a potential loving, caring partner, but there was something about him I couldn't quite put my finger on—something which caused me to withhold emotional commitment.

I began writing about Allen in my journal.

Allen loved to swing dance. Most of our dates revolved around dancing and socializing with his dance buddies. But when I suggested that he take me out to dinner or to a movie he blew me off.

I asked him why we never did the things I like to do. He responded, "You've never mentioned you wanted to go out to eat or to the movies."

"That's not true," I retorted. "I did ask you." (I knew that I had asked him and he refused, because I wrote in my journal.)

At this point, I'm questioning Allen's reliability.

Allen offered to help me plant flowers in my garden on a Saturday morning. I wrote it down on my calendar, "Allen plant flowers." When he didn't show up, I asked him what happened. He said, "You didn't tell me you wanted me to help you. I was with my friends at Starbucks!"

Allen cancelled our dinner plans, saying he had an evening appointment with a client. I wrote in my diary, "Allen cancelled dinner, client appointment." I called Allen to leave him a message during his session (he always kept his phone on silent when he was with a client). To my surprise, he answered his phone and I could hear rattling glasses, muffled voices and music in the background.

"Where are you," I asked.

"I'm at Fitzgerald's having a beer with the dance club chairman."

"You told me you were seeing a patient tonight," I said.

"She cancelled. I told you that!" he barked.

Yeah. Right. In Allen's world, I can never remember anything and he is never at fault.

My notes validated my quasi-instinct that Allen was a selfish, inconsiderate and inflexible jerk. I got the drop on Allen; I ditched him before he could dump me.

Mark was a handsome long-distance truck driver. Zoe was a working single mom of two teenagers. Mark took one look at Zoe at a wedding reception and wholeheartedly pursued her. Zoe was smitten by Mark's attention, constant flattery and barrage of gifts. He won over her teenagers with birthday shopping trips to the mall. He took Zoe grocery shopping, he cooked for her and he made small repairs around her house.

Mark told Zoe that his wife died ten years ago in a car accident, and he raised his two grown children without a mom. He showed Zoe wallet photos of his 20-year-old son, an Army communications specialist stationed in Iraq, and his 22-year-old married daughter living near OKC and pregnant with her first baby. He told Zoe he had purchased a $2 million, 60-acre horse farm in Kentucky, and he paid $60,000.00 cash for his 18-wheeler big-rig.

Zoe was lonely and looking for love. Mark painted Zoe a portrait of marriage and financial security. But something gnawed at Zoe's gut. Mark seemed too good and too quick to be true. Having dated a pathological liar, she instinctively kept a small diary of the things Mark said and did.

Weeks passed and Zoe ran into Mark's longtime friend, Bruce. Zoe stepped out of her comfort zone to ask Bruce about Mark. She learned that Mark's 18-wheeler was a company owned rig. Two weeks later Zoe and Mark were having dinner at her sister's and brother-in-law's house. After a couple of martinis Mark's tongue loosen, saying, "I'm ex-military but my crazy, depressed ex-wife gets half of my pension."

Zoe's Woman Within knocks over her Kamikaze, *What the crap did he just say?*

Zoe referenced her dairy, confirming that Mark had said he paid $60,000.00 cash for his truck, and he said his wife was deceased. With a little investigation she found out that Mark's wife was alive and living in Arizona with his 8-year-old twin sons.

Zoe confronted Mark about his truck and his Arizona wife and twin tykes.

"I never said I owned my truck, my company owns it," Mark exclaimed. And, "I never told you my ex-wife was dead. I said she was injured in a bad car wreck and she was on disability."

Zoe asked him about the wallet photos of his 20-year-old son and 22-year-old daughter.

"That's not what I said," he screamed. "Those are my brother's children."

Mark repeatedly referred to his ex-wife as his "wife" in casual conversation. Zoe called his attention to it: "Why do you call your ex-wife your wife?"

"Oh, did I say that? I'm sorry. It's a habit," Mark replied weakly.

Suddenly the puzzle pieces fit together. Mark was married with two small boys.

Zoe's Woman Within looks around for a body bag.

Zoe was head over heels in love with Mark, and although he was incredibly convincing, she couldn't deny the facts she recorded in her diary. Zoe put on her big-girl high heels and she broke up with Mark.

Dr. Dirtbag was a wizard at zinging me with his veiled insults, making it difficult for me to prove his malicious intent. He claimed he was "only joking," or he "didn't mean it," or I "misread" what he said. His explanations were plausible, making it hard for me to contradict him. I began writing his hurtful remarks verbatim in my journal. The more I documented his snide remarks, the more I realized his "jest" was a sinister cover-up for his ridicule and sarcasm. He would

blindside me with a disparaging wisecrack, and then he would mock me for reacting to his abuse. Once I understood what he was doing, I stopped second-guessing my gut and I stood up to his verbal manipulation.

Journaling helps a woman stop second-guessing what her intuition already knows.

Journaling is writing down facts. What a man says or what a man does—*is a fact*. You didn't make it up in your head. You didn't imagine it in a moment of hormonal hallucination. If a man is blaming, spiteful, selfish, criticizing, withholding or discounting—*that is a fact*. It doesn't matter if he offers you world-class, bulletproof excuses for his malicious conduct—*the fact is*—you are the recipient of his hurtful behavior.

Document what you were thinking and feeling when your partner hurts your feelings.

The thoughts you think and the feelings you feel are also factual. No amount of cajoling, justification or denial can change what you "think" and what you "feel" as the result of someone's inconsiderate or demeaning behavior. A partner, who is blaming, self-serving or abusive, will try to confuse you, manipulate you, and talk you out of your feelings. He will offer you a suck-it-up apology. He will tell you "you misunderstood," or "you're too sensitive," or "you're over-reacting," or he'll say your memory of the incident is flawed. It's possible your bruised emotions did cloud your discernment—or maybe, instead, he is denying your reality to take the focus off his insensitive, deceptive, toxic behavior. Maybe he wants you to suppress your anger and tears and accept responsibility for the problems in your relationship.

There is a reason you feel the way you do.

When a man, or anyone, hurts your feelings, and then tries to befuddle your brain with their conflicting explanations and blaming accusations, that is your signal that ALL IS NOT RIGHT in your world. When your gut churns and your mind reels after an altercation with your boyfriend or husband, that is when you need to step back and get in touch with your core. Journaling will help you validate your perception of the event, confirm his inconsiderate and harmful behavior, and consequently, legitimize your diminished, rejected, wounded feelings.

When you deny the logic—your intuition knows the truth.

Lindsey and her boyfriend Daniel had different views on life. Lindsey liked to spend her evenings sharing a glass of wine with conversation, cooking and eating dinner together, and then cuddling with Daniel on the sofa while watching TV. Daniel wanted to arrive at Lindsey's house, grab a beer out of the refrigerator, mimic conversation for five minutes, eat dinner in silence in front of the TV, maybe help with the dirty dishes, and then retire to Lindsey's office to surf on the computer until bedtime.

Lindsey tried to talk to Daniel about his rude behavior, but he became defensive, shifting the responsibility for his neglectful behavior onto Lindsey.

"You were talking on the phone," he exclaimed. "You were walking the dog." "You were busy washing dishes." And, "I was answering emails from work." Daniel wanted Lindsey to believe she was being unreasonable for questioning him about his withdrawn, boorish behavior.

Lindsey couldn't shake the feeling that Daniel had minimized her feelings. She tried harder to express her emotions. Daniel continued to trivialize her grievances. He became angry, they argued and Daniel shouted irately at Lindsey to shut her down.

Blame-shifting seeks to transfer responsibility onto another.

Daniel left Lindsey's house in a huff that night and he didn't call her for days, waiting for her to just "get over it." When they finally did talk by phone, he didn't apologize for his belligerent behavior and he accused her of instigating the argument.

Lindsey was profoundly frustrated. She loved Daniel—but she wasn't ignoring the fact that a relationship with him could mean heartbreak down the road. She asked me, "Do you think I am over-reacting?"

"Absolutely not," I asserted. "This is not the first time you've complained that Daniel minimized your feelings and then punished you with his brooding silence. The problem is: he keeps talking you out of your feelings and you keep giving him the benefit of the doubt. It's what we do as women. We minimize and forgive the despicable behavior of the men we love. My advice is to journal the things he says and does during an argument. If he repeatedly exhibits his hurtful behavior—you'll have your answer. Then you can deal with the real problem."

Blame-shifting is an attempt to deflect accountability.

Facts are truth. Truth is a fact. You can't turn a lie into the truth. You can't turn facts into a lie.

Feelings Matter

Regardless of what anyone tells you, it matters what you are thinking and feeling, because what you are thinking or feeling—is a fact!

Maybe you are overly sensitive to someone's "dry wit" or constructive criticism. Perhaps you need to "woman-up" and stop impulsively reacting to the opinionated, sarcastic personalities who come and go in our lives. That being said, there is a reason we feel the way we do. If someone hurts your feelings, the likelihood is, someone did say or do something, possibly unintentionally, more likely deliberately to offend you. If for some seemingly unknown reason, you are mistrusting or apprehensive of someone, chances are, they are genuinely a menace to your well-being. Self-absorbed people will tell you that you misheard or misunderstood something they did or said, and that you are over-reacting to their nasty comments. They will try to convince you that your imagination is your worst enemy. I say: our intuitive spirit is far, far shrewder than a conniving, berating, self-absorbed, narcissistic personality.

Facts reinforce what your gut instinct is trying to tell you.

If a man makes your heart ache and your gut grind, that is your intuition telling you SOMETHING IS WRONG!

Journaling will illuminate the pattern of a person's hurtful behavior (be it a boyfriend, girlfriend, co-worker, boss, husband or family member) and help you to understand the reality of a relationship with that person.

I know it hurts to stop seeing a man you like, but the discomfort from eliminating the wrong man from your life, in the early stages of dating, is nothing compared to how much you will hurt if you fall in love with him, sleep with him, and commit to a man who denies your feelings and your reality. Likewise, I know it feels like death to divorce a man you love, but the emotional consequence of staying with a man who maltreats you can cause lasting, and even irreparable damage to your well-being.

Remember, people will lie to you and your bleeding heart may mislead you—but facts are grounded in truth.

Journal Your Thoughts

Practice intellectual decisions versus emotionally induced actions.

First and foremost, writing down what you were thinking and feeling during an argument or hurtful event will validate your feelings. Right or wrong, it's important that your feelings are validated.

Journaling will help you to better understand yourself, your man, and your relationship with him. When you argue with your boyfriend or your husband, write down the details of the altercation. Write down his criticisms, spiteful jabs and so-called "jokes" directed at you. Write down what seems like evasive, manipulating, controlling behavior. Write down his refusal to communicate, his punitive actions, flimsy excuses and far-fetched explanations. Note how an argument started. Did the argument seem to come out of nowhere? Did it start over something insignificant and then escalate to a demeaning, berating episode? Did you feel like you were set up for a bruising event?

Journaling can help you work through your confusion and self-doubt. If your boyfriend's or husband's eruptive, fault-finding, combative behavior happens over and over, journaling will help you to recognize a pattern to his malign behavior and see through his shifty, self-serving actions. You will realize that you weren't wrong, you're not crazy, and you did hear him accurately. You will understand that his blaming, accusing behavior is an attempt to cover up his deliberate, hurtful, immoral conduct. Sadly, you will realize that he did intend to demean you and wound your spirit.

Journaling can help you improve your communication skills, especially when it comes to presenting a sensitive, emotive subject to your partner. If your approach sparks his defense mechanisms, rewrite your words to help you avoid an accusing confrontation. You may discover that your disagreements are nothing more than a couple working their way through a relationship curve. And then again, you may discover that your partner is argumentative, controlling and uncompromising.

With facts you can reason the probability of the truth.

If you are a single woman, journaling can help you realize it is in your best interest to quit dating a man, and wait for a more suitable man to appear. If you are a married woman or a woman in a committed relationship, and your husband or boyfriend is controlling, deceptive or abusive, journaling can help you find the courage to stand up to his hurtful behavior.

Use your journal as a path of personal growth. Take responsibility for your life and your happiness. Don't blame a man for your personal problems. Take accountability for your negative attitudes and dysfunctional behavior.

💔

Tattoo this on your forehead:

If you feel it in your heart and you think it in your head, chances are—you're right!

13 Intuition: A Woman's Supernatural Knowing

"God gave women intuition and femininity. Used properly, the combination easily jumbles the brain of any man I've ever met."

—Farrah Fawcett

Where do life's worst mistakes come from? You know, the ones we look back on, we regret, we grieve over and we say:

If only I had done things differently.

If only I had taken a different path.

If only I had asked more questions and thought things through.

If only I had listened to my heart and followed my gut instincts.

If only I had just said—NO!

Intuition is knowing without thinking.

Intuition is a powerful, supernatural, subconscious process which senses the truth without thought, knowledge or rationale. It is the divine ability to discern the underlying nature of people. If they are genuine or phony. If they are honest or dishonest. If they have concealed self-serving motives. Sometimes it is the uneasy vibes of our sub-conscious telling us something is wrong. *"I felt it in my bones,"* you say.

Tracie Dean drove 300 miles out of her way to follow up on a gut feeling she had about a little girl she encountered in a convenience store while traveling in rural Alabama. The little girl seemed frightened of the man in whose care she was. The look on the child's face told Dean that something wasn't right. Dean took down the man's license plate number. Four days later, back home in Georgia, Dean was unable to find the girl's picture on any of the missing children's databases on the Internet. Dean then got in her car and drove 300-hundred miles back to Alabama. She persuaded the convenience store owner to let her view the surveillance tapes of the day she met the little girl. While viewing the tapes, a sheriff's deputy walked into the store. Dean convinced him to view the tapes with her and to look into the matter. He did. Clues led the deputy to a mobile home in Alabama where the horror story of extensive child abuse at the hand of a convicted sex offender began to unfold. When asked what made her drive back down to Alabama, Dean said: "It was a God thing. It was in my heart just to keep driving."—NBC News Atlanta

Intuition Is Our Glimpse Into the Future.

Intuition is the secret weapon of many successful entrepreneurs. Business pioneers will tell you their unparalleled decisions came from a "hunch." It is how Bill Gates founded Microsoft, how Jack Canfield created *Chicken Soup for the Soul*, how Oprah built her media empire and how Fred Smith envisioned FedEx. It is how the Google guys conquered the Internet, how Mark Zuckerberg imagined Facebook, and how Walt Disney created a fantasy kingdom. Steve Jobs, one of the most renowned innovators of our time, followed his gut instincts. Despite his tough life of being put up for adoption as an infant, dropping out of college after six months, sleeping on friends' floors and returning coke bottles for five-cent deposits to buy food, he trusted his instincts and went on to pioneer Apple Computers and Pixar Animation Studios.

"Have the courage to follow your heart and intuition," said Steve Jobs. "They somehow already know what you truly want to become. Everything else is secondary."

If only women could be so discerning when it comes to men!

Women Who Lack Discernment

Everyone has intuition—*it's just that some have never developed it.*

When I was growing up I heard statements like, "You shouldn't feel that way. You're over-reacting," and, "You're being too sensitive, Nancy." While these statements seemed harmless and insignificant, it was put-down phrases like these which told me my feelings were incorrect and taught me to doubt, deny and stuff my feelings. Consequently, I grew up with a weak sense of self. I doubted my self-worth. I questioned my understanding of a difficult relationship.

The awful truth is: as women, we are typically slaves to our emotions. We choose feelings and attraction over logic. We ignore our internal compass. We mistrust our judgment about men.

When I dated a new guy I was always on my girlfriend's doorstep crying and begging her for advice. "Do you think he likes me?" I whined. "What should I say or do next?" "Do you think he'll call me again?" And, of course, "Why did he stop calling me?" and "What did I do wrong?"

The problem was: I lacked common sense and I doubted my ability to understand people or a difficult situation. I repeatedly made bad relationship choices. I got my heart broken frequently, and I became jaded about men and dating.

Mind Games That Undermine a Woman's Intuition

When I was with a man, I was afraid of saying or doing the wrong things. I was afraid to ask for the things I wanted and needed in a relationship for fear of a man's rejection. I was scared to stand up to a man's criticisms and controlling actions because I might provoke him. I was afraid to accuse him of drinking too much because I might offend him and push him away. I was afraid if I exposed his lies and deceit he would blame and penalize me with his punishing behavior.

I was accustomed to the accusing, confusing, disparaging statements that a man would hurl at me during an argument. He'd say, "That's not what I said," or "You heard that wrong," or "I don't remember saying that," or, "Lighten up, will ya? I was just kidding." When those digs failed to squelch my spirit he'd use his well-honed jab, "You're over-reacting"—code for: *"What's wrong with you?"*

A man's discounting, dismissive, blaming statements are designed to make a woman doubt her ability to reason and understand a difficult situation.

I began to wonder, was I crazy like he said I was? Was I being overly sensitive to his seemingly spiteful, wounding remarks? Could I have misheard or misinterpreted what felt like a hard slap in the face? Am I the one who is unknowingly destroying our relationship—*like he says I am?*

And then I began to ask myself: If I misunderstood what he said, or if he didn't say it, as he claimed, or if I heard something completely different from what he did say: ***Why then did I hurt so bad inside?***

Am I that much out of touch with reality?

My Intuitive Woman Within's resounding answer was: ***NO! I'm not wrong!*** *I DID NOT misconstrue what he said. I am NOT over-reacting to his manipulative, disparaging comments. I DID interpret his demeaning remarks correctly.*

Dr. Dirtbag insulted, berated and wounded me to boost his self-gratifying ego. He blamed me to avoid responsibility for his insensitive, malicious behavior. And then he had the balls to tell me I'm the one who was crazy!

He Could Fool My Heart—But He Couldn't Fool My Gut

It was on my second date with Dr. Dirtbag that I had an intuitive warning moment.

Dr. Dirtbag and I had enjoyed a lovely evening of dinner, wine and conversation. It was late and he was driving me home, when suddenly he pulled off a two-lane residential road into a vacant church parking lot, stopped the car and turned off his car lights—and then I saw a police car zoom by.

"What's wrong?" I questioned him, thinking he was dodging a certain DUI.

"There's a drug raid going down tonight," he said, "and I don't want to get in the way of those guys [the police]."

"What?" I snickered. "How do you know there's a drug raid going down?"

Dr. Dirtbag, clearly insulted, threw back his bald head, puffed out his chest and babbled something about his covert dealings with the police and the CIA—and then he turned the car around, punched the accelerator and sped off down the street.

CIA, I thought. How utterly absurd!

Malcolm Gladwell presents the power of first impressions in his book, *Blink*. He states, "There is a wonderful phrase in psychology—'the power of thin slicing'—which says that as human beings we are capable of making sense of situations based on the thinnest slice of experience." Gladwell says "thin slicing," that is, our first sub-conscious, split-second, knee-jerk reaction, is our most intellectual and accurate observation, and that it is the feeling we should trust. He refers to thin slicing as "rapid cognition." It's making very quick decisions with small amounts of information in the "blink of an eye."

Persons who have benefited from thin-slicing are: firemen making life-threatening, split-second decisions about a burning building. Policemen who have a "gut feeling" something is wrong. Stock traders on the exchange floor get a feeling about the market. A retired soldier's thin-slicing intuition reportedly outwitted the supercomputers of the US Armed Forces.

Gladwell gives an intriguing example of thin slicing and snap judgments in his book.

A sixteenth century BC art sculpture, called a *kouro*, was brought to the J. Paul Getty Museum. The art dealer's asking price was $10 million. Experts examined the sculpture for hours and deemed it as real, while several art experts looked at the sculpture and immediately decided there was something wrong with it. Test results proved the statue was, in fact, a fake. The thin slicers were correct, based on a gut feeling.

Gladwell states that one must practice and perfect the skill of rapid cognition. Taking in a very thin slice of information and making an accurate prediction or assessment, requires "knowledge, experience and skill that instinctively excludes confusing and unimportant incoming data that can lead to a bad decision." E.g.; Dr. Dirtbag's charm, braggadocio and exciting personality caused me to discount the obvious fact that he was, in fact, a flagrant, lying douchebag.

A year later I realized that my knee-jerk, unconscious reaction to Dr. Dirtbag's "CIA" comment was a flash of insight, or "thin slicing." His claim to have inside information on a drug raid caused a split-second pause in my thinking and a distinct thud in my gut. The problem was, I was already smitten with Dr. Dirtbag, and I was unwilling to look at reality. I told myself, "Oh, he's been drinking. He didn't mean it. It was just his little inner boy boasting a tale. Forget about it." I discounted his bizarre behavior, telling myself, "Well, it could be possible... he is a well-connected doctor. He could have had a trivial interaction with the CIA." And then I made the worst self-deceiving mistake of my life. I gave Dr. Dirtbag the benefit of the doubt because I wanted to date him. I wanted to be in love. I wanted to marry a doctor, who was also falling in love with me.

A woman's foolish, reckless decisions damage her confidence and self-esteem.

Somewhere just below our consciousness, our intuitive voice pleads to be heard. She tries earnestly to warn you. She murmurs, *You know the truth. You suspect he's lying. You sense he is shifting the blame to conceal his own bad behavior.* But you want him. You love him. And you don't want to give him up. So you tune out your knowing voice. You disregard the truth. You reject your intrinsic need for self-preservation. And you stay in a relationship that promises to break your heart.

So Powerful is Our Intuition—It is Called the Sixth Sense

Do not forsake wisdom, and she will protect you; love her, and she will watch over you.

—Proverbs 4:6

Within each newborn baby girl, God implants a small spiritual voice known as "Intuition." Intuition's sole purpose in life is to guide you, protect you, and influence you to make decisions that are in YOUR best interest. As a woman matures, hopefully so does her intuition. But a woman, who repeatedly ignores, compromises and suppresses that part of her spirituality, will be governed by her illogical emotions. She will have a weak sense of judgment. She will be naïve, gullible and vulnerable.

A woman who mistrusts her intuition turns control of her life over to another.

A woman who is controlled by her emotions will struggle to understand life's problematic people and difficult situations. She does not trust her assessment of men. She buys into a man's deceptive nature. She gets involved with the wrong man, and she struggles to expose his deceit and defend herself against his manipulative, blaming remarks. She is unable to understand the ugly truth about her relationship, that it is unhealthy and destructive, because her emotions rule her reality.

A woman who trusts her intuition enriches her self-worth.

Intuition is a feeling, an impression, a clairvoyant understanding of the unknown. It is uncanny insight into the complexities of people and circumstances which seem to have no easy solution.

A woman who listens to, honors and follows the direction of her intuition—her gut feeling—will trust her ability to make sound judgments. A self-trusting woman will recognize the silent signals of someone who tries to deceive, manipulate and control her.

❤

When others may mislead, exploit or betray you, your intuitive spirit knows only to influence decisions that are in your best interest.

After 11 years of marriage, Trudy's husband was still doting, reliable and active in their relationship, but her instincts told her something was amiss in their camp.

Trudy was a 34-year-old international flight attendant. Lonnie was a handsome, 6-ft-2, New Jersey, Irish-Catholic lawyer. Trudy and Lonnie met at a singles golf tournament, dated on and off for two years, and then they married.

Life was good with Lonnie. They had plenty of money. He was attentive, outgoing and stable. He managed their checking account and he paid their bills. He loved to cook and he prepared elaborate dinners for them. He orchestrated their social life and golf vacations. Although their sex life was plain vanilla and infrequent, Trudy believed her marriage to be practical and worthwhile.

Trudy's career was exciting; she flew almost every week to Europe, with layovers in Paris, Rome and London. Lonnie was supportive of her career. He always insisted on driving Trudy to the airport for her departure, and he picked her up on her return flight. Lonnie always made Trudy write down her travel itinerary. Trudy's previous boyfriends never bothered to ask where she would be or what hotel she would be staying when she traveled. Lonnie's concern made Trudy feel valued and special.

Four years passed and Trudy and Lonnie had not had sex. It was the unmentionable elephant in the room. Trudy knew that Lonnie was not that interested in sex before they married. She concluded that he had a low libido or erectile dysfunction. But he was affectionate; he held her hand in public, he hugged and kissed her and he cuddled with her on the sofa while watching TV. He told Trudy regularly that he loved her, but her core couldn't shake the gnawing feeling that Lonnie might be up to something.

Lonnie kept his desk drawers locked at home. He kept his cell phone on silent in his pocket and he took it with him everywhere he went, even to the bathroom. Trudy convinced herself he was entitled to his privacy. Then one day she got the mail first and she pried into his phone bill. His statement listed a number Lonnie had called repeatedly. Trudy told herself she had an overactive imagination, but her instinct told her to write the phone number down.

There was a 6-hour time difference between Trudy's New York City home and her overseas flight destinations. Lonnie always called Trudy the minute she walked into her hotel room. He would say, *"Hi, sweetie! How was your trip? I miss you. I love you. Had a long day;*

going to bed early. I'll call you tomorrow." After they hung up Trudy would have dinner at the hotel with the flight crew and then go to bed around 10 o'clock so she could fly out early the next morning.

Trudy flew to Paris, and as always, Lonnie called her on her arrival, telling her he would call her the following morning. But this night Trudy decided to check up on Lonnie. She set her alarm to call him at 11 p.m. New York time. She called Lonnie repeatedly, but he never answered his phone. When she got home she confronted him. Lonnie got angry, he accused Trudy of checking up on him, and he told her he turned his phone off when he went to bed because the email and Facebook alerts kept him awake at night.

Trudy's Woman Within screwed her face.

The following week Trudy faked a trip, telling Lonnie she had picked up a last minute overnight flight to London. She woke at daybreak, she packed her flight bag and put on her uniform, and Lonnie drove her to the airport. In the car he held her hand and he toyed affectionately with her wedding ring. He told Trudy to write down her travel itinerary, and he talked enthusiastically about going out to dinner and attending an art show when she returned home. Lonnie pulled up to the departure curbside, jumped out of the car, handed Trudy her luggage, hugged and kissed her and said, "Love you, babe. I'll be right here to scoop you up when you get back."

Trudy walked into the airport, hopped onto a terminal train to car rentals, she rented a car and she drove to a Brooklyn coffee shop. Sitting at a table sipping an espresso, she pulled out a piece of paper and she stared at the phone number she had written down from Lonnie's phone bill.

"Hello." The woman's voice was deep and gruff.

"You don't know me, but your phone number showed up repeatedly in my husband's phone activity," Trudy said nervously.

Deafening silence permeated the phone receiver. Trudy felt nauseous.

"What's his name," the deep voice asked.

"Lonnie."

Silence.

"I'm a flight attendant. I've felt he's been cheating on me for some time. I won't be mad at you. I just need to know the truth," Trudy whimpered.

The woman told Trudy that she met Lonnie in a B&D (bondage and discipline) chat room, and that Lonnie claimed he was single. She said they dated for nearly two years. She was Lonnie's dominatrix, or *Domme*, and he was her submissive partner, or *sub*. She punished and dominated Lonnie during sex, and he submitted. She said that was how Lonnie got sexually aroused: she would restrain him with a dog collar and handcuffs, he would lie at her feet handcuffed to her chair, and she would whip, demean and power over him.

Trudy drove around in a trance for hours, and then late that night she drove to her house, parked her car in the driveway, unlocked the front door, walked into the house, opened the partially closed bedroom door and she saw Lonnie lying on the bed naked, tied to the bedposts with a man, dressed in fiendish black leather attire, standing over him doing 50 Shades of nasty.

It's amazing what a cheater will do to cover-up his (or her) infidelity. For 11 years Lonnie took and picked Trudy up from the airport so she wouldn't unexpectedly show up at their home and catch him with one of his masochist lovers.

Gut check!

If your boyfriend's or husband's penis is working, and he's not trying to have sex with you—trust your gut instincts that he's having sex with someone.

Pay attention to the knot in your stomach.

Louise met Victor at a San Antonio bar and grill, where singles gathered to listen to local musicians jam to old tunes. Victor, a Chicagoan, was working in San Antonio on a six-month consulting assignment. Louise went to dinner with Victor. He was charming, worldly and generous. He was open about the details of his past life and his divorce. He told Louise that he divorced his wife because he caught her in bed with another man. He talked candidly about his single life. He cooked Louise dinner in his temporary apartment, and he spoke of Louise in his future. Louise slept with Victor and they became a twosome. They played house in Louise's two-bedroom condo, he cleaned her hot tub, and they grocery shopped together. Everything seemed peachy—until Louise had an intuitive moment.

Louise tells her story:

The first week of dating Victor I asked to see a photo of his two grown children. He pulled a worn snapshot out of his wallet of his son and daughter. They were youngsters wearing matching swimsuits standing next to their mom (his ex-wife). I asked him, "Why do you still carry a photo of your ex-wife?"

Victor ruffled his banty feathers and exclaimed, "It's my favorite photo of my kids. I'm not going to cut their mother out of the photo just because we're divorced!"

I had a skeptical gut reaction—but it sounded logical—and so I believed him.

Weeks passed and Victor's behavior was unpredictable and questionable. He disappeared for a weekend. He didn't call me, and he didn't answer his phone. I became suspicious so I Googled him. His Chicago past and current business checked out. I did a people search; a 56-year-old woman named Arlene was repeatedly listed as a possible relative. I did an internet search for Arlene and she popped up as a Chicago real estate agent, complete with her photo, cell phone and business contact information. I stared in disbelief at Arlene's photo, realizing it was the woman in Victor's photograph with his children—only older. I confronted Victor about Arlene and he shamelessly confessed that he was married.

Victor was a master liar. He created the façade of a successful single man working out-of-town on a temporary consulting assignment. He haunted San Antonio's known singles hangouts, and he actively dated single woman. Victor wooed Louise's heart with his charm and ardent pursuit, but her intuition "blinked" at Victor's explanation of why he had his ex-wife's photo in his wallet. Had Louise acknowledged her discerning voice, she could have avoided intimate involvement with a married scumbag.

What's the no. 1 rule about dating a man with unreliable, suspicious behavior? *Trust your gut!* What rule no. 2? *Do your frikkin, fracking homework!*

When I stopped listening to the biased, self-serving, manipulating statements of others, and I looked inward for my answers: I found wisdom. I ceased to be a constant slave to my emotions. I began to see people as they were, not as I imagined or hoped they would be. I was no longer victim to a man's charm, deceiving words and empty promises.

7 Steps to Develop Your Intuition

1. Intuition is like a muscle; the more you exercise it, the stronger it gets. The more you listen to your internal voice, the more audible becomes the message, the wiser becomes the counsel, and the more significant is the advice. Soon it will become second nature.

2. Listen to your internal conversations. Pay attention to your feelings of anger, fear and resentment; examine the root cause of these feelings. Is the culprit your negative mindset, or the damaging influence of someone else? Discard the negative comments of others and follow your gut.

3. Trust your first instincts about a man's (or anyone's) questionable or inconsiderate behavior. Pause in your thinking. Be cognizant and silently question his words and actions. Don't be swayed by his flimsy excuses or his boasting, flattering words.
4. Reserve emotional and intimate involvement during the early stages of dating. Sexual intimacy can drug your internal knowing, causing you to play down a man's undesirable behavior and character flaws.
5. Intuition is no good without the courage to act on your gut instincts. When you think a man is lying, twisting your words and manipulating you, step out on faith and expose his hurtful behavior. Each time you realize you were right, your confidence and self-esteem will increase.
6. If you feel in your heart, and you think in your head that something about a man doesn't sound or feel right, stop immediately and ask yourself, *"Why?"*
7. True personal power comes when you can depend on yourself to make the important decisions in your life. Apply intuition to your decision-making process and exert that power.

Trust your hunches. They're usually based on facts filed away just below the conscious level.

—Joyce Brothers

14 Positive Attitude: A Woman's Aura of Influence

The power of our thoughts form our entire life's experiences.

What would your life look like if your aura seemed to supernaturally attract friendships, opportunities, success, happiness, and even true love? What if accomplished, interesting, quality men enjoyed your company and ardently pursued you for a serious relationship? What if women admired you, sought out your friendship and promoted your interests? What if the people and things you needed to attain your dreams of success seemed to magically present themselves to you? If this were your daily reality—would your life be significantly different?

I have wondered all my life how some women instinctively gain a man's interest, devotion and respect.

Let's face it—some single women know how to push a man's testosterone buttons, inspire men to jump through burning hoops to get a date with them, and cause men to desire them, woo them and propose marriage to them without delay. And these women accomplish this—it seems, with little to no effort.

In my book *Secrets of the Ultimate Husband Hunter* I tell the true story that opened my eyes to my negative, self-defeating mindset, and how the power of positive thought magically transformed my life. The abridged story is worth repeating.

My girlfriend Camille attracted almost every man she met. I couldn't understand what men saw in her. She was attractive, but not gorgeous. She didn't have a job. She didn't have money. She was demanding, outspoken and self-serving. She boasted, "I can get any man I want when I put my mind to it." She was as cocky as she was confident—and yet, men took her to the finest restaurants and elite parties. They gave her flowers, gifts and jewelry. They swept her away on fabulous vacations. Men respectfully and ardently pursued Camille for a serious relationship.

What was she doing that got her this kind of attention?

I pondered my miserable single life. Why am I unable to attract the sincere interest of a quality man? Why do men stop calling me? Why do I repeatedly commit to men who are so very wrong for me?

Truly I was fascinated with Camille's magic allure. One day I asked her, "How do you attract all these men?"

She laughed, not fully realizing her special allure, and she said, "I just love men. I love the way they look, the way they act, the way they smell. I like the things they can do for me, and how they make me feel. I love them because they are very different from women."

At first I thought she was cracked. How could she possibly love all men? I couldn't stand most of the men I knew. And then the rocket went off in my head and parted the clouds above.

That's it! I get it! I understand! Camille attracted a multitude of men because she accepted and valued each man for his unique qualities. It was Camille's open-minded, approachable, inviting aura which drew men to her. It was her genuine interest and affirming, approving mindset which caused them to stay. Men sought Camille out because they felt good about themselves in her company.

I considered the possibilities of this unprecedented, unorthodox mindset. I thought: If loving all men will make me an alluring, intriguing, irresistible babe—then, *bring it!*

I re-entered the single world armed with a fascinating dating strategy. I named it the "Love-All-Men" philosophy, which succinctly meant, give all men a chance to reveal their best and more enduring qualities.

I deliberately dated a wider range of men with the hope of finding, dating, even marrying the love of my life. I told myself, I will accept, appreciate and value the men that cross my path. The more men I accepted and respected—the more men I attracted. The more men I attracted—the more confident I became. The more confident I became—Hallelujah! Praise the Lord! Amen!—the more men I again attracted.

When you judge another, you do not define them, you define yourself.

—Dr. Wayne Dyer

The irony was: when I ceased criticizing others, I also stopped criticizing myself and I quit doubting my self-worth. It was the gift of confidence and self-esteem for which I had been searching all my life. My Love-All-Men dating philosophy made me realize my negative mindset was robbing me of the things I wanted most in life.

Look for the good in people and you will recognize the good in you.

The Law of Attraction

The Law of Attraction is one of the better known universal laws. The theory is: we create our own realities by virtue of our thoughts and actions. We attract the things we want. We also attract the things we don't want. Negative thoughts draw to us problematic people, troublesome situations, financial difficulties, and even poor health. Positive thoughts magically attract opportunities, success, our favorite possessions, and meaningful relationships. Succinctly put—like attracts like.

What the mind of man can conceive and believe, it can achieve.

—Napoleon Hill

My book Secrets of the Ultimate Husband Hunter *was published and Valentine's Day was fast approaching. I needed publicity. In three short weeks I met four people, strictly by accident, on four different occasions, who were instrumental in my landing three TV appearances and a radio interview to promote my book and seminars, which in turn helped me gain regular TV and radio appearances. I contacted a local print newspaper and I asked them for a small article promoting my book and upcoming seminar. A reporter invited me to her office and interviewed me. She published a half-page article with a large full-color photo of me and my book on the front page of the newspaper. I was astounded! I was told later that the reporter did it because she "liked" me.*

I practice, preach and believe in the magical power of positive thought, but even I was flabbergasted at how much free publicity had materialized for me. My girlfriend Patty said, "Geez, Nancy, you're spooky. It's like you think about something you need and it just shows up."

Indeed, my life seemed supernatural.

Thread of Supernatural Attraction

"Six degrees of separation" is the theory that everyone is approximately six introductions away from meeting any other person in the world. Meaning: a chain of "a friend of a friend" multiplied by six (or fewer) can gain you the business or personal connections you seek.

Brenda, a divorced woman living in Nashville, had a 4-year-old son with a brain tumor. She took her son to St. Jude Children's Research Hospital in Memphis for treatment. While she was there she wandered into the hospital lobby boutique where she overheard two women talking excitedly about a new dating and relationship book. Brenda asked the women the name of the book. She bought the book and she read it while caring for her son at the hospital. She liked the book so much she called her girlfriend, Terri, in Nashville.

"Terri, you've got to buy this book," Brenda exclaimed over the phone. "It's awesome!"

"What's the name of it," Terri inquired, skeptically.

"*Secrets of the Ultimate Husband Hunter.*"

"No frikkin way," Terri exclaimed sardonically, "I'm not looking for a husband!" Nevertheless, Terri, having recently broken up with an abusive boyfriend, purchased the book.

Months went by.

Terri worked at a financial firm in Nashville. Her boss was organizing a health and wealth event for their clients. Terri's boss was looking for a relationship author to speak at the event. Terri told her boss about Nancy Nichols's book, and she implored her boss to book Nancy for the event.

"Her book changed my life," Terri exclaimed. "She would be awesome."

Terri's boss deep-sixed her suggestion, saying, "Nancy Nichols lives in Houston. We can't afford her."

Terri, disappointed, dropped the subject.

Unknown to Terri, I had recently moved back to my hometown Memphis, and I was making plans to move to Nashville in the upcoming year.

I booked a seminar at the Barnes and Noble in Franklin, Tennessee, just outside Nashville. I emailed a Nashville Meetup.com singles group, inviting the organizer, Aly, and her members to my seminar event. Aly responded to my invitation. I sent her my book and we became good friends.

A year passed and I drove to Nashville to scout out townhouses. I stayed with Aly in her lovely home. She took me to a Saturday night potluck dinner at a girlfriend's house, a riverfront 3-story log home sitting high on the bank of the Cumberland River. There were about 12 men and women sitting around a long, granite buffet bar, eating, drinking and chatting. I engaged in a conversation with one of the woman.

"What do you do," the woman inquired.

"I'm an author and motivational speaker," I answered.

A woman sitting across from us at the bar, abruptly, excitedly said, "I heard you speak last year at Barnes and Noble. You were really good."

Wow! My Woman Within is impressed.

A third woman, sitting across from us piped up, "Excuse me, I wasn't eavesdropping but I heard you say you are a motivational speaker. I'm looking for a relationship author to speak at my company's upcoming event."

Monday morning, back in Memphis, I received an email from an unknown woman. She wrote:

> **"I read your book. It changed my life. Have I got a story to tell you. —Terri"**

I was having a crappy, down-in-the-mouth morning. I had just learned that Dr. Dirtbag had married Bimbo. I didn't want him back—but I didn't want Bimbo to have my ex-dirtbag.

I emailed Terri:

> **"Call me. I would love to hear something uplifting..." and I sent her my phone number.**

Five minutes later Terri called me. She exuded excitement through the phone, telling me that her boss came into the office that morning, announcing that she had found a relationship author for their upcoming event, and her boss handed Terri my business card.

"That's my girl!" Terri shrilled. "Nancy Nichols! That's the author I told you about!"

Terri and I were both dumb-struck by the unlikely, linked events which brought about our magical connection. Over the following year we became close friends. I moved to Nashville and Terri introduced me to a gaggle of girlfriends and valuable business connections.

Let's Review The Supernatural Thread of Attraction:

- Two women were standing in St. Jude hospital talking about my book.
- Brenda, from Nashville, overheard the two women, asked for the name of the book, bought my book and read it.
- Brenda called her Nashville girlfriend, Terri, and insisted that she also read my book.

In the meantime…

- I met Aly, a Nashville "mover and shaker," through an online singles social group. We became friends. A year later I traveled to Nashville to visit Aly and she took me to a dinner party.
- At the dinner party a woman asked me about my book. A second woman at the party recognized me from my seminar in Nashville the year before. A third woman at the party, hearing our conversation, booked me to speak at her upcoming Nashville event.
- Two days later, Terri (whom I had never met) learned that I was speaking at her company's event and she felt compelled to email me.
- Over the next year Terri and I became good friends.
- A year and a half later I moved to Nashville and Terri introduced me to her circle of influence.

The Law of Attraction is like the frikkin energizer bunny…it just keeps connecting…and connecting…and connecting…

Your Attitude Defines Your Attraction

Two equally attractive, successful women with similar economic, social and parenting backgrounds experience life very differently. One woman gets along with co-workers, she has oodles of friends, she enjoys a satisfying career, and she has meaningful family and friend relationships. Men enjoy her company and they pursue her for a serious relationship.

The other woman dislikes her boss, she has conflict with her co-workers, she finds fault with most of her friends, she struggles to sustain business accounts, she has few dates, and her romantic relationships are short-lived.

What's the difference? In a word—it's ATTITUDE!

The Law of Comeuppance

Her smiles and compliments felt like a back-handed slap across the face.

Judith, a portly 57-year-old Tampa divorce attorney, befriended people with broken wings. She took them in. She gave them food, shelter and a listening ear. She beguiled them with her psychological mumbo jumbo, and when they emotionally bonded to her—she began to mistreat them. When her victims protested of her abuse, she blamed them for the relationship problems, she kicked them out of her house, and she told everyone they were impossible to live with. The men in Judith's life never knew what hit them. Sarah, on the other hand, realized that if a woman manipulates and maltreats men, she will eventually ill-treat her women friends as well.

Judith had a history of becoming intimately involved with her male clients. Andy, a 40-year-old divorce client, and a tool-toting, hard-body construction worker, became Judith's lover. He moved in with Judith in her country club home. He mooched off of Judith for five years, he borrowed large sums of money from her, and then he jilted her for his own boy-toy.

Judith began dating Marshall, another client going through a nasty divorce. Marshall moved in with Judith and he paid her exorbitant rent in exchange for kinky sex, her superb cooking, and pool and golf privileges. He took Judith to Italy and he bought her an exquisite handcrafted, 24kt gold embellished Venetian mirror for her bedroom dresser.

Both of Judith's lovers were mesmerized and were seduced by the listening, consoling ear of a seasoned counselor.

Judith and Sarah were new friends. Sarah lost her job. Judith told Sarah, "Move in with me. You can pay rent when you get back on your feet." During that time, Marshall was living with Judith. Judith provoked an argument with Marshall. She got in his face, he got mad and he pushed her shoulder with his hand. Judith kicked Marshall out of her home and she called the police. She told the police Marshall assaulted her. She changed the locks to her house, and she held Marshall's furniture for ransom, forcing him to pay hefty lease penalties.

Sarah settled into her new living arrangement with Judith, paying Judith $600.00 a month for her room and household privileges. They hosted dinners and pool parties for their girlfriends. They shared conversation and cocktails by the pool. It was the ideal setup for two single gals.

Sarah was at home much of the time scouting for a job. She cooked dinner for Judith and her, and she happily fed Judith's three dogs, a French Bulldog, an Airedale, and the newest family member, a rambunctious year-old alpha-male Goldendoodle. Sarah bonded with the brown-eyed Goldendoodle. She walked him, she obedience trained him, she bathed and brushed him regularly, and she occasionally paid for his professional grooming. Every night Doodle would jump in Sarah's king size bed to snuggle and sleep.

Life was great—at least—for the moment.

In the beginning Judith was a considerate, agreeable roommate. She included Sarah in her girlfriend's activities. She served Sarah dinner in bed when she was sick with the flu. She consoled Sarah over a recent hurtful breakup with her boyfriend. But it seemed the more chores Sarah did around the house, the more Judith took advantage of her. Judith constantly left her wet clothes in the washing machine. Sarah dried and folded Judith's clothes, so she could launder her own clothes. Judith left her dirty dishes piled in the sink for days. Sarah washed Judith's food-encrusted pots and pans, so she could cook in a clean kitchen. Judith asked Sarah to feed her three dogs in the mornings. Sarah tended to the dogs every morning and Judith began to shirk her dog owner responsibilities, ignoring the dogs' empty food and water bowls in the evening, and she ceased buying dog food. Sarah purchased a 50-pound bag of dry kibbles and she placed the receipt on the kitchen counter for reimbursement. Judith ignored the receipt—*and then it disappeared.*

Beware of friends who go out of their way to be nice to you, and then want to fix you.

The dogs became a big contention between Sarah and Judith. Sarah cut back on her constant dog chores. Judith became annoyed and retaliated. She scrutinized Sarah's makeup and clothes, and she mocked Sarah's mannerisms in front of their friends. Sarah called out Judith for her ridicule. Judith told Sarah she was "over reacting," and she claimed her insults were "constructive criticism" and harmless "jokes."

The more Sarah protested, the more passive-aggressive Judith became.

Normally Doodle jumped into Sarah's bed every night to sleep—suddenly he disappeared into Judith's bedroom at bedtime. Sarah was perplexed by Doo's sudden altered nighttime behavior.

Sarah questioned Judith, "I don't understand; Doodle always wanted to sleep with me. All of a sudden, he wants to sleep with you."

"That's because I feed him snacks to keep him in my bedroom at night," Judith snickered, jeeringly.

Judith's passive-aggressive behavior escalated.

Judith worked overtime to aggravate Sarah. She threw the living blinds open at daybreak so the dogs would bark loudly, insanely at the people walking by on the sidewalk, wakening and provoking Sarah. She allowed the three dogs to lounge on Sarah's nice sofa. She turned a blind eye to Doodle digging in the kitchen trash can, strewing slimy, discarded food and soggy coffee filters all over the floor. Sarah finally ignored the filthy mess, and Judith stepped up her game.

It was a Saturday afternoon. Sarah had spent two hours bathing, blow-drying and brushing Doodle. When she finished Doodle was a fragrant, huggable ball of fluffy ecru fur. Three hours later Judith knocked on Sarah's bedroom door.

"Come here. I got something I want you to see," said Judith. "You're not going to like this," and she smirked.

Sarah followed Judith to the kitchen back door. Torrential rains had poured the past two hours. There was Lil' Doodle, standing outside the glass door, his fur soaking, dripping wet, covered from head to toe in black sludge, his tail wagging and his face pleading to be let into the house.

Judith, pleased with her shenanigans, grinned at Sarah and giggled.

"That's it. I'm done," Sarah exclaimed sternly. *"He's your dog! He's your responsibility! You bath him,"* and she turned on her heel and left poor Lil' Dirty Doodle to fend for himself.

Judith vented her rage at Sarah. She told Sarah she was bi-polar, she needed to go to a psychiatrist, and she was impossible to live with. Sarah stood up to Judith's abuse, giving Judith the excuse she needed to boot Sarah from her home. The following week Judith's newest boyfriend, a client divorcing his wife, began moving his things into Judith's home.

The universe has a way of delivering someone their just desserts. Doodle made sausage out of Judith's brand new Louboutin high heels. Her $4,000.00, one-of-a-kind, Venetian mirror was demolished in shipping. Her newest, married boyfriend-client went back to his wife and his wife filed a malpractice complaint against Judith.

We Are Our Attraction

The people and things we are attracted towards, tell a lot about us.

It's not always the prettiest woman in the room that captures a man's attention. *No, indeed!* The woman who projects an aura of confidence, exuberance and approachability can own the room.

Lauren, a 49-year-old widow, was an average-looking woman. Standing 5-foot-4, she was plain-featured, shaped liked a pencil, and her jaw-length, naturally curly red hair was tedious and frizzy. She barely wore makeup and her style was ordinary—but men were drawn to her like a bear to a honeycomb.

I watched Lauren in envy and amazement as she mesmerized men with her wit and charm. I finally realized why men were attracted to Lauren. She was confident, cheerful, friendly and approachable. She could converse with any man about anything, especially about sports and politics. She genuinely complimented, affirmed and boosted a man's ego, making each man feel special, regardless of his appearance, stature or position in life. It was easy for Lauren to flirt with men because she truly liked men.

In other words, to attract the right man—you must *first* be the right woman.

We attract the negative aspects of our life.

A frequent question I hear from women is, "Why do I keep attracting the wrong man?"

There's a reason for the type of people we attract into our lives. Attractive women who are looking for a meal ticket will hook-up with a successful man who is narcissist and abusive. Women who are hyper-critical and demanding will find a man they can dominate—and then they are unhappy because their guy isn't "manly" enough. Women who are needy, insecure and codependent will habitually gravitate to men who are manipulative, overbearing and controlling.

Jill repeatedly attracted and committed to men who mistreated her and dumped her. After I got to know her, I understood why.

When I first met Jill, I was drawn to her meek, warm personality. We quickly became inseparable friends. I took her under my wing. I introduced her to my social circle. I became her protective big sister. But as I got to know her, she was hypersensitive and emotionally unstable. She was jealous of me having women friends, and she set out to sabotage my friendships with her veiled comments. She told me this woman was a bad influence on me, and another woman was using me. I believed her assertions and I pulled away from two of my women friends—a decision I gravely regretted later.

More than once, Jill got upset with me over an insignificant comment or a petty situation; she erupted into irrational, wailing fits of anger, and after her outburst, she withdrew in feigned helplessness. Her hot and cold behavior created a web of confusion, friction and codependency between us. One minute she was my best-friend-forever—the next minute she was a lambasting she-devil—and the next minute she was sorry her tantrum.

Jill eventually trashed me for a man. Sadly, this was not the first time a woman friend had knifed me in the back.

I asked my girlfriend, Annie, "What's wrong with me."

"You don't think things through," Annie said sternly. "You take people at face value. You naively expect everyone to be genuine and considerate. You let them get close to you without really knowing them. And when they don't live up to your expectations, you are disappointed and you feel betrayed."

I moaned, knowing she was right.

"Everyone is not worthy of your energy and trust," said Annie. "Some women are only meant to be social acquaintances. Some men should remain pals, instead of becoming lovers. You need to take time to truly know someone before you invite them into your inner sanctum."

"You're right," I groaned. I sensed she was recalling my inventory of hit-and-run men.

"Jill could still be a social friend and a business connection, had you not rushed in to rescue her. You were drawn into her poor-pitiful-me saga. You tried to fix her. She turned on you like a wounded viper, and you became the unsuspecting victim."

Another negative mindset that perpetuates unhappy circumstances is to dwell on the aspects of a past hurtful relationship.

I had moved 600 miles away to escape Dr. Dirtbag's maiming, abusive behavior, and yet, I regurgitated the pain, anger and resentment of our relationship on a daily basis. It infuriated me, that even with the distance between us, he still held power over me. I knew he had moved on with his life. He had a new squeeze, a new luxury automobile, and a beautiful new house. I was dead to him, but I kept him alive in my head and my heart because in some sick way it gave me comfort to anguish over him and hate him. I desperately wanted to let go of my hurtful images of him.

> I lived 600 hundred miles from Dr. Dirtbag and yet, I clung to his bad karma.

I pretended to open a cardboard box and I stuffed it with the haunting memories of his lying and abuse. I taped my imaginary box shut, and I mailed it to him, where those malign feelings belonged. One day I'll get to heaven and I'll see Dr. Dirtbag (pray that he makes it there), and I'll ask him, "Hey, Dirtbag, did ya get the box I sent you?"

Everything that's coming into your life, you are attracting by virtue of the images you are holding in your mind. And that includes a lying, cheating, abusive dirtbag.

Negative Thoughts Beget Unhappy Circumstances

Scarcity thinking is another form of negative energy and influence.

Scarcity thinkers feel there is not "enough" to go around. They spend their lives complaining about their problems and bad luck. They fixate on their lack of money, the problems within their relationships, or no relationship and being alone. Scarcity thinkers are mistrustful and self-absorbed. They are afraid they will not get their share of money, recognition, fun, possessions, love and happiness. They're afraid to share their knowledge, contacts or empathy because someone might take advantage of them, or someone might get ahead of them. Scarcity thinkers feel entitled and fearful. They are afraid to include others in their friend group, because someone may outshine them.

She Needed to Be the "Main Attraction"

I met Shannon through my Nashville friends. She was attractive, gregarious and a lively conversationalist. Shannon invited me to go to happy hours with her girlfriends. Sitting amid her friends at a bar or a table, she was engaging and witty, and seemingly the center of attention. I thought of her as the "social director." When I joined her and her friends at a bar, she would pat her hand on a stool, and say, "Here, Nancy, you sit here."

Shannon and I quickly became close friends. We were both fun-loving, vino drinking, visionary spirits. She seemed to attach herself to me; she called me first when she wanted a girl's night out. I called her when I got tickets to a special event, and I babysat her Jack Russell when she traveled out of town on business.

When I met Shannon, she was unemployed. Eight months later she went to work for my good friend, a successful businessman. Four months later she decided she didn't like her job and she passively-aggressively got herself fired. She openly discredited my friend. Cornering me at happy hour she bad-mouthed his business ethics in front of our friends. It was as if she were trying to pick a fight with me. I told her I was uncomfortable with her surly remarks about my guy friend. She was miffed because I refused to participate in her character assassination.

Shannon quit inviting me to happy hour and she declined my invitations to meet for a drink. Then one Saturday afternoon Shannon accepted my invitation to meet at Whiskey Kitchen.

I arrived early to save bar stools for Shannon and her good friend, Geena. The bar was packed with happy hour enthusiasts. Sitting at the bar, I struggled to hold two empty bar stools for Shannon and Geena. I put my Brahmin clutch on the seat of one stool and a glass of ice water in front of the other stool, pretending my wingwomen were alive and present.

Thirsty customers standing behind me asked me, "Are these seats taken?"

"Yes," I chirped.

The bartender glared at me, leaned his surly face over the bar and he snarled, *"Ya can't save stools with people waiting to be seated!"*

I screwed my face and I told him my friends were on the way.

"Are they in the parking lot now?" he growled.

"No."

He planted his hands on the edge of the counter, leaned his face into my space and he snarled, *"Then ya can't save 'em a seat!"*

I relinquished my two empty seats to a couple hovering behind me. Seeing two empty bar stools open up at the end of the bar, I grabbed my wine glass and my purse, I jumped to the floor and I quickly commandeered the empty seats. Sitting on one stool, I placed my purse in front of the unoccupied stool, marking my territory. A crusty old man sitting two seats down barked at me, *"What's wrong with you? You can't save chairs! People are waiting to sit down!"*

Geena arrived just in time to claim the empty stool. I gave the crabby old man a kiss-my-expensive-Brahmin smile. Geena ordered a glass of wine and she began sharing the details of her busy week. Suddenly, Shannon is standing behind me, her hand on her hip, her eyes narrowed, glaring at me wild-eyed.

"Why didn't you save me a seat!" she demanded.

Her indignant aura knocked me backwards.

"I tried to for thirty minutes," I exclaimed. "The old man at the bar growled at me and the bartender made me give it up."

Shannon hurled razors at me with her eyes.

"Here, take my seat," I insisted. I hopped off my stool and I motioned for her to sit down.

"No!" she retorted. "I'm not going to take your stool. I'll just go home."

"Don't go home," I pleaded."

I was frustrated that she refused to acknowledge that I worked hard to save her a stool.

"Please! Take my seat. I don't mind. I can stand behind you until another stool opens up."

"I'm going to the restroom," Shannon snapped, and she turned on her heel and stormed off to the back of the restaurant.

I gawked at Geena, astonished at Shannon's outrageous behavior. Geena gave me a crooked smile and shrugged her shoulders, as if Shannon's behavior was quasi-normal.

Fifteen minutes later Shannon emerged from the restroom. She arched her eyebrow, peered at me skeptically, put her fake Gucci purse on the bar, and she slid onto my bar stool next to Geena.

Ten minutes later a bar stool opened beside Shannon, and I quickly sat down.

I sat next to Shannon at the bar the rest of the evening, her back turned to me while she engaged Geena in a lively conversation. The restaurant was noisy; I strained to listen, but I could only catch a whiff of what they were saying. Every once in a while Shannon would turn and look at me with a half-smile, allowing me to be a part of her privy conversation. Shannon acted as if nothing had happened. I was bewildered and wounded.

Her hurtful behavior was off the Richter Scale.

Shannon quit calling me. I called her on occasion to invite her to this or that. She always declined, and I began seeing her at happy hour sitting at the bar, huddled in a conversation with our mutual friend, Farrah. Shannon flashed me her ex-girlfriend smile. It was obvious that I was history and Farrah was Shannon's newest, greatest BFF.

When I first met Shannon, she told me she had "fired" her previous girlfriends because they all had negative attitudes. I wondered: Had she fired me because I didn't save her a bar stool at Whiskey Kitchen?

Six months passed and I was invited to have drinks with girlfriends. I arrived, I sat beside my girlfriend Janice, and I put my purse on the empty bar stool next to me to save it for our next arriving girlfriend—and in walked Shannon.

Shannon walked up to me, forced a synthetic smile and said, "Do you mind if I sit in the middle?"

What the crap? Shannon wanted me to give her my stool so she could sit between me and Janice.

I paused, and I said, "I want to sit in the middle too. When you sit in the middle you turn your back to me and I can't hear the conversation."

"Well, I can't hear either," Shannon exclaimed.

"Tell you what, I'll scoot my stool back so we can have 3-way conversation."

My Woman Within leaned over and whispered in my ear, "She wants to sit in the middle so she can control the conversation."

Wendy and the Disappearing Wallet

Scarcity thinking causes us to be self-interested, manipulative and greedy. She is the first person in line. She is a stingy tipper, and she complains about the cost of wine or dinner. She shows up empty-handed at a party. She will ask you for a favor, but when you ask a favor of her, she is too busy, or allegedly too broke to reciprocate.

Wendy, an attractive 45-year-old, twice-divorced brunette, was a talented interior designer. With her abilities, looks and gregarious personality, she should have had a lucrative career—but instead she struggled with job stability because Wendy spent all her time looking for a man to take care of her.

Johnson was Wendy's latest and greatest man discovery. He was a tall, assertive, suit-and-tie guy who shaved his head to accent his polished, manly persona. Johnson was the CEO of a high-end furniture manufacturer, and he traveled the United States and Europe extensively.

Wendy was all aglow after sleeping with Johnson on their second date. She bragged of his sexual endowment, his six-figure income, his expensive Fort Worth home, and his upcoming job transfer to Chicago.

She said, "This guy is going to take care of me for the rest of my life."

I thought, *Wow, how can she make such a declaration so quickly?*

In the following months Wendy traveled with Johnson. She should have been scheduling customer appointments, but instead, she was concocting surprises for Johnson. She shopped for provocative lingerie. She bought him lush bath towels engraved with his initials. She treated him to champagne bubble baths. She served him elaborate candle-lit dinners. Wendy had a plan. It was to capture Johnson for his adoration and her personal security.

And then without rhyme, reason or warning—Johnson suddenly and abruptly dumped Wendy.

You won't find love in a man's wallet.

It didn't make sense. Wendy and Johnson seemed like the perfect couple. Johnson acted as though he worshiped Wendy. All of her friends thought they would eventually marry. One day Wendy was talking about selling her condo and moving to Chicago with Johnson—and the next day, Johnson flipped the switch and walked away.

I thought about Wendy's past relationships. Her twelve-month fling with Frank also ended abruptly without a plausible explanation. She blamed their breakup on his emotional baggage. And Jerry, her seven-month matinee, was an ugly slap in the face. He ditched her through an email saying he tried—but he just wasn't in love with her. And her second husband—she divorced him after only eight months of marriage because he cheated on her.

Then I considered Wendy's relationships with her girlfriends. She never seemed to have money. When I met her for cocktails and appetizers, I somehow always picked up her check. She would be short of cash, or she just wouldn't go for her wallet. When the girls got together for a potluck dinner, she would bring a cheap bottle of wine or a head of lettuce. Wendy was always borrowing something; an expensive blouse to wear on a hot date, furniture to fill up an empty corner of her condo, fine crystal and silverware for a party, and, of course, money. Wendy constantly complained about not having money. Her girlfriends bought her event tickets. Her long-distance girlfriends bought her plane tickets so she could visit them. One girlfriend felt sorry for Wendy and bought her a 40-inch flat screen television for her new condo.

Then one evening it all came together. When the dinner bill arrived at our table—Wendy pretended it didn't exist.

Wendy and I were having dinner with a group of her friends at a restaurant. We sat next to a married couple—Meg and what's-his-name. When the separate checks were presented, Wendy grabbed my arm as I reached into my purse for my credit card (somehow we both knew I was buying her dinner).

Wendy leaned over and whispered in my ear, "Wait, don't pay yet; see if Meg's husband picks up our check"—which he did as a generosity gesture to his wife.

Wendy turned her head sideways, covered her mouth with her hand and murmured, "See, I told you so."

Holy crap! My Woman Within is struck with a wave of clarity and understanding. That's why Johnson dumped her. That's why the men in her life tired of her—and that's why I always felt compelled to pick up her tab. Wendy methodically, deliberately, and selfishly manipulated her friends and romantic interests to pay her way through life. I felt, as I am sure her boyfriends did, betrayed and exploited.

The opposite of a scarcity thinker, is an abundance thinker. Abundance thinkers believe the universe has plenty to go around. They are givers and they are grateful for all they receive. Their hearts are full, their thoughts are large, and their exuberance is contagious. They believe the Universe is generous and the things they need to succeed in life will show up exactly at the right time. They are quick to share their time, knowledge, resources and connections because they believe it will come back to them magnified. Abundance thinkers are astounded, and grateful for their amazing good fortune.

7 Habits of Positive Thought

A positive mindset is at the core of prosperity, success and happiness.

1. Learn to look for the good in people. Treat everyone with respect and courtesy. Forgive the shortcomings of others, and you will soon forgive your imperfections.
2. Be sincere in your actions. Be honest, enthusiastic and friendly. Express your genuine feelings in a considerate and caring manner. This is your best self. Your best self will bring out the best in others.
3. Be open-minded to the thoughts, opinions and ideas of others. You may be unexpectedly inspired. Don't let prejudices or pre-conceived notions blind you to opportunities.

4. Develop an attitude of gratitude. Make a mental list of the things that you appreciate about your life, small and large, and give thanks for these blessings. The Universe recognizes a grateful heart and will bring you more of what you desire.
5. Be a giver; not a taker. Give of your time, money and wisdom. Give from a place of generosity. Don't expect anything in return. It is the intent of the heart, not the amount, which manifests prosperity.
6. Continually think about the things you want, not what you don't have. Visualize the things you want in life; believe that it is yours. It's the feeling that creates reality, not just the thought.
7. Pay attention to your dreams. Follow your gut instincts. Draw upon the wisdom that is within you. This is your spiritual guide pointing you in the right direction.

Practice thoughts of acceptance, generosity and gratitude and you will receive equal or greater amounts of the same—some people call it luck.

15 Personal 10 Commandments

We can't change the past, but we can change the future by making right choices today.

–Joel Osteen, *Become a Better You*

Once upon a time my low self-esteem issues wreaked mayhem in my life, causing me personal difficulties, relationship discord and heartbreak. Part of my personal growth was to acknowledge and correct my faulty, judgmental mindset. I wrote my "Personal 10 Commandments": a list of the actions, habits and qualities that I felt personified the confident, considerate, engaging woman I wanted to be. Before I left the house to go on a date or meet my friends, I reminded myself of my intentions: To rebuke the critical thoughts I had about others, and instead offer compliments and understanding. To squash my tendency to talk too much and be a good listener. To curb my tendency to gossip about superficial my girlfriends. To project a welcoming aura that would attract friendships, opportunities, success, and hopefully a quality man.

It's easy to backslide into our negative thought patterns.

Years passed and confidence and self-esteem were no longer an issue for me; I was instead opinionated, outspoken and self-absorbed. I neglected my family and friends. My constant socializing hindered my writing career. Dating was again a huge disappointment for me.

I was a magnet for liars, married men and players. The guys I had a crush on weren't interested in me—or, the guys that acted like they were "into" me, didn't call me for a second date. Once again I asked myself, *What am I doing wrong?*

❥

When I was 21-years-old, I rededicated my life to Christ. I was joyful and starry-eyed about my renewed spirituality. My dad, a devout Christian, said to me, "It's easy to do what's right when you're excited about your faith, but in time, life's daily grind will diminish your enthusiasm. When that happens, don't act on feelings. Do what's right because it's the right thing do."

It's the one piece of advice I remember my dad giving me, "Do it because it's right."

Another year slipped away; dating, men and happy hours interfered with me finishing my second book. I succumbed to depression. I didn't know why I was depressed—I just knew that I was. I picked up a book that had gathered dust on my nightstand, *Become a Better You* by Joel Osteen. I began to read it.

How high do you want to rise? Osteen asked. *Do you want to continue to increase? Do you want to see more of God's blessings and favor?*

"Yes, Lord," I answered. "I want to finish my *Never Date a Dead Animal* book. I want to help women attain confidence, self-esteem and relationship wisdom. I want to have a successful motivational speaking career. I want to have a wonderful loving man in my life."

Joel continued:

When He brings matters to our attention, if we want continued success and blessings, we have to be willing to face the truth about ourselves and take the corrective measures God commands.

In other words—we must do the right things.

Sometimes a dose of reality is the best therapy.

Osteen's words pricked my heart. His message was exactly what I needed to hear to shake my depression, squelch my self-doubt, pick myself up by the boot straps and rededicate myself to finishing my book. But first, I needed to update my "Personal 10 Commandments."

My Personal 10 Commandments: Revised

Commandment No. 1: *Broaden my circle of influence.* Attend social and business networking groups, gaining me new friendships and valuable connections. Promote the interests of others, especially my women friends. They will support my efforts and I will realize my dreams.

Commandment No. 2: *Don't brag; don't boast.* A pompous spirit is unattractive. It creates the disfavor of others.

Commandment No. 3: *Be a good listener.* If I am doing all the talking, not only am I an irksome bore, I'm not learning about the person in front of me. Concentrate on what someone is saying. Say their name three times in conversation. They will be flattered and I will be more apt to remember their name.

Commandment No. 4: *Don't talk about anyone in a negative way.* Idle gossip makes me look insecure, spiteful and untrustworthy.

Commandment No. 5: *Don't procrastinate.* Get off my computer, iPhone and iPad and take care of personal matters. Take time to whiten my teeth, get a pedicure, pay my bills and clean my bathroom.

Commandment No. 6: *Don't neglect family and friends.* Take time to connect with my loved ones and buddies. If I don't, there may come a time when I will be alone and forgotten.

Commandment No. 7: *Exercise regularly.* Set my alarm clock an hour earlier for morning exercise. Power walking and lifting weights strengthens and tones my body. The endorphins I get from exercise invigorate my mind and spirit.

Commandment No. 8: *Stop over-spending.* Spending money I don't have creates debt. Debt creates guilt, anxiety and fear, the genesis of negative energy.

Commandment No. 9: *Don't blab my personal business.* Don't tattle my age, how many times I've been divorced, or if I've had plastic surgery. Every time I tell a man my age he starts examining my crow's feet. There's plenty of time for self-disclosure.

Commandment No. 10: *Drink in moderation.* Don't drink and drive. Don't drunk dial. Wine doesn't love my figure or my face and it exacerbates my large personality.

Do what's right and I will be right with the world.
Thanks, Dad.

Your Personal 10 Commandments

It's your turn! Write your Personal 10 Commandments that will improve the quality of your life.

Commandment No. 1:

Commandment No. 2:

Commandment No. 3:

Commandment No. 4:

Commandment No. 5:

Commandment No. 6:

Commandment No. 7:

Commandment No. 8:

Commandment No. 9:

Commandment No. 10:

💔

My College-Dropout Woman Within whines, I work full-time. It'll take me six years to get a nursing degree at night school. By the time I graduate I'll be 57!

I frown and I ask her, How old will you be if you don't get your degree?

16 Change Your Thoughts; Alter Your Destiny

"How you feel about yourself will have a tremendous impact on how far you go in life and whether or not you fulfill your destiny."

—Joel Osteen

What keeps us from realizing our dreams? What is at the core of our harmful decisions? What makes us believe we are less than our best? What causes us to think we are unworthy of happiness and success?

Most of our internal programming is the result of how we were raised. As children our parents molded us to the image of their personalities, beliefs, values, fears and prejudices. Our teachers and authority figures strived to affect our opinions and character. Our classmates and friends influenced our decisions and behavior. Later in life, a boyfriend or a husband contributed to our mindset.

If the people and influences of our past were disapproving, disparaging and demeaning, our thinking became contaminated. We cling to the memory of a punitive father, a hyper-critical mother, or the remarks of a reproachful school teacher. We brood over a girlfriend's unkindness. We obsess over a boyfriend's or husband's cruel words and infidelity. These toxic images manifest into repetitive thought patterns that grieve our emotions, distort our reality, affect our behavior, and impair our ability to maintain healthy relationships.

The voice in your head is not who you are.

—Eckard Tolle

Eckard Tolle says that the voice in our head will tell us sad, anxious, or angry stories about ourselves, our lives, other people, and about past, future or imaginary events. The voice will be blaming, accusing, complaining, imagining, and we identify with whatever the voice says, and we believe its distorted thoughts.

In other words, our negative, disparaging thoughts create our sad reality.

When I was in high school my negative inner voice told me I didn't fit in with my classmates. She said, "You're ordinary. You're plain-looking. Your personality is annoying and boring. Your face is freckled and your hair is drab, dishwater blonde. Your clothes are an embarrassment. The popular girls don't want to be your friend. The guys don't want to date you."

My Teenager Within throws her hands in the air, *Praise Jesus your orthodontic braces came off before high school!*

I looked at the "popular" kids, you know, the preppy cheerleaders and the football players, the hot-shot fraternity brothers and the snooty sorority sisters, the homecoming queen and her Gidget-Tammy-Funicello bouffant court, and, of course, Mr and Miss Most-Beautiful-Most-Popular-Most-Likely-To-Succeed—and I envied them. The guys were testosterone beefcakes. The girls were gorgeous, flighty and cliquish. They were the super-students destined to go to college, have successful, exciting careers, travel the world, marry well, hatch curly-towheaded children, and live in the burbs in a two-story, white provincial house.

Next to them I felt insignificant, tattered and flawed.

I despised lunchtime in high school. Standing in the middle of the cafeteria, holding my lunch tray, I desperately scanned the room for classmates who wouldn't shun me for sitting at their table. My Teenager Within told me: *You're not good enough to sit at the lunch table with the sorority girls. You'll feel out of place. They'll snub you. Sit at the table with the other dweebs, geeks and no-names—or better yet, sit by yourself so you don't say something stupid.*

I listened to my negative inner voice.

I graduated from high school and my negative inner voice continued to squelch my confidence and self-esteem. In my 20s and 30s she told me I wasn't as smart as my co-workers, and she told me I was an oddball within my friend groups. She told me I wasn't worthy of a boyfriend who would love and respect me, and so I dated men were who less than what I wanted and deserved, and I married a man who slugged me.

When I reached my 40s my negative inner voice was full throttle. I felt third-rate, unattractive and unloved. In my 50s my negative voice jumped on her AARP soapbox. She complained: *Your hair is thin and lifeless. You need Botox, a breast lift and a tummy tuck—and for God's sake, when are you going to start exercising!* She taunted me, *What are those humps on your thighs? Is that cottage cheese on your butt? Jesus, are you growing a mustache?* She was quick to point out the attractiveness of younger women. They had long, thick hair, flawless porcelain complexions, perky DD tits, and concave stomachs. My negative inner voice said, *Men want to date younger women. You're past your prime. Go ahead, enjoy your margaritas and cheese enchiladas, and get yourself a moo-moo tent dress. Men aren't going to ask you out.*

My Core Woman Within is awakened from a 35-year comatose slumber. Shocked at the inconceivable, condescending thoughts ravaging through my mind, she screams: *Who put this garbage in your head? It certainly wasn't me! And it certainly wasn't your Maker!*

You're Fat, Ugly and Undeserving

Angie developed severe body image issues as a child. Growing up she watched her mother struggle with a constant weight problem. In college her mother was a beauty pageant winner and a runway model. When her third child died in childbirth, she succumbed to depression and she gained 80 pounds. Eating became her emotional crutch. She binged on sweets, she constantly dieted, and she complained bitterly about her overweight body. She hammered Angie about her developing, adolescent body. When Angie asked for a second helping of food at the dinner table, her mother snapped, "Haven't you had enough to eat, little piggy? I can't afford to keep buying you fat-girl clothes." Angie's mother limited her food intake to fruits, vegetables, tuna fish, chicken and salads, allowing her an occasional slice of pizza and dessert. Angie felt deprived. Late at night, when everyone was in bed, Angie would sneak into the kitchen and gorge on fried chicken, cookies, cake and ice cream. Food sedated Angie's feelings of being unloved, low self-worth and loneliness.

In high school Angie stood 5-feet-2, weighed 145 pounds, and she wore a size 14. She wore baggie shirts and big coats to hide her round figure. She couldn't afford, or fit into stylish clothes like the other girls. She bought her clothes at Goodwill and Walmart. The kids made fun of her, calling her "Mamaw" because she dressed like a grandmother.

Angie made good grades in school, but she instinctively knew that she didn't fit in with the popular kids. She joined the yearbook staff, because she was comfortable hanging out with the "nerds." She didn't try out for cheerleader, because she wasn't pretty or slender. She hated dressing out for her gym class, because she felt dumpy and inferior next to the slender pom-pom girls. She didn't date, because she was too self-conscious. Her mother told her, "You need to lay off the sweets. No man will want you with that wide load."

Angie consoled herself with food. She consumed jelly donuts, fried onion rings and Twinkies in the school cafeteria. She inhaled Big Macs, milk shakes and French fries on the weekends. Walking home from school, she stopped at the convenience store and she stocked up on candy bars, cupcakes and potato chips, secretly binging in her bedroom until bedtime. Food comforted Angie, momentarily; after her food frenzy she felt heavy, guilty and worthless. She avoided looking in the mirror, because her demeaning inner voice reminded her that she was fat, ugly and undeserving. She skipped her high school prom, because she wanted to disappear.

In college, Angie started smoking pot and chugging beer and vodka shooters. She gained 25 pounds. She flunked out of college and her life spiraled out of control. Her family doctor prescribed her Buspar, and she gained 10 more pounds. She switched to Prozac, totally sedating her emotions. She took diet pills and she lost 50 pounds.

Men began to notice Angie and sex became her new comfort food. She indiscriminately slept with guys, trying to fill the void in her heart. Afterwards, she felt used and dirty. She fell in love with a salesman at work and she got pregnant. He didn't want to get married; he dumped Angie and she got an abortion.

Angie was devastated over the loss of her baby and her boyfriend. Her negative inner voice told her, *You need to lose weight. You know he's attracted to slender women.*

Angie practically stopped eating. During the day she ate celery, carrots, rice cakes and crackers. She constantly drank sweet ice tea, diet Cokes and coffee to kill her appetite. At night she ate sliced tomatoes, salads dressed with vinegar, a slice of turkey and sugar-free Jell-O. She stopped drinking beer and wine and she switched to Scotch and water. She was obsessed with counting calories, measuring food portions, and weighing herself at least twice a day. She refused to go out to lunch or eat in restaurants and she stashed fat-free candy in her bedroom. If she ate the wrong food, or she overate, she stuck her finger down her throat to make herself vomit—and she ran extra miles.

Angie's girlfriend warned her she had lost too much weight. Angie stood in front of her full-length mirror in her bra and panties and stared at her gaunt, skeleton-like body. Her cheeks were sunken and her eyes were hollow. Her collarbone and sternum bone protruded through her rawboned skin. Her pencil arms were veined and wispy. Her hip bones were sharp corners jutting out the top of her bikini underwear. Angie weighed 90 pounds soaking wet.

Her hyper-critical inner voice told her, *You're fat! You need to lose 10 more pounds*!

My Jealous, Disparaging Inner Voice

It was a hot summer Friday night. My guy and I were at a neighborhood Sushi restaurant, sitting at the bar enjoying each other's company. I was sipping on a champagne cocktail, he was enjoying a Dirty Martini. We nibbled on cucumber wrapped lobster and cream cheese crab rolls. My guy looked handsome in his white linen shirt and silk shorts. I felt sexy in my Calvin Klein seersucker sundress. My tan shoulders, arms and bare legs glistened. My man eyeballed my décolletage as if it were his next nibble of Hamachi.

Life is good!

I casually glanced over my shoulder at an attractive mature couple seated at a table sipping martinis and engaged in an intimate conversation. The couple oozed of style and success. I turned, I smiled softly at my guy, and I took a sip of my champagne.

I looked sideways again to nonchalantly study the woman. I impulsively critiqued her, sub-consciously comparing myself to her. She was more petite than I; her tight white jeans looked two sizes smaller than my size 8. Her sheer, long-sleeve top was classy couture. Her pastel plaid, sling-back, peep-toe wedge heels were the essence of summer panache. Her coiffure was short, sassy and more dazzling blonde than mine. Her French tip nails were immaculate. Holy mascara! Look at her round impressive eyes—she's got to be wearing false eyelashes! Her complexion was flawless. Her glossy Lancôme lips looked like a collagen commercial. She was my age—but she looked like a Baby Boomer Barbie doll.

I innately disliked this woman—and I didn't even know her.

I felt my demeanor suddenly change. Envy heated my blood. My body flushed with negativity and my spirit plummeted. I felt old, frumpy and uncultured. I was no longer bubbly and beautiful.

I casually turned, looked at her husband and I appraised him, as well. He was delicious. He was in his early 60's; tall, toned and sophisticated. He appeared to be of Italian descent (you know what they say about Italian men). His olive complexion was bronzed from the sun (probably from a recent trip to an exotic beach). His thick, grey-tipped dark hair was stylishly combed back, a handsome broad smile spread across his chiseled jaw. He was dressed to the nines. He wore a Floridian shirt, flowing silk slacks, an impressive Rolex and a gold nugget ring. Hmm… that must be their silver Bentley Flying Spur parked conspicuously in front of the restaurant.

Jealousy and envy self-sabotaged my evening.

Suddenly my guy was no longer handsome and wonderful.

A gloomy, grey cloud washed over me.

My Woman Within downed her third glass of champagne and screamed, What's wrong with you—your guy is adorable, he's successful, and he's totally devoted to you. For crying out loud, he treats you like you were his prized Labrador!

One minute my world was perfect. My guy was handsome and amazing. I was happy-go-lucky and I felt special. Fifteen minutes later my negative inner voice undermined my confidence, sabotaged my feelings for my sweetheart, and ruined my Friday night.

I spent a lifetime listening to my blaming, belittling, hyper-criticizing inner voice. It told me I was not smart or pretty. It told me I was different and I didn't fit in with others. It told me I was unworthy of friendships, happiness and success. It told me I was not as capable as the other guy, and I didn't measure up in the workplace. It told me I needed a man to feel complete. It told me I didn't deserve the love and respect of a wonderful man.

I read Rick Warren's book *The Purpose Driven Life*.

"You are not an accident," Warren said. "God prescribed every single detail of your body. He determined the natural talents you would possess and the uniqueness of your personality. We were made to have meaning."

My Woman Within stirred. That's right! I was born with a perfect spirit. I was born with a spirit of joy, confidence and compassion. I was born with innate talents, a unique personality and a desire to be special. I would have developed my God-given traits and talents had I not allowed the undermining, influencing thoughts of others make me believe I was incapable and unworthy... and then I thought: where does it say that I have to live my life out believing the negative thoughts of others?

Where indeed?

I shut my eyes, I withdrew from the world, and with great intent I reached into my soul and I erased my faulty belief system that dominated my subconscious. I envisioned the person I could have been without the past negative influences in my life. I envisioned myself as a newborn baby whose mind was *tabula rasa*—blank. My mind was pure, untouched and void of negative thought patterns and it was hungry for information that would nourish my temperament, personality, character and talents. I pretended to fill my infant mind with positive thoughts that were wholesome, illuminating and uplifting. As I grew up my parents were loving, supportive, encouraging and positive-minded. I imagined myself a teenager; I mastered academics and social interaction. My grades excelled. I had lots of friends. I was happy, outgoing and confident—not the timid, fearful, self-conscious teen I had been in reality. In college I pursued a degree that would land me my dream job. I would be a lawyer, a doctor or the CEO of a large cosmetics company, or perhaps I would be a Hollywood celebrity or a noted TV personality. As an adult I surrounded myself with people and influences that strengthened my core being and bolstered my aspirations. I rejected and insulated myself from the people, dogmas and opinions that would taint my positive identity. I embraced my zany, high-spirited personality and I harnessed my cutting-edge creative talents. Maybe—just maybe—I would become an eminent self-improvement, dating and relationship author.

My Woman Within whispered in my ear, Maybe you never fit in—because you were supposed to stand out.

I was created for a special purpose. I was assigned unique personality traits and talents. My life was intended to have special meaning. My purpose is to contribute to the betterment of those around me. If this is true about me, then YOU must exist for a special reason, too. So who am I to judge and criticize the uniqueness of others—and who are they to criticize and judge me?

At long last, I realized the confident, powerful, purposeful woman God intended me to be—silencing my negative inner voice—*forever.*

Listen up!

- You are not the hyper-criticisms of your mom or your father.
- You are not the insecure teenager who was rejected by your classmates, who didn't make the cheerleader squad or basketball team, or got blackballed from a sorority.
- You are not the shame-based woman who slept with a string of men, seeking a man's affection and acceptance.
- You are not the little girl whose father abandoned or abused her, causing you to crave a father's love and validation.
- You are not the unkind words of your self-absorbed girlfriend, co-worker or boss.
- You are not the woman who drinks or does drugs to numb the pain of your past.
- You are not the demeaning put-downs of your abusive boyfriend or husband.
- You are NOT a punching bag!

Any questions?

17 Shut Up! Negative Self-Talk

"A belief is nothing more than a chronic pattern of thought, and you have the ability—if you try even a little bit—to begin a new pattern, to tell a new story, to achieve a different vibration, to change our point of attraction."

—Ester and Jerry Hicks, *Money and the Law of Attraction*

Twelve Examples of Negative Thinking, and How You Can Turn Them Around.

1. **Closed Mindset:** You categorize everything in black and white, no shades of gray. You have a kneejerk reaction to the comments, opinions and ideas of others. They're wrong. You're right. Instead of listening to the person talking, your mind rushes to respond with your point of view.

   Positive Solution: Listen patiently to the opinions and ideas of others. Be slow to share your comments and opinions. Ask questions. Consider that they may know something that you don't. Consider that there can be two rights, and no one is wrong.

2. **Self-doubt and Procrastination:** *I don't think I can do this, you think.* You are afraid you will fail so you postpone starting a project. You have great ideas, but you fear deep down that you are incapable of success, so you drag your feet, lose your enthusiasm and you fail by default.

Positive Solution: Commit your ideas and goals to paper, set a start date and a timeline for completion—and then just do it! Forget about being successful. Your goal is to execute small and large action steps. Your motions will motivate you. Your incremental accomplishments will empower you, pushing you closer to success.

3. **Comparing Yourself to Others.** We'll never be as pretty, as talented, as rich, or as successful as everyone else. We can always find someone we think is better, if we look hard enough. Comparing yourself to others zaps your confidence, creative energy and motivation to excel.

   Positive Solution: Stop comparing yourself to others and concentrate on your strengths, talents, accomplishments and successes, small and large. View your idiosyncrasies as unique, special traits. Love and appreciate who you are, right now, not who you want to become.

4. **Guilt-Induced Performance.** You beat yourself up for your shortcomings. We all fail from time to time. We under-plan, we over-estimate, and we miss the mark. We overeat and we overspend. We over-react and we respond poorly. We occasionally disappoint our friends, co-workers, boss and loved ones. Beating ourselves up for our minor infractions is counter-productive and creates a negative self-image.

   Positive Solution: Acknowledge your error. Put it in perspective and move on. "I spoke rashly to my friend." Apologize and let it go. "I overate and I didn't exercise." Skip dessert, exercise tomorrow and get your enthusiasm on track. Focus on your successes in your personal and business life in the last week, month, year, or five years. Keep a journal of your accomplishments.

5. **Self-Deprecating Dialog:** Your inner voice belittles and devalues your worth. You reject compliments and you underplay your accomplishments. You put yourself down in front of others. You say, "I'm so clumsy. I look fat. I'm not smart enough. I always forget things. If anyone can screw up, I will."

   Positive Solution: Immediately reject negative self-talk. Focus on the things you like about yourself. Focus on your talents and abilities. Acknowledge your accomplishments. Accept your imperfections; we all have them. Don't broadcast your shortcomings. Say "thank you" for compliments.

6. **Rationalizing With Your Emotions.** "I feel, therefore it must be true." You react to life and people based on your unhealthy, illogical and irrational emotions.

   Positive Solution: Base your perception on facts and evidence. It will illuminate reality.

7. **Over-Reacting:** You immediately go on the defense when someone insults or maltreats you. You feel the need to confront them and expose their insensitive behavior, e.g.; a girlfriend slights you to be with her new boyfriend. You take issue with her, she gets defensive, and the result is additional negative feelings.

   Positive Solution: Let the insults and negative actions of others roll off you. Don't let their problem become your problem. Lower your expectations of others, realizing no one is perfect. Take time to cool-off; you may decide it really was no big deal. Whatever the outcome—don't burn your bridges.

8. **Scarcity Thinking**. Scarcity thinking makes us overly competitive and greedy. Your sub-conscious tells you there is not enough to go around. You need to get this or that before the other guy does. You can't share your knowledge or connections because someone may take advantage of you. Scarcity thinking shuts down your resourcefulness and the generosity of others.

   Positive Solution: Learn to see success as something that can be shared. If I am generous and I help and support your efforts, you will, in turn, feel benevolent about promoting me. We each increase our chances to be successful.

9. **Pessimistic Point of View:** You see everyone and everything in a negative light. You look for the worst in others. You capitalize on their shortcomings. You complain about every situation. You openly express your negativity to everyone around you.

   Positive Solution: Negative chatter is an acquired bad habit that can be broken. Look for the positive aspects in every person and every situation in your life, and express those thoughts. You may be surprised that you like what you find.

10. **Unrealistic Mental Filters:** Your life is a negative journey. You dwell on what you don't have, and therefore, you are never happy in your present circumstances. You think you can't be happy until you reach a certain goal, certain lifestyle, certain relationship or a certain income.

    Positive Solution: Count your blessings for all that you do have and consciously enjoy those things. Live your life in the present.

11. **Assuming the Worst:** You jump to conclusions about others and situations. You imagine someone doesn't like you, or you assume the worst of a situation, without facts to support your reasoning. You anticipate the hurtful behavior of others before they have actually done or said anything. You over-react to a comment or minor infringement, e.g., your husband or boyfriend is in a bad mood; you automatically think you did something wrong.

    Positive Solution: Assume things are going well (that people like you, that you're doing a good job, and all is right in your world) until you learn differently. Assume that someone's hurtful behavior has nothing do with you. Realize life is not always about you.

12. **Generalizing.** You allow a single hurtful event to define your daily existence, even the outcome of your life. You let one negative remark ruin your whole day. You see one mistake as a deficit against your overall good performance. You view one failure as defeat.

    Positive Solution: One negative event, person or comment does not define your life. One error does not make you worthy or unworthy. See a single unpleasant incident as a bump in the road.

My Woman Within looks at herself in the mirror, *I love you and from now on I'm going to talk like it.*

Part Three

Find Your Authentic Self

"Your best self will bring out the best in others.
That's when others can truly enjoy your company."

— Nancy Nichols

18
Comfortable In Your Own Skin

People who are authentic write their own songs, sing their own music and march to their own band.

People want to connect with someone who is authentic. They want to feel they know the "real" you. They want to feel they can trust you.

People who are comfortable in their own skin know who they are. They know what they want—and what they don't want. They understand their limits. They are able to maintain healthy boundaries with their boyfriends and husbands, friends, grown children, family members and co-workers. They can walk away from situations that are objectionable or unsettling to them. They will not accept someone's unreasonable, inconsiderate or self-serving behavior. They will stand up to a person's passive-aggressive, manipulative, controlling behavior.

People who are comfortable in their own skin have realistic perceptions of themselves, of others, and the world around them. They have embraced their hurtful past. They have forgiven themselves for their past indiscretions and transgressions. They have privately, or openly, acknowledged their injurious behavior against others; hence, they live their lives free of guilt. The blame, accusations, criticisms of others roll off them like water off a duck's back. Because they have realistic expectations of themselves, they have reasonable expectations of others. Because they are accepting of themselves, they are less likely to criticize others. They respect the differences in people, regardless of someone's intellect, background, or social and economic status. They allow their friends to express their individuality.

They allow the contrasting viewpoints of others, and they are open-minded to new ideas. They don't feel they have to always be right.

People who are comfortable in their own skin are bold about their future; they are secure in who they are and what they are doing. They are independent thinkers and problem-solvers; they tend to be spontaneous and unconventional. They work to improve their weak points and they capitalize on their strengths. Their glass is half-full—not half-empty. They view their world with a sense of anticipation, appreciation and awe; simple experiences are a source of inspiration and pleasure. They are often motivated by a sense of personal responsibility, ethics and helping others. In times of difficulty, they understand it is a temporary setback, they are strengthened by life's challenges, and they remain determined, focused and optimistic.

People who are comfortable in their own skin emit confidence and independence, acceptance and approachability. Onlookers are intrigued and drawn to their welcoming, self-assured presence. They view life as an opportunity to make new friendships, enjoy social rapport and business connections. They relish the company of others, but they are equally content to spend time alone, pursuing their interests and developing their potential. They are willing to share of their time, knowledge and resources because they do not worry that someone will get ahead or take advantage of them.

For the most part, people who are comfortable in their own skin acknowledge a Higher Power. They rely on their Higher Power for guidance, encouragement, inspiration and stability. They give thanks for their blessings and they experience moments of intense gratitude and joy. Acknowledging a Higher Power keeps a person's ego in check. A realistic, humble ego is fundamental to being authentic.

When you are truly comfortable in your own skin, not everyone will like you, but you won't care about it one bit!

—Unknown

19 Your Best Self

Your best self will come out of the emotional pain you have conquered, the character flaws you have corrected, and the wrongs you have righted.

I have pondered my earthly existence for a very long time. I thought about who I turned out to be, and what I could have been in a perfect world. I wondered about the events that shaped me as a person; the people and experiences that influenced my mindset, and created my self-doubt, defense mechanisms and hyper-sensitive personality. I considered how my life could have turned out different—*had I done things differently.*

When I was growing up it seemed boys were special, and I was, well, a girl. As a tween I was a scabbed-kneed, tow-headed, freckled-faced kid. There weren't any girls my age to play with in my neighborhood, and so I played with my two brothers and six or eight obnoxious boys in our family's humongous backyard. There was Asa, a fair-complected, mild-mannered boy with curly dark-hair, who was an artistic prodigy. There was Kurt, a handsome, older, lanky, dishwater blonde 16-year-old boy, whom I dreamed of marrying one day. And Wendell, a skinny, icky kid who once tried to bust my head open with a brick.

My park-size, forest-like backyard was a magnet for the neighborhood kids. We had a clearing that served as a baseball-football field. We had apple and pecan trees to climb and eat the fruit. There was a jungle of mature trees and thicket to play kick the can, and to hide from my dad when I misbehaved, to avoid him whipping my bare legs with a razor-sharp tree branch. We had a concrete pad for a basketball goal and roller skating, and a massive 40-foot oak tree which supported a long, thick rope swing that flew frightfully high into the air.

With no girls to play with, boys were my adolescent role models. I shinnied up trees. I played a mean game of tackle football. I slammed home runs. I played guard in basketball. I raced my bicycle down the winding trails in our backyard and throughout the neighborhood. I swapped punches with the guys, and I threw apples at the neighborhood kids walking across the street. My older brother admittedly ran off the only neighborhood girl by throwing rotten apples at her—*thanks, Bro!* I hit my younger brother in the head with a large rock and a golf-ball size knot popped up on his forehead. *I thought I might have killed him!* He stabbed me in my ankle with an edging shovel—*I think I can still see the scar!* I slid down an icy driveway sitting on the end of a spade shovel, fell on my face, busted my lip and cracked my front tooth. It was all in a day's fun for a scrappy, freckled-faced tomboy with sun-white, poker-straight short hair.

My teen years were difficult for me in a family where boys seemed to have privileges—and I did not. My brothers shared a bedroom replete with twin beds, spaceship bedspreads, matching study desks and bookcases and shelves to house their books, sports paraphernalia and my older brother's do-it-yourself telescope and Van de Graff generator science project. My make-shift bedroom was the small dining room adjacent to the kitchen and the living room. My bedroom furniture was a faded seafoam-green pull-out sofa and a vanity-slash-desk and stool. I crammed my meager clothing and shoes into the narrow linen closet. Privacy in my so-called bedroom was a fantasy—a skimpy pullback curtain blocked my view of the kitchen and folding louver doors separated me from the living room. I was ashamed to invite my girlfriend over for a sleepover in my bastardized bedroom. Early Saturday mornings the loud clatter of dishes and loud voices would wake me, putting me in an ugly, fighting mood.

In junior high I didn't make the Marching Archers, but I rocked at high jump, track, baseball and basketball, and I shared notoriety with Asa and Wendell as our school's three most talented artists. Puberty was not my friend. My mom over-permed my short dishwater blonde hair, and she didn't let me have a training bra until I was in the 8th grade. One day I was flat as a fritter, and the next day I came to school sporting 32B knockers. I cringed as the boys turned sideways in the school hallway gawking at my full-figured sweater.

I finally shaved my legs in high school. I couldn't afford to wear nice outfits like the popular girls and I was embarrassed by my drab school clothes. I worked at the local Woolworth store after school and on weekends so I could buy cute clothes at the department store. I didn't make the cut as cheerleader and I was black-balled from an elite sorority. I had an anxiety attack during sorority rush and I forgot the name of a Sigma Sigma uppity sister—*whatever!* The same week Sigma Sigma repudiated me, and my new hot, super-popular boyfriend-of-two-weeks cheated on me with Wendy. He broke up with me and he confiscated his Pi Kappa Alpha pin—*whatever and love sucks!* It was one crappy week for a gawky, insecure, speckled-faced 16-year-old girl with colossal boobs and a bad perm.

I rebelled in my senior year. I smoked my first cigarette. I drank my first half of a half-pint of cherry vodka. I got shitfaced. I upchucked and I had my first hangover. I learned how to French kiss in the back of the neighborhood Park Theatre with a guy classmate. I was ousted from a Friday night matinee for ambushing my classmates with a water gun. The theatre manager grabbed my arm, escorted me to the office and called my dad. My dad picked me up from the theatre, drove me home in shame, and grounded me for a month from talking on the phone and going out with my friends.

After two weeks, of what seemed liked cruel and unjust punishment for a harmless juvenile prank, I threw a hissy fit. My militant dad came at me with a belt. I bolted out our home's front door and I fled down the street with him chasing me, his face blood-red, his eyes blazing, swinging his leather belt. I knew if he caught me I was dead meat. I outran him and I hid at my girlfriend's house all weekend. My parents finally caved in and pleaded for me to come home—that's when I learned the power of making my parents worry. After that, when things didn't go my way, I ran away from home until my parents repented of their badness.

Our family had one car, a tank-size, baby blue and white 1960 Oldsmobile 88, shared between three teenagers, all with brand-new driver's licenses. On the weekends my brothers wanted the family car to date girls. I wanted to pick up my girlfriend, Wendy (I eventually forgave her for making out my super-hot boyfriend), and drive through Shoney's, Sandy's and the Pig and Whistle, looking for my classmates and boys.

It was Friday night. My dad gave me permission to use the family car to go cruising with Wendy.

"I got the car!" I shrilled through the phone at Wendy.

An hour before I was to pick Wendy up, my mom announced, "Your brother has a date and he needs the car."

What the crap?!?! Don't my plans count?

Evidently not!

I didn't apply myself in high school. I struggled to fit in with my classmates. I battled with math and algebra, but I excelled in English, art and Home Economics. I butted heads with my teachers. My guidance counselor told me my grades weren't good enough for me to take French (code for: I was too retarded to speak a foreign language). My older brother learned to speak fluent German. My younger brother spent a high school summer in Italy, reciting, "*Ciao. Scusa. Grazie* and *mi capisce*?"

Was I not from the same gene pool?

❦

As a teenage girl I don't remember my parents ever saying to me:

> You're going to college; it's not an option.
>
> You can't get a good job without a college education.
>
> Learn to take care of yourself; don't depend on a man for your livelihood.
>
> Pursue your dreams. Have an exciting career. Travel. There's plenty of time to get married, say, when you're forty and *gawdawful* rich.

It seemed my brothers were earmarked to go to college so they could earn a good living to support their wives and children. They both graduated from college with Masters in Physics (and I am quit to brag on them). While I, the girl, was destined to follow in my mom's footsteps; possibly attend college for a year or two, get a desk job, marry, have children, go back to work to help support the family, whilst raising the kids—*and live happily ever after?*

I graduated from high school and I immediately looked for a job. My tidy handwriting and outgoing personality landed me my first job as an advertising secretary. I saved my paychecks for a year for a down-payment for my first car. At age 19, I bought a shiny new, red 1967 Camaro Rally Sport convertible with an automatic 327, 4-barrel V8. For the first time in my young life I felt as if I had a noteworthy identity—I was the feisty blonde driving the coolest machine in East Memphis. I had wheels, I had money in my pocket, and I drank Pabst Blue Ribbon to mask my insecurities and bolster my lack of confidence.

I went on to fulfill my life's destiny, dragging my low-esteem issues with me. In my twenties and my thirties I was foolhardy and desperate for love. At age nineteen I married a high school classmate to escape my unhappy home life. We drank and we argued. I had a baby. He slugged me and I divorced him after one year of marriage. Ten years later I married the red-neck-from-hell. We fornicated like bunnies, drank like largemouth basses, and I had my second child. I knew he was bad news before I married him. He was verbally and physically abusive, he quit paying the bills and our house went into foreclosure. I divorced him after 10 years of marriage.

I started ironing out in my forties. Ten years after my second divorce, I married my third husband and father figure, thirteen years my senior. He was a decent man, who spoke to me on special occasions. I landed my first major career in cosmetics and I traveled extensively. I matured. I outgrew my husband emotionally and I divorced him after ten years without conversation, foreplay or intimacy.

I started ironing out in my forties.

In my fifties, I was quasi-stable and fun-loving. But I struggled with a drinking problem that sabotaged my relationships and bended my fenders. And then came the coup de grâce—I fell hook-line-and-sinker for a clinical, narcissistic sociopath.

💔

I grew up feeling like the "female black sheep" of our family. I felt second-place to my brothers. I felt inferior to my high school classmates. I felt flawed, insignificant and undeserving as an adult. I regretted not finishing college. I struggled to find a decent job and I struggled financially. I questioned my abilities and I felt inferior next to my co-workers. I felt out of place, inept and second-rate in social settings. I wrestled with low self-worth in my relationships, and I allowed men into my life who maltreated me. I married three times, to the wrong men, for the wrong reasons.

Don't be afraid to be different—different is good!

It was my son, wise beyond his years, who inspired a healing moment in my life.

I was 57-years-old, struggling to heal from Dr. Dirtbag's toxic abuse, going through an emotional crisis, and lamenting my hurtful past. Talking long-distance on the phone with my son one night, he sensed my mental anguish. He said to me, "Mom, your family didn't understand you when you were growing up because you were different from them. They were reserved, intellectual and introverted. Your brothers were compliant and studious. You were extroverted, adventurous, creative and headstrong. Your mom and dad didn't know how to handle you." And then he said, "Mom, you don't understand. You're more intellectual than both of your brothers. They got their smarts from books. You make your stuff up."

Everything you need is within you.

Wow! I thought—from the mouth of the next generation. Tears streamed down my cheeks.

That was a precious awakening moment for me. In essence my son was saying, "Mom, you don't understand, you have everything you need inside you to create the life you want and deserve."

20 Recipe for Trouble

"Nobody is good at everything, and no one is called to be everything."

—Rick Warren

Our best self includes our unique flaws, our shortcomings, our physical imperfections and our eccentricities with which we struggle.

If ever there were a recipe for discontent, unhappiness and failure—it is comparing ourselves to others.

Women are notorious for comparing themselves to other women. We compare ourselves to another woman's physical features and outer dress. We compare ourselves to another woman's abilities, her career, her social status, her possessions, her husband and children, her boyfriend, and other relationships. Without realizing it—when we compare ourselves to another woman—we define ourselves.

If you go looking for trouble, you will find a woman who will make you feel inferior.

All my life I compared myself to others. My negative self-talk was quick to tell me I didn't measure up to the next gal (or guy), saying I wasn't as intelligent, or as talented, or as attractive as someone else.

I was once a director for a multi-level skincare and cosmetic company. My income and promotions came from selling product and recruiting others into the business. My unit director, Carla, was a crackerjack salesperson. She was consistently a top seller and top recruiter in our company. Carla's down-line recruit and best friend, Frieda, was equally successful. Every year at our company's annual national convention, Carla and Frieda pranced across the stage to collect their newest promotion and awards. They won eye-popping jewelry, fabulous trips and Titanic Cadillacs (silver—not pink). They were exceedingly irritating with their air of victory and tight-knit friendship. I was "eat-up" with jealousy over their accomplishments.

> **The ego lives through comparison. How you are seen by others turns into how you see yourself.**
>
> **—Eckhart Tolle**

Comparing myself to Carla and Frieda played havoc on my self-worth. My envy and resentment poisoned my motivation. I loved the business and I valued the women in my down-line, but I was discouraged trying to outsell and outwit this hateable dynamic duo. I was a heartbeat away from quitting the business.

I was one of Carla's star performers. My second year in the business I won a trip to the Bahamas as her top seller and top recruiter. In the Bahamas I shared a hotel room with Carla and her irksome BFF, Frieda. The three of us were unpacking in our room, Carla and Frieda were sharing a bottle of wine, and I listened to them talk freely about their lives. They both despised their husbands and they talked disparagingly about them. Their children were selfish hellions. Frieda was a recovering drug addict. Carla struggled with smoking, a constant weight problem and low self-esteem body issues.

They badmouthed their sister directors, and they criticized the hierarchy of our company. They sniggered at their shifty selling and recruiting tactics. Their thinking was self-absorbed, condescending and twisted. Their behavior was catty and helter-skelter. Their lives were chaotic and unhappy. In a nutshell, these dingbats were two of the most dysfunctional, unpalatable females I had ever encountered.

I had put Carla and Frieda on a Mary-Kay-Amway-Pampered-Chef-Tupperware pedestal. I measured my competency, intelligence and performance by their accomplishments. I had allowed these misfits to intimidate me, make me feel jealous and doubt my abilities.

Don't be envious of the runner in the lane next to you; just focus on finishing your race.

—Rick Warren

I was a changed woman after spending four days in the topsy-turvy, malfunctioning world of Carla and Frieda. Before my Bahama trip, I thought I couldn't measure up to the super business skills of these female fireballs. After the trip, I realized I was much more talented, much more discerning, and much more competent than these two dizzy directors glued together.

I quit looking sideways, comparing myself to Carla and Frieda. I focused on building my multi-level marketing business. I concentrated on my talents. I applied my abilities. I trained and motivated my sales force. I worked my plan and I kept my eyes locked on the prize. Six months later, in record time, I was awarded top sales and top recruiter in our region. Several months later I walked across the stage at our annual national convention in front of thousands to receive a promotion, a car, and an exquisite diamond and sapphire ring as one of the company's top ten nationwide directors.

Hey, Dynamic Dizzy Duo—eat my pink dust!

God created us in a perfect image. He doesn't look down from heaven at you and say, "Why can't you be more like your sister? Why can't you be more like Angelina Jolie?"

—Rick Warren

Note to Self:

✓ Comparing myself to others fuels my insecurities and low self-esteem issues.

✓ Comparing myself to others damages my spirit and discourages me.

✓ Comparing myself to others impairs my talents and abilities.

✓ Comparing myself to others creates unrealistic expectations of me, and of my loved ones, friends and co-workers.

✓ Comparing myself to others is the impetus for my criticisms, envy and jealousy.

21 The Things That Don't Kill You, Make You Stronger

"Your most effective ministries will come out of your deepest hurts. The things you're most embarrassed about, most ashamed of, and most reluctant to share."

—Rick Warren

Les Misérables, translated means: *The Miserable Ones, The Wretched, The Poor Ones, or The Victims.*

Les Misérables, an 1862 French novel and 1998 movie, is the story of Jean Valjean (Liam Neeson) an outcast ex-convict who finds redemption in a kindly old priest, and consequently becomes a force for good in the world. Valjean rises to the rank of a wealthy factory owner, and he is appointed mayor of his adopted town of Montreuil-sur-Mer—but he cannot escape his dark past.

Fantine (Uma Thurman) is a beautiful, illiterate unwed mother, who lost her factory job because of the local attitudes about her illegitimate daughter. The destitute Fantine turns to prostitution to care for her daughter, and she is arrested and tortured by the fanatic Inspector Javert (Geoffrey Rush). Valjean rescues Fantine from her unjust imprisonment and she becomes gravely ill. Valjean shelters and cares for her, and as she lay on her deathbed he promises to raise her small daughter, Cosette. Fantine felt unworthy of Valjean's benevolence; moved by his kindness she wept and said to Valjean:

"But you don't understand. I'm a whore, and Cosette has no father."

Valjean replied tenderly, "She has the Lord. He is her Father. And you are His creation. In His eyes you have never been anything but an innocent... and beautiful woman."

Guilt, Shame and Restoration

"The wounded recognized the wounded."

– Nora Roberts, *Rising Tides*

Warning: This true story contains sexually graphic language.

The absolute worst and abominable is the parent who physically or sexually abuses their children. Truly there must be a purgatory hot seat waiting for them on judgment day.

Jenny grew up on the wrong side of Boston. Her father, a factory worker, was a chronic alcoholic and her mother was cold, distant and severely depressed. Her father drank every night and her mom and dad had knock-down drag-out fights. Her mother would get mad and hurl a drinking glass, an ash tray or a plate full of food at her dad. Her dad would become violent and hammer her mother with his closed fists or his thick leather belt and buckle, lacerating and bloodying her mother's face and body. If Jenny were in striking distance, her dad would lash out and beat her. Jenny learned to hide with her younger sister in the bedroom they shared, waiting for the sound of raging voices and breaking glass to stop. Jenny's mother stayed in bed most of the time, and her father began molesting Jenny at age 5.

Jenny shares her story.

When I was 5, my dad told my mom he was going to give me a bath. He took me in the bathroom, he undressed me, he put me in the tub, and while he was bathing me, he put his finger inside me. I remember that it felt weird and I felt awful, but I thought it must be okay, because he was my dad. That went on for years. My mom never questioned my father's suspicious, inappropriate behavior.

When I was 10, my dad began to talk to me about sex. He put me on his lap, he ran his hand up my skirt and he touched me between my legs, telling me, this is where a man inserts his "dick." Chills ran up and down my 10-year-old body and I felt a weird, alarming sensation under my underwear.

My mom started working away from home. My dad came into my bedroom, he sat down on the side of my bed beside me and he exposed himself to me. He took my hand and he made me touch him and his penis swelled up in front of me. I didn't know what he was doing and I was scared, but he was my father and so I yielded to him. He told me to take my clothes off and lay down on my bed and he raped me. He hurt me and I cried. He told me it was natural for a father to show his affection to his daughter to prepare her for her relationship with a man and marriage. When I got older, I begged him to stop. He told me I was lucky to have a father that loved me as much he did, and he accused me of not loving him. I instinctively knew what he was doing was a terrible secret. I kept my mouth shut because I was afraid my mother would blame and punish me.

School was a way for me to get out of my home. I walked 3 miles to high school every day in the worst of weather. I didn't mind. It was three hours that kept me from being sexually abused by my dad. I was ashamed and self-conscious in school. I felt like everyone knew I was a sexually molested child. I felt like that my being born was a horrible mistake.

When I was 12, I ran away from home to go live with my grandmother. My dad forced me to come back home and he threatened to beat me if I ever ran away from home again. My grandmother told me, "Jen, God loves you. One day you will find someone who will love and care for you."

When I was 14, I tried to tell my mom what my dad was doing. She called me a liar and she told me not to anger my dad. My mother couldn't deal with the truth and she shut her eyes his abuse. My dad sexually molested me until I left home after graduating from high school.

It became my mission in high school to get out of my house, away from my dad's sexual abuse, move away from my impoverished neighborhood, and make something out of my life. I knew college was not a reality for me and so I took typing, shorthand and I got my cosmetology license.

At age 18, I moved in with my aunt and I got a job as a hair dresser. I worked hard, I saved my money and I attended cosmetology events. I landed a makeup artistry and hair stylist position with a major hair care corporation. I traveled every week. I was lonely and I began drinking excessively. I craved a man's acceptance and affection. I hooked up with men in hotel lobby bars and I took them back to my room and I had sex with them. I was conditioned to submit to a man sexually. I afraid to say "no" because I needed a man to love me. After a man left my hotel room, I felt used and vulgar.

In Boston I frequented happy hours. Men bought me drinks and they told me I was beautiful and desirable. I wanted to believe them and I followed them to their homes, I had unprotected sex with them—and I never heard from them again. I was sitting at a restaurant bar when a handsome man approached me. He was in town for business. He brought me drinks. He expressed a genuine interest in me and he invited me back to his exclusive hotel for a nightcap. We took a taxi to his hotel, we went straight to his hotel room and we had sex. When we finished, he told me he had an early morning meeting. He put on his pants, he pulled out his wallet, he handed me a $20 dollar bill and he said, "Will this be enough to cover your cab?" "Sure," I said coolly, masking my wounded soul. I felt like a paid prostitute.

More than once, I was tested for genital herpes and AIDS. And I got pregnant and I had two abortions.

By the time I was 40, I lost count of the men I had slept with, and I didn't remember some of their names. I felt damaged, soiled and unworthy. I believed that a decent man wouldn't want me. I wondered if God could forgive me for my immoral behavior. I clung to the words my grandmother told me as a child, "God loves you. One day you will find someone who will love and care for you."

I began seeing a psychologist. She dug into my perverted past. I was consumed with guilt and shame. I believed that I did something to cause my dad's sexual abuse. I was ashamed of having sex with an unnumbered parade of men. I grieved my abortions. My psychologist gradually helped me to understand that I was not the depraved things that happened to me, I am instead a cherished creature of God worthy of respect, love and happiness. She helped me to realize that I didn't have to live the abused, destitute life of my mother; I could create a life full love, security and happiness.

I threw myself into my work, presenting hair care product training and working with hair and makeup artist teams nationwide. I worked two years with the CMT Flameworthy Video Music Award, working behind the scenes doing makeup. I worked behind the stage at the CMA Music Awards. I rubbed shoulders with Martina McBride, Shania Twain, Tammy Wynette, Garth Brooks, Willie Nelson and Johnny Cash. They were nice to me, they liked me and they complimented my work. For the first time in my life, I felt valuable and worthy.

After I left home I worried about my little sister still living at home with my father. I wanted to protect her, but I lived over 900 miles away. She graduated from high school and she came to stay with me for a summer. She confided in me that our dad began molesting her at age 12.

It took decades for me to forgive my dad for the sexual abuse he inflicted on me, and to forgive my mother for turning a blind eye to his heinous behavior. I told myself, he didn't kill me, he made me stronger. His abuse gave me an abhorrence for the mistreatment of children and women, or anyone. My emotionless mother made me value my extended family and friends. My deprived past made me determined to achieve financial security and to be caring and generous to those less fortunate than me. Every day I try to appreciate the small things in life and I tell the special people in my life, I love them.

I volunteered for Dress of Success, an international organization that prepares disadvantaged women for job interviews. These women come from bleak, depressed backgrounds. They're poor and they lack education. They've been abused, rejected and abandoned and they struggle to care for themselves and their children. Dress for Success is their only hope of achieving a better life.

As I applied lipstick and foundation to these women's faces, and I looked into their eyes, I felt their pain and suffering. I wanted to tell them, you are not what happened to you. You are God's daughter, and His plan for you is not to harm you, but to give you a life of hope, love and prosperity.

My Avenger Woman Within hands Jenny's stepdad a helmet, jock cup and knee pads. Bend over and grab your ankles, you child molester—The Maker is going to rip you a new one!

It is estimated approximately that one-third of abused and neglected children will eventually victimize their own children.

– U.S. Department of Health & Human Services

Moms and dads, do you really want this to be your child's life?

The abused grow up to abuse—or they themselves become

victims of abuse—passing the destructive behavioral pattern down to the next generation ... and to the next generation ... and to the next ... until a mom or dad seeks counseling and breaks their dysfunctional, toxic, maiming behavioral pattern.

I experienced hurtful sexual events, as a child and as an adult, which damaged my self-worth and evoked my promiscuity. As I was writing my book, a repressed memory came forth.

> *I was 7-years-old, playing in the driveway of my home, when a strange man riding a motorcycle through my neighborhood, stopped and convinced me to hop on the back of his motorcycle and take a ride with him. He drove me to the nearby isolated woods where he exposed himself to me. He wanted me to touch him. I was confused not understanding what this man was doing or what he wanted from me, I was instinctively frightened and I refused. Amazingly he returned me home untouched and unharmed. He stopped his motorcycle at the edge of my driveway, I jumped off, and he sped away. My mother saw me disembark the strange man's motorcycle. She grabbed me, dragged me into the house, thrust me into the bathtub and she washed me from head to toe. I felt dirty, not from sitting on the forest ground, but like I was soiled and vulgar inside—and I didn't know why.*
>
> *In high school I was sexually naïve and afraid of boys. I was a virgin, untouched and barely kissed. Several of the boys I dated tried to score with me—but I rejected their seduction. I suppose my dad thought differently because his sex "talk" was accusing, demeaning and humiliating. "Keep the guys' hands out of your pants," he barked at me. My dad mortified my innocent, feminine self-esteem.*

In my twenties and my thirties I was desperately looking for love. I married at 19, thinking a man, any man, would fill the void in my empty soul. My husband and I were an immature mismatch with bad tempers. I had a baby and I divorced him. I was acutely lonely, raising a baby without the emotional and financial support of a husband. I craved a man's companionship and affection. I became intimately involved with a string of men. My needy, inebriated behavior ran off every guy I dated. I was in one ugly word: promiscuous.

I was 27-years-old, divorced and living in my Memphis apartment with my 6-year-old daughter, when I had a life-threatening experience. After a late night of night-clubbing with my boyfriend, we returned to my home, and as I was unlocking my front door, two armed men suddenly appeared and forced entry into my apartment. They robbed us of our money and jewelry, ransacked my apartment, tied our hands behind our backs, put us in separate bedrooms, and then they proceeded to rape me at gunpoint. Lying on the bed they held a pillow over my face, pressing it hard against my mouth to keep me from screaming during the assault. I couldn't breathe. I thought I was going to suffocate and die. All I could think about was my young daughter growing up without her mother.

My bourbon and coke was a Godsend that night. I was in shock after the brutal assault, but my inebriation impaired my recall of my near-death experience. Through the years my fuzzy memory helped me to repress the painful event—or at least, that's what I told myself.

A tear slides down the cheek of My Woman Within and she embraces me, *You're lucky to be alive to tell your story.*

"You are no longer defined by what you did or what someone did to you. God has taken care of your past and a wonderful future awaits you," states Joyce Meyer.

There was a time in my life when I felt like damaged goods. I slept with men to gain their love and acceptance. I married men looking for financial security and the love of my father. Two men sexually assaulted me at gunpoint. My husbands and boyfriends mistreated and abused me. I was a three-time divorcee with a succession of broken relationships. But in God's eyes, regardless of my previous transgressions and the injustices I endured, I have never been anything but a beautiful, valuable and special creature. To see myself as anything less, is contradictory to His will.

We are healed to help others. We are blessed to be a blessing.

—Rick Warren

22 Find Your Purpose. Find Your Authentic Self.

Your security, happiness and self-worth cannot be found in a man. It is realized within your authentic self.

Dr. Phil McGraw states that our authentic self is who we were created to be; while, our fictional self is defined by our jobs or roles. The fictional self draws its identity from its function in life or social station. For example: when a person is asked who they are, they will answer: "Well, I'm a mom." "I'm an attorney." "I'm a wife." "I live in Beverly Hills." But this is not who we are; this is what we do.

Our authentic self is our "real, true, genuine identity," states Dr. Phil. It is the part of us not defined by our occupation or role, but can be found at our "absolute core" and is the "composite" of all our unique gifts, skills, abilities, interests, talents, traits, insights and wisdom that is uniquely different for every person. A person who denies their authentic self, who ignores their true gifts and talents, and does not realize their ambitions and dreams, while performing "assigned" and "inherited" roles, may find themselves "feeling incomplete," as if there is a "hole in your soul."

> **If you want to find your true purpose in life, know this for certain: Your purpose will only be found in service to others, and in being connected to something far greater than your body/mind/ego.**
>
> **—Dr. Wayne Dyer**

I Found My Purpose in Writing

I am not what happened to me.
I am what I chose to become.

Expressing the intimate details of my life on paper has been a healing force in my life. Throughout my life I felt defective, unworthy and unlovable. I grew up surrounded by negative emotions. I was a victim of shame-based thinking. I believed there was something inherently wrong with me. I was afraid to share my true thoughts for fear someone would criticize me. I stuffed and suppressed my hurt feelings. I was terrified of intimacy and rejection. I acted out my fears by throwing hissy fits and erecting self-protecting walls that sabotaged my relationships. I felt dowdy and undesirable, even though men told me I was attractive, and even beautiful. I felt like an outsider and inferior to others, causing me to be withdrawn and shy and suffer from acute loneliness. I was hyper-critical, a perfectionist, and I expected others to be perfect. My shame manifested itself as suppressed anger and defense mechanisms of denial, projection, blaming and striking back at those who offered me the slightest criticisms.

I lived in fear that someone would see through my happy-go-lucky façade and expose the dirty, damaged, frightened girl that lived inside me. At age 45 my counselor helped me to gradually, slowly, and with much introspection debunk my irrational, demeaning beliefs I had about myself, and progressively dispel my feelings of low self-worth.

To forgive ourselves—is healing. To confess our fears, transgressions and immoral behavior to another person—is liberating and empowering.

> **If we can share our story with someone who responds with empathy and understanding, shame can't survive.**
>
> **—Brené Brown, *Daring Greatly***

Years ago part of my healing process was to attend a recovery group. After listening for weeks to a small group of men and women share the private, intimate and humiliating details of their lives, I found the courage to bear my soul. I revealed my dark, sordid secret of promiscuity, going from man to man, craving his love, acceptance and affection. As I told my story uncontrollable tears poured down my cheeks. My wet tears and runny nose drenched wads of tissue. My chest heaved as a lifetime of guilt oozed out me in front of men and women, who with unconditional compassion and concern, validated me as a valuable human being.

Confessing my shame and my guilt in front of this small trusted group of men and women was a gargantuan healing moment. I felt my oppressing, persecuting demons float out of my body and evanesce in the midst of our circle, releasing me from a lifetime of self-degradation and self-loathing. Time passed and I found the courage to share more and more about my hurtful past. At first I opened up about small things: my insecurities and my lack of a college education. My self-worth increased. I joked about my multiple divorces. I came clean about my drinking problem. I shared my dark secret, suppressed for over 40 years, of being raped by two men at gunpoint in my home.

George Whitefield, an eighteenth century English Anglican preacher, famous for spreading the Great Awakening in Britain and the American colonies, knew how to respond to a pointing finger. When he was falsely accused by his enemies and received a vicious letter accusing him of wrongdoing, his reply was brief and courteous:

"I thank you heartily for your letter. As for what you and my other enemies are saying against me, I know worse things about myself than you will ever say about me. With love in Christ, George Whitefield."

For those of you who will accuse me of foolish, disorderly, wicked behavior, I thank you heartily, but I know worse things about myself than you can ever imagine.

God loves to use imperfect, ordinary people to do extraordinary things in spite of their weaknesses.

—Rick Warren

I have sacrificed much to pursue a writing career. I have exposed myself to public scrutiny, sharing my relationship blunders, my personal shortcomings and the hurtful events of my life. I turned down major job offers, and I worked mediocre part-time jobs so I would have time to write my books. I was often lonely. I declined social invitations and I isolated myself for long periods of time, committing myself to finishing my books. I spent large sums of my own money to publish and promote my books. I worried about money and my future. But, alas, finding a real job, or a husband or a boyfriend, became secondary to fulfilling my purpose.

When someone is doing what they love to do, no one has to motivate you. When someone is passionate about their work, they will say, "I would do it for free if I could. It's not about the money." That's because they are living their dream.

I believe our passion in life emerges from our natural talents and innate abilities. I believe our purpose in life begins to form when our talents and abilities benefit someone or something other than ourselves.

God have given each of us the ability to do certain things well.

—Jeremiah 1:5

I was born with an artistic, adventurous, curious nature. I believe I was created to be a catalyst of energy and inspiration for women. My creative, inquisitive, analytical nature has helped me to be an informative and engaging writer. My animated, mischievous, out-of-the-box personality has enabled me to be an entertaining motivational speaker. My life's experiences have shaped me as an encourager, self-improvement author and empowerment spokeswoman.

Never in my wildest dreams did I ever think I would, or could write a book. Never did I imagine that one day I would be speaking to thousands of women about the power of logic, intuition and positive thought. Never did I envision that women would look to me for guidance, understanding and encouragement. Never did I ever fathom that women would tell me that my message transformed their lives.

I came to understand that my quirky, outgoing personality was my biggest asset. Without my vibrant presence, I would be a humdrum lecturer. Without my artistic, offbeat mindset, I would be a tedious writer. Without my hurtful past, I could not feel compassion for women who struggle with low self-worth issues. Without my prior naivety, I could not understand or have empathy for women who are gullible and weak-willed about their relationship problems. Without my headstrong traits, I would have given up my writing career years ago.

God gave my brothers and my son the aptitude of math and logic. He gave my oldest brother the gift of teaching and service. He gave my younger brother the gift of determination and stability. He gave my son the gift of discernment and perseverance. He gave my daughter the heart of motherhood and compassion for others. He gave my girlfriend, Terri, the gift of bringing people together to bolster their careers. He gave my friend, Annie, the gift of insight, accountability and encouragement. He gave my dear friend and editor, Denise, the gift of generosity and good deeds. He gave me a lifelong desire for truth and self-expression. He bestowed on me the insight, abilities and compassion to inspire women who seek emotional stability, relationship understanding and a higher sense of well-being.

Anytime you use your God-given abilities to help others, you are fulfilling your calling.

—Rick Warren

7 Steps to Finding Your Authentic Self

1. Do what you love; love what you do. Knowing what you want, need and desire (not what someone tells you what you should want or do) is essential to self-discovery.
2. Develop an open mind about everyone and everything. Don't make snap judgments about people or possibilities. Don't automatically poo-poo the suggestions of others. A closed mind will blind you to the endearing qualities of others; undermine your abilities, energy and creativity and thwart your opportunities and push away people that might otherwise have assisted you. Begin each day open to the possibility of new friendships, ideas and connections.
3. Face your fears. Forgive your shortcomings. Forget your failures. Move beyond the negative influences of your past. Get rid of your mental garbage to make room for your Higher Power's blessings.
4. Never compare yourself to anyone. It will erode your confidence and self-esteem. It will blind you to your best potential.
5. Stop concentrating on what you are not and what you don't have. Take an inventory of your innate talents and unique traits, and the abilities and strengths you have earned by living life. Focus on these qualities—therein lies your best self.
6. Stop worrying about what others are thinking. It's wasted energy that will rob you of your personal power. Rarely is someone thinking what you think they are thinking.
7. Trust your gut. It is the gate keeper of your authenticity.

Bonus Authenticity Tip: Have a sense of adventure. It's where vibrancy and opportunity come together.

23 Supernatural Assistance

"Are you there, God? It's me—Nancy."

Joel Osteen talks about living your "best life" in his book *Become a Better You.* He tells us to practice positive thoughts, form better habits, develop better relationships, embrace where you are, develop your inner life, stay passionate about life and keep pressing forward.

A walk in the park, *right*?

I have wondered why God has been silent the times in my life when I needed his intervention most. When a divorce or a relationship break-up brought me to my knees. When I desperately needed a job to pay my bills and take care of my children. When loneliness enveloped and suffocated me. At times, when my heartbreak seemed unbearable, I pleaded to God to deliver His miracle. I felt I was deserving of His assistance. I tried to do the right things. I strived to be open-minded and non-judgmental. I tried to stifle my gossiping tongue and limit my cocktails. I said my prayers at night; I asked forgiveness for my screw-ups, blessings for my family and friends, and mercy for my backstabbing I'm-so-over-it-girlfriend. I tried to overcome my disappointments. I endeavored to ignore the know-it-alls and naysayers. I tried to project a hopeful, upbeat attitude. But sometimes, as I lay dejectedly in my bed at night, my distraught, downtrodden Woman Within would look up and yell at the ceiling, *"Helloooo—is Anybody up there?"*

My first book took five years to write and publish. My second took another three years of my life—and my third book took three more years to complete. I was approaching my eleventh year of craziness. I labored day and night, often writing ten to twelve hours a day, five to seven days a week. I spent tens of thousands of dollars of my retirement funds for publishing, travel and promotions. I sold my home and I moved to Nashville to be in a progressive, media-forward environment. I curtailed my social life. I squelched my relationship longings. I felt I was doing everything humanly possible to realize my dreams and generate the income I so badly needed. Many nights I wept on my pillow, begging God for a sign, a business connection, a source of finance, a supernatural happening.

I wailed to God, I've done everything I can do. I'm frightened. I'm weary. I'm out of money and ideas. What else can I do?

I had put my life on the line for my writing career. I was worried about failure. I was frightened about the outcome of my future. I was afraid of becoming a bag lady and falling through the cracks.

I wondered: *Had I made the worst, most harebrained mistake of my life in pursuing a frivolous writing career?*

I crumpled to the floor, raised my eyes to heaven and I wailed, *I've done everything I can do. I'm frightened. I'm weary. I'm out of money and ideas. What else can I do?*

This could be the day I see God's miracle.

—Joel Osteen

To be our best self we need timely doses of God's inspiration. But to receive His supernatural assistance we must be in agreement with Him—and that may require some of us to "clean up" our dirty backyards.

God examines our hearts, our actions and our motives before releasing his supreme blessings. Meaning: We may need to replace a negative, critical attitude with a positive, accepting mindset. We may need to let go of the anger, resentment and bitterness we feel towards someone. We may need to apologize for an unkind deed or right a wrongdoing. We may need to reach out to a loved one or a friend to mend a broken relationship. We may need to seek treatment for an anti-social personality disorder that wreaks havoc in our lives and the lives of our loved ones. We may need to conquer a drug, alcohol or other addiction that damages our body and spirit, hampers our personal growth, and prevents us from being in agreement with God.

I have always been a Paul.

> **When I want to do good, I don't. And when I try not to do wrong, I do it anyway.**
>
> **—Romans 7:19**

My brothers would say as an adolescent-teenager, I was Sister Satan; I was always throwing temper tantrums and causing turmoil in our family. My version is: I revolted against my mother's and father's critical, straitlaced parenting. My older brother and I fought like tabby and bull terrier. My younger brother hid under his spaceship bed to avoid flying fists. Nevertheless, blood is thicker than cherry vodka, and my brothers are bright stars in my eyes.

As a teenager I was rebellious and headstrong. I started smoking and drinking when I was 17. I felt cool with a cigarette perched between my two fingers, sucking in a draw, smelling and watching the musty vapor float from my mouth. I loved the giddy-buzz that Budweiser and Boone's Farm gave me, how it amplified my fun at parties and embodied my teenage defiance. In my twenties I chose to party instead of finishing college. As I got older Scotch buffered my social insecurities, lubricated my conversations and bolstered my confidence with men. By the time I was 30, I was a high-functioning "social" drinker. I lived a normal life. I kept a clean home and I took good care of my daughter. I excelled at my job and I rarely missed work. My bosses considered me to be talented, dependable and hardworking. My co-workers liked and respected me. My friends viewed me as clever and intelligent.

No one suspected that my self-deprecating, insecure mindset tortured me and provoked my drinking. When I met someone for a business lunch, I consumed multiple cocktails to bolster my confidence, and then I returned to my desk blitzed. Or I would drink too much at happy hour, and the next morning I called in sick for half a day, saying I woke up with flu symptoms or food poisoning. I turned 40, and then 50. Cocktails were a fundamental part of my life. At the end of a long work day, Cosmos melted my stress, while wine helped me to cope with my loneliness, depression and anxiety—at least, momentarily. I had pre-dinner cocktails at home, and I had multiple glasses of wine at restaurants. I frequented happy hour and I imbibed at social and networking events. For the most part, when I drank, the visible effects were trifling. But when I drank excessively, I was loud and outspoken, my face flushed and my eyeballs swimmed, and I spilled wine on myself and others. Occasionally I would need to leave my car at a restaurant; a friend would drive me home, and I would politely pass out in my bed. The next morning I had a banging hangover and limited, or no recall of the previous night's conversations.

> Research has shown that the brain is still developing during the teen years and a young person's emotional maturity can stop developing at the age they start abusing alcohol or drugs. For example: A 40-year-old woman, who began drinking excessively at age 16, will remain at the maturity level of a 16-year-old. As an adult she will struggle to cope with the demands and problems of life; consequently, compounding her low self-esteem issues, her life's difficulties and her unhappiness. If and when she quits drinking or drugging, she will do what is called "thawing out." With abstinence and counseling she can begin to "get in touch with her feelings," deal with her repressed issues, and resume the maturing process.

And so it was with Sista-Satan. Drinking had become my psychological crutch. Drinking had stunted my maturity. Drinking was blocking God's supernatural assistance.

Are you blocking God's supernatural assistance?

The negative aspects of our lives block our creative brainwaves, damage our relationships, undermine our abilities and obstruct God's blessings.

Gene, a handsome, 60-year-old successful entrepreneur and devout Christian, will never reach his greatest potential until he corrects his belligerent attitude.

When I met Gene I thought he was the sweetest, most considerate man I had ever met. I even considered him for a serious relationship. But as I got to know him, I saw him to be rigid and condescending. He complained about everything and everyone. He became irritated and verbally obnoxious in traffic. He griped strongly when we had to wait more than ten minutes for a table in a restaurant. He nitpicked the menu and he protested the prices. He criticized every topic I introduced into our conversations. Everything had to be his way or the highway. No wiggle room. No compromise. He watched only the movies he wanted to watch. He wouldn't eat pizza if it wasn't thick crust. He wouldn't accompany me anywhere that didn't interest him. He told me it had been fifteen years since he had been in a serious romantic relationship because he couldn't find a woman worth dating.

I quit dating Gene because his negativity was oppressing and exhausting. It was clear that his gloom and doom interfered with his relationships and his blessings in life.

Allison was a demanding, complaining princess-diva. In her mind the world revolved around her whims and highness.

After twenty years of being employed as a hospital administrator, Allison lost her job on her 50th birthday. She presented a carefree, picture-perfect exterior to her friends, but secretly she was discontent with her life. She was disgusted with the corporate world.

She was regularly at odds with a girlfriend. It had been ten years since her last meaningful romantic relationship.

Allison questioned her life's path. She wondered: did she have a purpose? She began to fanaticize of a new career as a pastry chef.

Allison was a talented baker and pastry maker. She created melt-in-your-mouth French baguettes, éclairs and scrumptious pies with handmade crimped crust. She expressed her artistic talent in her theme-decorated birthday cakes and cupcakes. She basked in her friends' praise for her confectionary creations.

With time on her hands, Allison dreamed of owning her own boutique bakery shop. Her vision included an online retail store, shipping her sweet confections direct to customers and nation-wide brick-and-mortar stores. She imagined herself appearing on the "Shark Tank," gaining notoriety and financial backing, and she toyed with the possibility of her own bakery reality show. What was stopping her?

Allison's conflicts in life were always someone else's undoing. Her boyfriends never measured up to her standards. She pooh-poohed the suggestions and ideas of her girlfriends. She flew off the handle at a girlfriend because she felt "slighted." She trashed that girlfriend, attached herself to another girlfriend, and then she complained about the previous girlfriend to her new girlfriend. She manipulated her friends into doing things her "way" or she would refuse participate.

Be forewarned: don't hold your breath waiting for an apology from Allison, because you will asphyxiate.

Allison's ideas were exceptional and her talent was substantial. She had the brains, moxie, looks and money to accomplish her heart's desire. The problem was: Allison's self-concerned, small-minded mentality thwarted her muse, who inspires creativity, innovation and success. The bigger problem was: Allison consciously, or otherwise, refused to own up to her negativity.

💔

Joyce Meyer was a most unlikely candidate to become a famous international author and speaker. An ex-housewife from Fenton, Missouri with a 12th-grade education, she said she was once an angry, depressed and bitter woman. Her father began molesting her as early as age of five. His sexual, mental, emotion and verbal abuse continued until the time she left home at age 18. She married the first man who showed her any interest. Her husband was a womanizer, drunkard and thief, and when Joyce got a job in the accountant's department of a firm, he persuaded her to write fake checks which he would then cash. When Joyce told him she was pregnant, he went to live with a mistress. Joyce got a divorce, became a chain smoker and started having short flings with strange men. At age 23, she was a single mother and bankrupt. A year after her divorce she married David Meyer, a devout Christian, and although Joyce gave her life to Jesus Christ when she was nine years old, as an adult she was depressed, stubborn and verbally abusive. Her insecurities and anger spilled over into her marriage.

There was nothing in Joyce's walk of faith that marked her as a future Bible teacher.

Joyce Meyer is living proof that God still chooses the "weak," the "low" and the "despised" to deliver his word to the masses. God convicted Joyce of her "judgmental... suspicious... harsh... fearful... controlling" behavior. Thirty-five years later she built one of the largest Christian ministries in the world.

When God puts a dream in your heart—
know that you can do it.

God wants to give us his favor and blessings. He wants to increase our talents, passion and accomplishments. He wants our intellect and abilities to contribute to our world. He wants our unique personalities to shine. He wants us to realize our greatest potential. He wants us to have a life filled with love, joy, peace and fulfillment. He wants our authenticity to bless others.

When we step out in faith to rid ourselves of the negative strongholds in our lives, God will pull up the slack. He will open our minds. He will change our thoughts. He will refresh our hearts. He will illuminate the way. He will put the right people and the right situations in our paths. He will do exactly the right thing, at the right moment, to help us realize our dreams.

> **God will help you, but you cast the deciding vote. If you choose to stay focused on negative elements in your life, if you focus on what you can't do and what you don't have, then by your own choice you are agreeing to be defeated... On the other hand, if you'll get into agreement with God, your faith can cause God to show up and work supernaturally in your life.**
>
> **—Joel Osteen**

And so the final questions become:

What is your dream?

What is your passion?

What are your career ambitions?

What are your relationship aspirations?

What are you willing to give up or change that keeps you from realizing the things you want and so richly deserve in your lifetime?

> **Get into agreement with God, and He'll do more than you can ask or think.**
>
> **—Joel Osteen**

Part Four

Supernatural Sobriety

I don't like the word "alcoholic." I like to think of myself as an advanced drinker.

—Chelsea Handler

Party Time

I learned the hard way what works, and what doesn't work.

If I could change three things about my life: I would have never taken that first puff of a cigarette. I would have finished college. And I would have never drank one beer, one cocktail or one glass of wine.

I have lived a colorful life. I was impetuous, gutsy and foolhardy. Through the decades I struggled with addictions. I began smoking when I was 16, and I didn't quit until I was 39. I started drinking when I was 17, and I didn't quit drinking until I was 66. By the time I reached age 30, happy hour was a frequent and habitual part of my life. Through the years, when my drinking got out of hand and my life became unmanageable, I would quit drinking and clean up my act. Several months later I would resume drinking, swearing to control my intake, limiting myself to two glasses of wine whenever I was behind the wheel. But then a girlfriend would invite me to happy hour or a special event, two glasses of wine turned into three glasses, and three glasses turned into a bottle and a hangover. Regretting my depraved behavior, I would abstain drinking for a day or two, promise again to limit my cocktails, and then the happy hour bell would chime.

I was a happy hour alcoholic.

The truth was: I didn't want to quit drinking. And I didn't want to eat while I was drinking and ruin my lipstick and my buzz. But I regretted getting drunk. I regretted acting unladylike and turning a man off. I regretted being verbose and obnoxious in front of my friends. I worried that I would taint my reputation with business acquaintances.

My 45-year love affair with cocktails dominated and contaminated every aspect of my life.

I confessed my penchant for cocktails to my psychologist girlfriend. She hypnotized me, planting the subliminal suggestion that I stop drinking after two glasses of wine. Her voodoo worked one time—but my inner demon got thirsty, ordered the third glass of wine, and I was quickly back up to speed.

Driving plus cocktails added another layer of misfortunes to my life.

Being a girl I finagled my way out of speeding tickets and I eluded DUI's. I was 26 when I struck out after a night of drinking to visit my boyfriend some 260 miles away. Barreling down the moon-lit interstate, I squinted one eye to keep from seeing double. A highway patrol car, cruising in the opposite direction, did a neck-breaking u-turn, bounced across the grass median strip, leaped onto my side of the interstate and with his blue light blazing, he overtook me and pulled me to the side of the highway.

The officer pointed his Maglite into my pie-eyed face. I was blintzed. Befuddled. Thick tongued. The officer scowled and demanded my driver's license. I mentally prepared myself to be handcuffed. Suddenly his 2-way radio summoned him to a more serious crime. He twisted his face (knowing I deserved to be punished), he handed me my driver's license begrudgingly, told me to *slow it down*, and his blue light vanished in the night.

I went on to use up my nine lives, gleefully consuming beer and gin in my 30s. I had (and still have) a lead foot. On two occasions policemen pulled me over for speeding, both times the officers, realizing that I was tipsy, allowed my passenger girlfriend to take the wheel of my car and drive us home.

I made it to 40. It was Friday happy hour at my favorite watering hole, I knocked down two glasses of wine on a growling stomach, and then I hopped into my Mazda RX7 to meet my girlfriends at a new restaurant catering to the singles crowd. Wheeling down a busy 6-lane boulevard, in 5 o'clock traffic, I blindly cut into the far right lane. Suddenly the right side of my red sports car was juxtaposed to a white car. I caught a split-second glimpse of a screaming woman white-knuckled to the steering wheel of her car—and *snap*—I jerked my car back into my lane.

Stunned. Surreal. What happened? Our cars never braked. I didn't hear the crunch of metal. It happened so fast I wasn't sure if we collided, or not, because I was deliciously buzzed.

The white car zoomed away. I assumed all was well. I veered onto the off-ramp and an ominous blue light flashed in my rearview mirror.

My stomach clenched.

I pulled to the side of the interstate and I rolled down my car window.

"Did I do something wrong, officer?" I purred, cringing in my bucket seat.

"Are you kidding me?!?" the police officer snapped angrily. *"You sideswiped that car back there!"*

My heart jolted.

I jumped out of my car and I followed the officer to the right side of my car, fully expecting to see an ugly gash in the door of my shiny red Mazda, followed by a failed sobriety test and a trip to jail.

To my amazement, and to the double-double amazement of the police officer, there wasn't a scratch on my car. The police officer frowned and released me, and I met my girlfriends for round 2 of happy hour.

The next morning I couldn't stop thinking about my near-miss with the white car. I went outside to inspect my Mazda. I was proud of my racy sports car. I hand washed it weekly. I knew every ding and scratch on it. I bent over sideways, examining the right side of my car. My heart pinged—there it was, a faint white hairline on the passenger door. The policeman did not detect the minuscule blemish—but I knew I had in fact made infinitesimal, nanosecond contact, sideswiping the white car.

A sane person would have bent over, kissed their lucky stars and quit drinking. The following week I met my girlfriends for drinks.

💔

It wasn't my first divorce that prompted me to evaluate my life. It wasn't my string of failed relationships that made me want to change my evil ways. It wasn't my second divorce which sent me yelling and screaming to a psychologist. It was a rebound relationship with the devil-reincarnate that dropped me to the ground and sent me crawling to a therapist.

It took me months to get an appointment with my counselor Stan.

In the beginning Stan didn't say much. Week after week he sat in his comfy leather chair, his hand cupped under his chin, his eyes narrowed, listening intently to my ranting and wailing and blaming my ex-husbands and ex-boyfriends for my relationship failures and misery. Stan would raise an eyebrow, nod his head and mutter, *"Hmmm."*

Eventually Stan addressed my drinking.

"I want you to stop drinking," Stan said. "I want you to stop drinking and I want you to sign a contract pledging that you will abstain from drinking."

What?!? My Happy Hour Woman Within is horrified.

Stan and I discussed my teetotalling future. Wanting to adhere to his guidance, I signed his abstinence contract—and then he told me he wanted me to quit dating for a while.

My Woman Within snarls, *Nuh-uh! I'll give up my vino but I ain't giving up men!*

Stan and I continued to talk; he admonished me about my quasi-suggestive apparel, insinuating that my aura was attracting the wrong kind of attention from men. I was embarrassed and I was offended by his comment.

I quit drinking and I traded my tight dresses, spiked heels and cleavage in for a white long-sleeve Lauren shirt, knee-length pencil skirt and conservative 3-inch heels—and I began dating Richard, a handsome, attentive, 50ish businessman who enjoyed fly fishing and scotch.

I resumed drinking while dating Richard. A month later Stan asked me, "How are you doing with your drinking?"

I was blindsided by Stan's direct hit. I hemmed. I hawed. And I stuttered, *"I had a drink."*

"I knew you would," he said candidly, compassionately. "Don't you understand? Alcohol controls you. You don't control it."

That was my come-to-Jesus moment and I stopped drinking completely.

Without wine to self-medicate, and with Stan's help, I thawed out and I shook off a couple of layers of low self-esteem. Stan opened my eyes to my faulty mindset: that I wanted to blame everyone and everything for my problems. Within months my mental fog began to lift exposing my life's hurtful realities. I embraced my frightened, angry inner child. I dealt with my harsh upbringing and my dejected teen years. I faced my feelings of inferiority, resentment and self-loathing. I dealt with my suppressed shame about my rape and my promiscuity. I released the demons of my abusive relationships. I tore down my impenetrable barriers of self-protection. I forgave myself.

Eighteen months later I felt reborn. For the first time in my life I felt blameless and valuable, desirable and pretty. I started exercising; five mornings a week I jumped out of bed at 5:30 and I ran three to five miles before going to work. After work and on Saturdays I went to the gym, I worked on the machine circuits and I did step aerobics. I knew I was obsessed with exercising, but it gave me something to pacify my addictive personality and mitigate my anxiety. At age 43 my body looked like a 20-year-old.

I continued my non-drinking lifestyle and I married my third husband, a moderate drinker. He was a decent man but he was withdrawn and rigid. Our social life revolved around an organization that promoted constant libations. "The party with a cause," they claimed. I started drinking so I could relax around my husband and enjoy our relationship. Drinking glued our marriage together for ten years. When the glue lost its glow, I divorced him and my drinking kicked into fifth gear.

I entered my 50s. I fell in love with Dr. Dirtbag, a charming but erratic alcoholic. Living 100 miles away, Dr. Dirtbag was able to conceal the extent of his drinking. Our relationship progressed; by day I knew him as a caring doctor and loving partner—but when he drank (almost every night and on weekends) he morphed into a crazed, abusive monster. Who am I kidding! I closed my eyes to his excessive drinking because I relished my 5 o'clock cocktails, and I made excuses for his bad behavior because he was a doctor and he was rich.

I broke up with Dr. Dirtbag after eight months in purgatory and I moved to Houston, a melting pot of big money, fast cars, chichi restaurants and night clubs. I met my friends for frequent after-hour drinks and I chalked up drinking mishaps. I plowed my BMW into the front of my apartment garage, knocking a hole in the drywall and dislodging my bumper. I gouged the sideskirt of my car on a raised curb in my girlfriend's underground garage, setting me back a nasty $1000.00.

After a night of drinking, I rolled out of bed in the middle of the night to go the bathroom. I thought I was sitting down on the toilet, but I instead fell backwards into the tub. I hit the back of my head on the ceramic soap holder. I blacked out for a minute or so. When I woke I was dazed, disoriented and scared, wondering why I was submerged in the bathtub, wrapped in a shower curtain, my legs splayed over the side of the tub, and a sharp pain in the back of my skull.

Sitting up in the tub, I reached my hand to the back of my head, fingered my hair and I felt a wet, sticky gash in my scalp. The wound felt deep and my fingers were bright red from blood. I pulled myself out of the tub, leaned over the vanity sink, cleaned the blood out of my hair and clothes, wrapped my head in a large towel with an icepack, and I crawled into bed, terrified I would die in my sleep.

The next morning I went to the doctor, he told me I was fortunate that my injury had bled outward, otherwise I could have died. The following week my girlfriend told me her 50-year-old sister had died from a fall in the tub. Like me, her sister went to the bathroom in the middle of the night, half-awake, half-asleep, she lowered herself to sit on the toilet, but instead, she plummeted backwards into the tub whacking her head hard on the porcelain edge. Her blow sprouted a goose egg. She dismissed the seriousness of her injury. The following day she complained of a severe headache, nausea and vomiting. A day later she consented to go to the doctor. The doctor told her she had a subdural hematoma, an injury that bled internally. He hospitalized her for observation. Five days later she died of intracranial hemorrhaging.

I shuddered. I knew I had survived a near-death experience.

Four days later I covered my cranial laceration with blonde hair extensions and I met my new Match.com man for cocktails.

25 Sooner or Later—It Will Catch Up With You!

"The problem with drinking and driving is the mourning after."

—Author Unknown

I started writing my second book, *Never Date a Dead Animal,* I packed my luggage and my wine bottle and I moved to Nashville, famous for The Grand Ole Opry, Tennessee Walkers, Blake Shelton, CMA Awards and the AT&T 33-story Batman Building.

I immediately plugged into the large Nashville social scene, meeting new girlfriends for happy hour, three, four and even five evenings a week swigging wine and designer cocktails. It was expensive and it was exhausting.

Another year passed and my Dead Animal manuscript gathered dust.

I chastised myself, What's wrong with you? You moved to Nashville to finish your second and third book. Your goal was to get high on helping women with their relationship problems—not ginger-infused martinis. You squandered two years in Houston at happy hour. You frittered the past year in Nashville emptying stemware. Where's your brain? You don't have money to burn on cocktails. You're getting older. Your drinking is wearing out your face. Your writing career is slipping away! Get a grip! It's do or die! Now or never!

Months passed. *Never Date a Dead Animal* was published and I continued writing on my third book. I met a girlfriend for happy hour, I ate an appetizer, I drank three glasses of pinot grigio and then I hopped into my Beamer to drive myself home. It was dusk. I turned a wide curve at 35 miles per hour when suddenly my body jolted and my mind snapped when the driver's side of my car catapulted onto a median strip exploding my two left tires. I yanked my steering wheel to the right, bounced back into oncoming traffic and I slammed my car to a menacing, grinding halt. I was shocked and dazed wondering *what the hell* had just happened. I leaped from my car, burnt Michelin smoke billowed from my wheels. My two left tires and rims were decimated.

I called my guy friend (a convicted DUI criminal).

"Get out of there *now*!" he implored. "Leave the car. Just get out of there!"

I left my car, hiked 7 blocks to my apartment and I called a tow truck and they hauled my car to the BMW dealership. The next day I had to purchase two new tires, two aluminum rims and had my front end realigned. It was a $1700.00 cocktail.

The following morning I lay in my bed with a pounding headache, recalling the harrowing details of my collision. A sickening, nauseating feeling gripped me, realizing I had momentarily blacked out while driving down a major street. Tears filled my eyes. I was grateful that I wasn't arrested for a DUI. I was thankful that I didn't hit another car. I was grateful that I didn't injure myself or kill someone.

I lifted my eyes to the ceiling and I cried, "Oh, Dear God, please fix me! My life is a mess. I hate what wine does to my body. I hate my nauseating hangovers, my queasy, bloated stomach and the weight gain. I hate looking in the mirror at my dehydrated, wrinkled face, the bags under my peepers and my road-map eyes. I hate how drinking warps my personality, glazes my eyes over, slurs my speech and loosens my f-bombing tongue. I hate how wine zaps my energy, demotivates me and interferes with my writing. I hate how drinking intensifies my loneliness, lowers my inhibitions and causes me to succumb to a man's seduction. I hate how alcohol impairs my ability to reason and causes me to over-react to

I hated looking like a bar stool ornament.

someone's trivial, inconsiderate behavior. I hate driving under the influence, knowing that any minute I could total my car, be arrested for a DUI, jeopardize my driver's license and lose my gun carry permit. I hate how drinking damages my relationships. I hate looking like a bar stool ornament. I hate feeling guilty when I drink too much. I hate my life. Please help me to stop drinking—*or at least to not drink as much!*

God screwed his divine face and said: Daughter, what the Moses are you thinking? That's not why I created you—to wake up in the mornings with a hangover, to go around all day with your mind in a fog, feeling depressed, tired and defeated. I didn't bless you with health, beauty and intelligence for your martinis to desecrate your femininity, shrink your brain and pickle your organs. I didn't send you to Nashville to waste your talents and forfeit your destiny. I sent you to Nashville to be a noted self-help author, to be a riveting motivational speaker and a charismatic radio and TV celebrity. I sent you to be an inspiration to your friends, to be a respected community leader, and most of all, to help women who struggle with low self-esteem issues and relationship problems. I didn't send you to Nashville to fall off your bar stool, drunk dial and wreck your Beamer.

I gravitated to men with a penchant for booze.

In Nashville I signed up for Match.com and I dated a series of men who enjoyed cocktails and upscale dining. Wayne, a charismatic, successful salesman, could easily knock back a bottle of good merlot. Anthony, a handsome, white-haired retiree, professed the three most important things in his life were scotch, cigars and golf. Larry finally confessed he was convicted of a DUI and the court ordered him to install an ignition interlock device (breathalyzer) in his SUV. Lonnie, a short, good-looking, cocky Italian, tried to impress me and my girlfriends one night, buying us bottomless drinks while he socked down umpteen Manhattans. Later that night, driving home, he was arrested for a DUI. And then there was Ralph, a reformed alcoholic, who wanted to dine at 5 o'clock. I wanted to start drinking at five and suck cocktails until twilight. I decided we didn't have anything in common and I stopped dating him.

My Woman Within orders her third Mojito. *For crying out loud, why do you keep attracting losers?*

By the time I moved to Nashville I had built up a tolerance to wine. I quit buying wine by the fifth, I instead bought two Barefoot Pinot Grigio magnums at a time so I wouldn't run out. I got into the habit of drinking almost every night. I drank two to three glasses of wine at home to help me unwind and lift my spirits. I drank three or more glasses socially to get my desired "buzz." Most times no one realized that I was blitzed, because before I fully morphed, I managed to get home, take off my makeup, put on my pajamas and pass out in my bed.

My drinking model looked something like this:

One drink: I am an effervescent butterfly.

Two drinks: I am a vaudeville comedian and the center of attention.

Three drinks: I become a Martini Warrior. My banter is loud, salty and obnoxious. The stranger sitting next to me becomes my long-lost friend. I spill red wine on your white silk blouse. I'm touchy feely; I grasp your arm, look at you doe-eyed and I say, "*I love you, man,*" when I really don't. I promise to call you next week for lunch, but I don't because I can't remember your name. I insist (and believe) that I am okay to drive home, but I'm not. When I leave I forget to pay my bar bill.

Four drinks; the point of no return: Confiscate my car keys. Strap me to my bar stool. I'm bulletproof.

I gave up dating and I hung out with my girlfriends, haunting happy hours at Stoney River, Bricktops, J Alexander's, Puckett's, Bluebird Cafe, Red Pony, JJ's Wine Bar, Virago, Sambuca and Saffire.

Fifteen months had passed since moving to Nashville and my third book was still incomplete. I received an email from a Match.com man expressing his interest in me. His profile said he owned a farm with horses and cows. My Nashville fantasy was to put on my field boots, walk out my front door to the stable, saddle my friend and gallop over rolling hills of chestnut oaks and cattails. And although he didn't look like my type (a Boss-jacket-designer-jean, silver-haired bad boy), I thought I might get to ride a horse and pet a cow.

Leon was two years older than me. He was reserved and considerate. His clothes were dated and drab. Sitting in front of him at dinner on our first date, I flinched at his mothball wardrobe, but I sensed that he was the "real deal," genuine and normal. Leon was a moderate drinker; he sipped a glass of red wine with his dinner. I limited my wine to two glasses to maintain my feminine composure.

Dating Leon was novel and down-to-earth. We visited his farm. He introduced me to his two barn cats, Morris and Brooks. I fed carrots and apples to his two horses, Cinnamon and Annie. In the afternoons we rode his gator over his 300 acres, drinking wine out of Solo Cups while surveying his 50-plus herd of premium Angus cattle. I liked the fact that Leon was a breeder, not a hamburger grinder.

Leon pursued me like no other man. He took me to a new restaurant almost every night. Wine flowed, foie gras appeared, filet mignon disappeared and Frangelico was guzzled. I quit counting my drinks because Leon always drove. After going out with Leon, there was always a pounding headache and nauseated stomach the next morning.

Leon and I were perfect for one another. He fell in love with my vivacious personality. I was his arm candy: an effervescent fashionista, community lifestyle writer and an author with a promising career. I fell in love with Leon's heart. He was the strong silent type, enduring, intelligent and a bulldog businessman with a talent for negotiating a lucrative land deal. He adored me and he indulged me. He took me to nice restaurants. He surprised me with gifts. He painted me a future full of love, frills and security. Everything he said and did fulfilled my core necessity in life—security. I helped him spiff up his wardrobe and I made him homemade blueberry muffins.

26 Don't Drink and Argue

"I was drowning my sorrows but they learned to swim."

—U2

Leon lugged a trunkful of problems into our relationship. One by one his personal issues began to surface. His wife's abandonment and his prolonged divorce, his dicey finances, his codependent relationship with his irresponsible adult alcoholic daughter and his pricey white elephant house. His personal issues complicated our relationship and ruffled my feathers. I confronted him about his inability to stand up to his manipulating soon-to-be-ex-wife and him enabling his rent-utility-free boozing daughter. He shuffled his feet and he promised to get his life in order.

Six months passed. Prince Charming sprouted warts and he discovered the broom parked in my garage. Leon's procrastination grinded on my patience; he tap danced around his divorce and he indulged his deadbeat daughter. He kept saying, *"I'm waiting on her [the wife] to submit her affidavit. I'll take care of it. Trust me." And—"She's [the daughter] got 30 days to stop drinking, get a job and start paying rent or get out of my house. I'll take care of it. Trust me."*

Leon dragged his boots and I hammered him about his passive aggressive behavior: Double talk. Stonewalling. Convenient loss of memory. Evasive, contradicting excuses. His ambiguous behavior infuriated me and I niggled him, *"Are you going to wear that? Whiten your teeth. Exercise. Put the toilet lid down."* Leon became withdrawn, moody and brooding. I pouted and I punished him with my silence. I kept telling myself, *Things will get better. When he gets his divorce. When a land deal comes in. When he boots his vodka daughter out of his rental house.*

Mixed with wine, Leon and I were a ticking grenade.

I poured myself a glass of pinot.

Our arguments escalated—and so did our drinking. I knew we were drinking too much—but I was unwilling to give up my carefree, entertaining lifestyle. We met new friends at bars, locally and afar. We sat at beachfront restaurants sipping cocktails, laughing about the money we saved on half-priced happy hour drinks and appetizers. We relaxed on our patio in the evening, sharing wine and conversation.

Leon got his divorce, his windfall came in and his daughter moved out of state. But the waves of conflict and bickering had taken its toll on our magical relationship. Our personalities changed. He was stoic, closemouthed and distant. I was angry, resentful and unhappy.

It was a balmy summer evening in Naples, Florida. Leon and I sat at the bar of our favorite restaurant, dining on grilled sea bass and consuming copious amounts of pinto grigio. Leon downed two shots of Sambuca and ordered a cappuccino-frosted brownie. Normally we shared a dessert. The waiter placed his brownie in front of him. I reached for a fork and he snapped, *"You can't have any!"* and he shoveled his dessert into his mouth while staring blankly at nothing in front of him. His comment was laced with acrimony. I grabbed my purse, stomped outside and I sat on a bench in front of the restaurant. Fifteen minutes later Leon emerged from the restaurant, rage frothing from his 230-pound walrus body.

We climbed into his SUV. He peeled out of the parking lot, speeding and driving recklessly down a busy street, and then he abruptly, mistakenly veered left, near missing a median strip. I shrunk from his anger. At home I went directly upstairs to the guest room, locked the door and I went to bed.

The next morning Leon begged or my forgiveness. He blamed his unconscionable behavior on his excessive drinking. I loved him. I believed him. I forgave him. After all, blind-drunk behavior was nothing new to me.

Two weeks after I married my fourth husband he packed his bags and left me.

A month and a half later Leon and I married. Leon moved into my house. Two weeks after our wedding Leon's violent behavior erupted again.

It was the evening of July 4th, Leon and I consumed an inglorious amount of wine at a country club party. Leon sunk into one of his silent, sullen moods, shunning me in front of our new friends. When we returned home he gushed with affection at our two new Goldendoodle pups, petting them and purring to them, *"Hey pretty girl, are you a pretty girl? Hey, big boy, Who's ya daddy. Whos's ya daddy?"*

His blubbering regard for the dogs infuriated me.

"Oh, you won't talk to me all night but you'll talk to the dogs," I stabbed.

Leon's eyes bulged and his nostrils flared. *"That's because you're a fucking bitch!"* he screamed. *"You're a fucking bitch and I'm leaving."*

Leon angrily packed his belongings into his SUV and he drove away to his white elephant house—and just like that—*POOF!* My marriage was over!

In all my years of pain and suffering, I choose the wrong medication.

Drinking plus relationships have never worked for me; through the years wine has cost me a multitude of relationships. I ran men off with my loosey-goosey inebriated behavior. I dated and married men who mirrored my propensity for cocktails.

Large drinkers tend to be immoderately dysfunctional; the outcome was never pretty. When my boyfriends and husbands drank, they were insensitive, deceptive and often abusive. Drinking made me hyper-sensitive, irrational, confrontational and explosive. Drinking had an adverse effect on my friendships. I lost three

Nashville drinking gal pals: one because a girlfriend got mad at me because the bartender wouldn't let me save a bar stool for her in a jam-packed restaurant; the second, because I couldn't endure her constant babbling, self-serving braggadocio; and the third, a party-down girlfriend ditched me for a schlong.

My fourth marriage disintegrated in front of my eyes. I sunk into a pit of hopelessness and depression. Everything that I dreamed of, worked for and struggled for—was gone. I would be known as the boozing, self-help author whose brand-new husband dumped her. I felt like an imposter. A four-time loser. My life was a sham. My author career was over. Ten long writing years down the drain. How in God's name could I possibly explain this mucky, awful mess?

I dated and married men who mirrored my penchant for drinking.

I poured myself another glass of wine.

I holed up in my house, I avoided phone calls and I told no one that my marriage of two weeks tanked. After two weeks in isolation I felt like a zombie and I decided to go out to dinner.

It was Wednesday happy hour at the Red Pony featuring half-price martins. I slinked up to a bar stool, glanced up and down the long oak counter, hoping no one knew me, and I ordered a soothing pink martini. Sitting at the bar alone I felt like a gigantic red "L" was flashing on my forehead. I inhaled my vodka anesthesia and I ordered a second transfusion. My angst mellowed and I struck up a conversation with a woman sitting at my elbow.

Vera was welcoming and conversational. She told me she owned several horses and she operated a luxury trail ride. I felt like I had met a special friend. We exchanged phone numbers and we promised to have lunch together. Unbeknownst to me, my shattered, desperate world was about to be transformed by a black equine spirit.

Two weeks passed. Leon texted me, professing his adoration and he apologized for his hurtful outburst—but our relationship had turned a murky corner. Our love was poisoned by mistrust, anger and uncertainty. My emotional pain was unbearable. I packed my suitcase and I drove to Charlotte to see my dear friend, Annie. Someone who understood me and even enjoyed my quirky personality.

I sat on Annie's patio drinking pinot grigio. Annie sipped. I guzzled. I glanced around her backyard, a wrought iron bench adorned with Nantucket blue and white striped pillows. Flagstone steps laid a path through her manicured lawn to her cutting garden of pink astilbe, Gerbera daisies and purple lavender. Picturesque. Peaceful. Relaxing. Her Boykin Spaniel, Barnie, laid contently at Annie's feet on the brick pavers. Her doting Carolina husband opened the screen backdoor, poked his head out and drawled, *"What time do you gals wanna eat? I'm cooking salmon."*

Everything seemed so—*stable!*

I confessed to Annie the events that led to Leon's unexpected abandonment. Annie said, "Nancy, you know drinking has always been a problem for you. The truth is, I like you better when you don't drink. You're funnier when you don't drink. You're more articulate. You're more charismatic and more attractive. But when you drink—"

I finished her sentence "*. . . it exacerbates my large personality."*

Annie pressed her lips in a firm line and nodded, "That's right. You're a better person when you don't drink."

My head drooped.

I laid in bed that night, ruminating Annie's words. She was right. I had a drinking problem. I had tried for many years to control my intake, to stop after one or two drinks, but no matter how much I wanted to quit, no matter how hard I tried, or how much remorse I felt, I couldn't because my wine and cocktails controlled me—I didn't control it. I was an alcoholic.

Two days later I struck out for home, stopping at a service station to fill up before hitting the interstate. I got out of my car, reached for the fuel pump nozzle and I saw an orange pocket-size New Testament Bible conspicuously sitting on top of the gas pump.

How odd, I mused.

I stared at the small Bible, momentarily, and then I inserted the nozzle into my car's gas tank. My hand squeezed on the handle and pungent liquid guzzled into my car. I stared at the small abandoned Bible and pondered, *Why is a Bible sitting on top of a gas tank?*

My Woman Within whispered, *It's a sign! It was put there for you. Pick it up. Take it. It's a new life. A better way. All you have to do is pick it up!*

Zap! Click! A switch went off in my head and a profound awareness permeated me. I knew I could no longer run from my drinking problem. I knew that was God's last warning. I knew if I didn't stop drinking He would turn me over to my free will, allow me to fully enjoy my folly, permit me to knock back bottles of pinot grigio, quaff ginger-infused martinis and swig pink cosmos. I knew unequivocally, if I rejected His unmistakable final warning to QUIT DRINKING—*completely and permanently*—He would allow me to demolish my cars, ruin my health, destroy my career and my reputation, wreck my friendships and my marriage, and drink myself into a stupid stupor.

Checkmate!

There would be no more kidding myself about my drinking problem. There would be no more intervening, invisible angels. No more close calls. No more minimizing and justifying my inebriated behavior. No more feeble excuses and empty promises. No more pleas for forgiveness. No more get-out-of-jail-free cards. I knew if I didn't quit drinking *tout de suite,* God would allow me to suffer the consequences of my irresponsible inebriated behavior. He would allow me to suffer from blackouts, develop cirrhosis of the liver and memory loss. He would let me climb behind the wheel of my car schnockered and be arrested for a DUI, plow into another automobile, maim and cripple myself, or kill an innocent driver and serve jail time. He would let me squander my chance to become a best-selling author and motivational speaker. He would let me endure my fourth divorce. I believed the small orange Bible was, indeed, a grim omen.

I was afraid to NOT stop drinking.

The party was over. My rock star lifestyle of bar stools, cocktails, extravagant dining and constant trips to the liquor store had gone up in flames.

My life had hit an all-time low. I felt powerless. Frightened. Paralyzed. I knew I had to stop drinking to receive God's deluxe, five-star, top shelf, Saks Fifth Avenue, Rolls-Royce, Gulfstream, Patek Phillippe supernatural assistance.

I got down on my knees, opened my hands and extended my arms, I looked towards heaven and I prayed:

Dear Lord, I want to stop drinking—but I can't. Wine controls me—I don't control it. I am helpless against this sickness.

After almost 50 years of irresponsible, indulgent drinking—*I quit.*

27 It's a Process! It's a Process! It's a Process!

I began to connect the dots.

I could trace every difficulty, every problem, every struggle, every mishap, every regret I have had in my life back to my drinking. I didn't finish college because I wanted to party with my friends. I shortchanged promising, steady jobs to live a frivolous, non-productive lifestyle. I dated and I married functioning alcoholics who were financially irresponsible, emotionally unavailable or abusive. I doled out thousands of dollars to fix my crunched fenders, cockeyed bumpers and speeding tickets. I pursued superficial drinking relationships with friends. Excessive drinking fostered conflict with my girlfriends, ran off my boyfriends and contributed to the demise of my marriages.

Drinking altered my core values. When I was single, drinking lowered my inhibitions causing me to indiscriminately sleep with men out of loneliness and desperation. When I was married, drinking would accelerate our arguments, exacerbate my misery and cause me to yearn for the good-looking man sitting at the end of the bar. I shortchanged my children because I had rather be out drinking with my friends, instead of attending a basketball game. I ditched church on Sunday morning because I was nursing a Saturday night hangover. My excessive drinking caused me financial difficulties, distressed my loved ones, affected my health and stunted my career. And yet, I was unwilling to give up the relaxing, sedating buzz I got from wine and martinis. I was unwilling to forfeit my fun times with my girlfriends. I was unwilling to surrender my psychological crutch.

I knew if I didn't quit drinking my life was always going to be a piece of crap. I knew my friends would eventually get tired of my uncouth, sloshed behavior and strike me from their social register. I knew my tainted reputation would catch up with me and business connections would withhold their endorsements and referrals. I knew I would continually struggle with my weight, I would be unhappy with the way my clothes fit and I would age prematurely. I knew I would fall short of my dream of being a noted self-help author and motivational speaker. I knew drinking would be the downfall of my fourth marriage.

The burning questions became:

How bad did I want it? What was I willing to give up and endure to get it?

❥

Leon and I both agreed to quit drinking to eliminate conflict and strengthen our marriage. Happy hour was indisputably my Achilles heel; I didn't know how to relax without a cocktail in my hand. We began eating dinner at 5 o'clock; a full stomach seemed to mitigate my craving for a glass of wine. We participated in activities that didn't promote drinking. We went to the movies, music events and art galleries. We began exercising and we inspired one another to get our middle-aged bodies in shape. I started reading at night, a luxury I couldn't comprehend with a fuzzy brain. In the beginning our non-drinking conversations were uncomfortable and feigned, but our dialog evolved into meaningful, witty, enlightening discussions. I fell in love with my husband's new teetotalling personality. He admired my determination to be a better person.

I didn't know how to relax without drinking.

My drinking psyche had deep roots. It was vital to my abstinence for me to comprehend *WHY,* every day when the clock struck five, a gnawing, empty feeling triggered my need to drink.

Leon told me, "You don't know how to relax."

Maybe.

My psychologist driveled, "In a normal family, evening hours are family time. If you didn't have that growing up you may carry that void into your adult life."

Nah!

I believe my internal 5 o'clock cocktail alarm stemmed from being a hyper-active, extrovert suffering from low self-worth.

I have always been a "driver" personality. I am assertive, competitive, action-oriented, a risk-taker and tenacious. Through the years I tackled numerous careers. I thrived on a challenge and I worked tirelessly to achieve recognition and success. During the day my business mind churned and my energy zoomed. At the end of the day I was mentally drained. Boredom encroached. Loneliness seeped in. Anxiety prevailed. I didn't know how to sit still, relax and just *b-r-e-a-t-h-e*. I needed something to decompress my brain, relieve my stress and placate my angst. A glass of wine sedated my restlessness, perked my spirits and amplified my nighttime fun. Except for work, everything I did, and who I did it with, revolved around drinking: casual drinks at home, happy hour with friends, wine with dinner, traveling plus cocktails, parties and social events. Drinking was a habitual, intrinsic, non-negotiable lifestyle.

I knew to quit drinking I had to alter my lifestyle.

Abstinence is a mindset. I can choose to drink wine or booze—or I can choose to drink soda pop or iced tea. When I am stressed, and my mind is assaulted by the thought of a soothing, sedating glass of pinto grigio—I can choose to entertain the thought, increasing the odds of me giving into my desire—or, I can deliberately redirect my thoughts.

Quitting smoking was one of the hardest things I've ever done. For me, smoking was like a heroin addiction. I smoked the first thing in the morning. I burned two packs during the day and I puffed on a cancer stick the last minute before crawling into bed. I secretly feared I would die of cancer—and yet, I couldn't kick the habit. After smoking for over 20 years, I quit cold turkey. I was riddled with anxiety. I suffered headaches and insomnia. I was nervous, irritable and explosive. I chewed NRT gum (nicotine replacement therapy) until my jaws ached. Six weeks after I quit smoking, instead of my withdrawal from nicotine becoming easier—it got worse. My doctor prescribed me a short-term prescription for Valium to soothe my mental and physical anguish. It took me six months to feel quasi-comfortable as a non-smoker. A year passed when I realized smoking was finally an afterthought, instead of a constant craving. I told myself, if I could quit smoking, surely I could kick a martini in the ass.

Quitting drinking for me required two things (1) a game plan, and (2) an unwavering, sacred commitment to abstain.

I got rid of temptation: I poured half-empty wine bottles down the sink and I stored unopened wine and booze. My new happy hour cocktail was club soda on ice with a big splash of grenadine and a twist of lime. Every day at five, when my alcoholic demon bawled, I chugged tall glasses of my red, low-calorie drink. I told myself: alcohol is packed with calories that contain no nutritional value. A large glass of wine contains the same calories as a slice of cake. Two or more drinks in an evening equals two donuts, three cupcakes and a colossal Hershey bar.

My Woman Within twists her head and glares in the full-length mirror at her thunder-thighs, *Lawdy Miss Clawdy, that's where that came from!*

Because I wasn't drinking, I woke early every morning bright-eyed and ready to tackle the day. I power walked 40 minutes to an hour almost every day. I hired a trainer to teach me how to use free weights and the exercise machines. I cut back on my carbs and I munched on fresh fruits and vegetables, and continued to guzzle grenadine club sodas. I lost weight, my flabby butt tightened and my brain cells fired on all cylinders. I took a mini-recorder with

I got high on endorphins instead of wine.

me on my walks to capture my spontaneous thoughts. Poignant revelations and introspection filled my recorder, thoughts so profound, my heart moaned and I murmured, *Thank You, Heavenly Father. Thank You for Your favor and blessings.*

But my nervous energy still craved a 5 o'clock Woo Woo martini.

Writing kept my mind busy in the daytime, but I needed something to subjugate my evening craving for wine. I continued to eat dinner early. I sucked on hard candy. I guzzled gourmet flavored coffee. I pounded the sidewalk with my tennis shoes. I treated myself to foods that I really enjoyed eating and I indulged in desserts. I threw myself into writing the final chapter in my book, "Supernatural Sobriety."

When 5 o'clock hit I had to keep my mind occupied and my body active.

I avoided situations that promoted drinking—except for my Women 'n' Wine group.

I was the founder of Women 'n' Wine, a popular Nashville social and business networking group. I was committed to organizing and attending our group's monthly get-togethers. A month after I quit drinking, I was driving to my Women 'n' Wine monthly happy hour, when suddenly, I was struck with anxiety, thinking about conversing with 25 imbibing women without a glass of wine in my hand.

I gripped the steering wheel and I acknowledged the stronghold alcohol had me. I told myself, *Wine controls me, I don't control it. It's a disease. A sickness. An illness. A killer.*

My Woman Within nodded in agreement.

She exclaimed, *You wouldn't eat something if you knew it would give you cancer, would you?*

No. Hell No!

You wouldn't drink rat poison, knowing it would kill you, would you?

Nuh uh! No way!

Well then, when you see a glass of wine—think of it as rat poison.

I got through the night drinking club soda.

Ten months passed and I refrained from drinking. There were times when my sober gremlin subconsciously craved a glass of wine: after a stressful work day, after traveling on an airplane, and when dining out of town. When it happened, I inhaled a deep breath and I reminded myself of the benefits of a clear head, a youthful face and increased energy, and I cringed, remembering my banging headaches, memory loss and mangled BMW. I poured myself a grenadine club soda with lime. I ate a light snack—and my happy hour craving subsided.

I kept telling myself, "I want a better life."

After I quit drinking, I worried about losing my girlfriends. The truth was—my gal pals rarely invited me to meet them for happy hour or dinner. I was always the one who initiated the invitation; sometimes they would show up, other times they declined. It made it easy for me to disappear from the happy hour scene.

After I quit drinking, I felt as if I had been driving through life asleep at the wheel, functioning in an altered hypnotic state. The cobwebs in my head began to clear, but I suffered from "brain fog." My thoughts seemed to dissipate in mid-sentence, or they were mushy. I struggled to express my thoughts in a conversation, to find the right word, to remember a name, to recall my zip code.

After I quit drinking, I felt incomplete, like a huge part of me was missing. I felt like I was floundering, searching for my life. I felt insecure and flawed, as if there was something wrong with me. I wondered if I appeared normal in front of people. I wondered if my non-drinking personality was acceptable, if I appeared approachable and if I was even likeable. I wondered how I would "fit in" with my new identity.

After I quit drinking, I discovered something surprising about myself. I realized that I enjoyed being alone. Surprising because solitude had always been my arch enemy. It was a dark place where

I felt restless, hollow and dejected. Before I quit drinking there was nothing I enjoyed more than sitting on a bar stool, sipping on martinis, medicating my anxieties, talking to my girlfriends, whiling my life away. I knew I had matured because after I quit drinking, I cherished my "me-time."

After I quit drinking, I realized I had convinced myself I was a "social" drinker—when in truth, I depended on martinis and wine to anesthetize my emotional pain, bolster my insecurities and accelerate my good times.

After I quit drinking, I realized my sobriety was a critical missing part of my book *God, Please Fix Me!* Without my sobriety I was fooling myself, shortchanging my relationships and duping my readers.

After I quit drinking, I became painfully aware of the activities and environments that triggered my craving for alcohol. When a waiter passed by me delivering a tray of long-stem glasses filled with wine. When a woman sitting at the end of the bar sipped on a martini with shards of ice and plump olives. When I walked down the grocery aisle and I spotted a cooler cradling rows of chilled wine. During the winter holidays, while shopping or traveling, a trendy restaurant bar would beckon me to celebrate with an Irish coffee. I loved to sip wine while cooking, or when I finished a long day of writing I wanted to sit in my courtyard with a glass of pinot grigio, and in stoic silence, listen to nature and admire my hydrangeas. It was especially hard to imagine being in Florida, sitting at an oceanfront restaurant without a cool one to enjoy the sunset. It was a gnawing, infernal itch I didn't dare scratch.

After I quit drinking, I had moments of weakening; a sudden unexpected urge when my soul craved a soothing glass of wine or martini. In those moments, I didn't know what to do with myself. I didn't know how to extinguish my restless energy, where to redirect my thoughts, how to be content with my life and live in the moment. I didn't know how to just be still—and *be.*

There was one thing I knew for certain: one drink would lead to four drinks and I would forfeit the success I had dreamed of having all my life.

How bad do you want it? My Woman Within whispered, soberly.

I inhaled a deep, calming breath. I fixed myself a grenadine club soda. I sucked on a piece of caramel-apple candy. I put on my tennis shoes and I powerwalked for 40 minutes.

28 The Miracle of Ready to Roll

"If we are not a little bit uncomfortable every day, we are not growing. All the good stuff is outside our comfort zone."

—Jack Canfield

Two months passed and my lips had abstained from wine and martinis. My new friend, Vera, invited Leon and me to a Saturday afternoon "Raise the Roof" event to raise funds to build a $1 million-dollar equestrian arena at Harlinsdale Farm in historic Franklin, Tennessee. The outdoor event included live music, appetizers and cocktails, horse demonstrations and a live auction. We were driving to the event when suddenly a knee-jerk mental picture assailed me. My my skin twitched and my pulse fluttered, envisioning outdoor bars serving wine and icy cocktails.

Man up! My Woman Within snapped. *You can do this!*

I inhaled a deep breath, sucking it down to my solar plexus and I pictured myself strolling through the grounds drinking a tall, reassuring glass of iced tea.

Leon and I pulled into Harlinsdale Farm and I quickly made my way to the outdoor food booths, heaping my plate with appetizers, salads, meat concoctions and lip-smacking desserts. I guzzled my iced tea, cleaned my plate and I went back for second and third helpings.

The main attraction was inside a large white party tent housing rows of banquet tables and a platform supporting a bluegrass band. Leon and I settled into our seats, the auctioneer stepped up to the microphone, and "Ready to Roll" was paraded by us.

Ready to Roll, a 5-year-old Tennessee Walker gelding, was donated as an auction item by Bill Harlin, a longtime TNW breeder and the original owner of Harlinsdale Farm. Ready was the offspring of World Champions, Midnight Sun and Gen's Major General. Standing 15.5 hands tall, and prancing at the end of his lead rope, he was solid black with a white star-blaze on his forehead and one white stocking. My eyes danced. I had never been that close to such a spirited, magnificent horse.

The auctioneer opened the bidding for Ready to Roll. Leon turned in his chair, looked at me and said, "If I get you this horse are you going to take care of him?"

"What?!?" I shrieked softly. "What are you talking about? I've never owned a horse! Are you kidding me? Are you serious?"

Through the years my history with horses was to hand a stable manager $20.00, hop on the back of a saddled, bridled horse, jiggle the reins and slap the horse's side repeatedly with my legs to get him to budge from the barn—and then poke along on a 1-hour trail ride. My experiences with a rental horse were: one lied down with me in a pond and two tried to take my head off by running me under a tree limb and an overhanging metal roof. I watched my girlfriend, Wendy, get her foot stuck in the stirrup when dismounting a horse; the horse took off, dragging and pounding her on the ground beneath him. My knowledge of a horse was to watch out for his teeth, stay away from his rear end, hold on to the saddle horn, and beware of low-bearing tree limbs.

I looked at Leon. My words said, *No! Maybe! I don't know!* But the expression on my face said, *All my life I've dreamed of owning a horse. Yes, I will take care of him!*

The stable door opened, Ready-to-Roll looked at me with curious, cautious eyes. My heart pulsed as I held my gloved hand up to his mouth, nervously cradling carrot and apple pieces. He sniffed and he rebuffed my offer.

"He's been stabled all his life," grunted the stable manager. "He probably doesn't know what a carrot is."

Ready had lived his entire life as a show horse, with minimum turnout, disciplined lunging exercise and professional grooming that didn't include veggie treats from a doting hand.

"Here ya go, fella," I purred. "Try it. You'll like it." I tentatively studied Ready's large black face hovering 12 inches from me. He took the apple wedge from my hand, chewed it skeptically, devoured it, and he jutted his head toward me, sniffing for more.

Three days later I left for Charlotte for a 12-day writing refuge.

I settled into my aisle seat on the plane, planning to work on my book. It was a two and a half hour flight, I wanted to spend my time wisely, reviewing my manuscript notes so that when I arrived at my condo rental I could shut out the world and immerse myself into the writing process. I buckled my seatbelt and I pulled out my iPad to check my emails before takeoff.

Damn!

"*Do you know how to get online with an iPad?*" I asked the woman sitting next to me.

"No, I'm sorry, I don't," she replied.

It was obvious she was also anticipating a flight without mindless prattle.

"Thanks," I replied, and I glanced at the book lying on her lap with the cover photo of a woman and a horse.

My mind rallied. Three days ago I could have cared less about a book about horses. Suddenly I felt a curious connection to the woman sitting next to me.

"Oh, do you ride horses," I asked clumsily.

"I used too," she replied. "I'm participating in my girlfriend's equine therapy program."

Huh?

Her name was Susan, an attractive, 40ish single woman returning home to Charlotte from a weeklong business trip in Nashville.

Susan knew a lot about horses. She explained equine therapy to me, saying when someone spends time with a horse, grooming him, stroking him and walking him, the interaction promotes emotional healing for troubled youths, abused women, special needs children, the elderly and wounded soldiers. She said horses can sense and will response to a person's emotional pain, and the connection between the horse and the person can be profound and spiritual.

"Wow!" I said.

I gushed to Susan about my new 5-year-old gelding, Ready to Roll.

"I've never owned a horse," I confided. "I'm terrified of him."

"He knows that," Susan said matter-of-factly. My senses told me she was grounded and perceptive.

"Horses are prey animals," she said pointedly.

"Prey animals! Seriously!"

"They are innately untrusting, suspicious and highly intuitive. He will mirror your feelings and body language. If you're afraid of him, he will be afraid of you."

Susan and I talked about horses the entire flight. We exchanged phone numbers and we met later in the week for dinner in Charlotte.

I arrived at my condo, I set up my office, I downloaded a book on my iPad about the mindset and behavior of horses, and I settled into my manuscript. I wrote every day from morning until dusk, stopping only to eat a quick lunch at my desk and take a brisk walk in the afternoon to resuscitate my creative juices. I gulped grenadine club soda with lime at 5 o'clock. Every night after dinner, I crawled into bed with my iPad to read about the enigmatic mind of horses.

I learned that horses are intelligent, highly social herd animals who establish a "pecking order" to determine which horse will dominant the herd, and which horses will be submissive. A horse establishes its dominance by biting, kicking and pushing other horses, making the other horses move their feet, surrendering their space. The dominant horse, a stallion or mare, gets priority over food, breeding partners or preferred space. Submissive horses depend on the herd leader for their safety, to tell them where to run in emergencies and which way to travel to find food and water. The law of equine nature is: submissive horses respect, obey and submit to the Alpha horse.

A horse sees his relationship with its owner the same way he sees it with another horse. He will respect and submit to a strong, skilled leader—or he will defy and walk all over you.

I finished reading my first book about the mindset of horses, and I downloaded a second book on how to train a horse.

To train a horse you must think like a horse, communicate like a horse and relate to a horse in terms that a horse understands. You must be confident and assertive, but gentle and understanding, using "pressure" and "release" training methods that tell the horse "no," but reward him often with "yes." Safety is crucial when working with a horse. You must establish clear boundaries on the ground, teaching your 1200-pound animal to stay out of your "bubble." To gain the trust of a horse you must be consistent and predictable, and you must remain calm and unafraid when he is fearful. When a horse respects your authority on the ground and he learns to accept and trust your leadership, he will respect your personal space and willingly submit to you under his saddle. When all of this is present an undeniable bond develops between a horse and his owner.

Every night when I finally closed my eyes, I imagined my relationship with Ready.

After 12 brain-wracking days in Charlotte I returned home.

Ready to Roll was boarded at a local riding academy and stable. I walked into the stable's grooming area and there stood Ready in crossties, looking tall, majestic and fearless. My heart swelled with love for this animal. I felt as if I had supernaturally bonded with him long-distance. I reached up, stroked his forehead, and I gazed at his face. His dark moon eyes were stern and questioning. I wrapped my arms around his large neck, I rested my head on his cheek, and a tear slid from my eye.

"Hi, big guy. How are you?"

Ready eyeballed me skeptically with his left eye. I looked at him in awe and I wondered why this magnificent horse was offered as an auction item. He had a small scar on his lower right foreleg. I wondered, *Did this little boo-boo disqualify him as a world-champion show horse? Too bad for his owner,* I mused. *Lucky me!*

"Okay, are you ready to ride him?" the stable manager asked as he lead Ready from the grooming stall to the indoor arena.

"Is he ready?" I asked hesitantly.

"Sure. Your guy is a smooth ride. I rode him. Your riding instructor rode him. He's ready to roll."

Ready was well trained for pleasure riding. I needed riding lessons. Twice a week I went to the stable to learn how to ride a gaited Tennessee Walker. Ready was intelligent and eager to please; he yielded to his bridle and to my leg pressure. He was compliant, but he was spirited and he spooked easily. In the indoor arena he rode like a digitally programmed Mercedes Benz. Riding him in the outdoor paddock, his turbos revved and he resisted his bridle. My gut sensed if I gave him free rein he would break the sound barrier.

Four weeks later we moved Ready to Roll to our farm. He settled into his new life socializing with Leon's two retired horses, having daily turnouts in his paddock, munching on carrot and apple treats from my hand, and slumbering in his oversized stall. But I was afraid of Ready. The first time I turned him loose in his paddock he bolted into a frenzied bucking gallop, shaking his head wildly, kicking intractably, and he charged towards me standing outside the fence. When I walked him from his stall to his paddock he pranced excitedly, he threw his head skyward and he shoved and pushed me with his shoulder.

I had never heard of "ground manners" but I instinctively knew Ready didn't have any.

I devoured more books about a horse's innate behavior. I purchased a library of horse training videos, and I hired Lucy, a talented natural horsemanship trainer, to teach me how to teach Ready to respect me as his leader.

Ready was sweet-natured, curious and he quickly learned how to respect my personal space. Standing on the ground with him I taught him to back up, move his front end, pivot his hindquarters, come to me with the waving motion of my hands, circle the arena with the point of my finger, and stop circling with my mere stare at his rump. The more I worked with Ready the more confident I became with him. I groomed him and I cleaned his hooves. I haltered him and I led him to the green pasture and I stood with him while he grazed. I filled his hay bag, I replenished his water bucket and I gave him grain. Each activity established communication and trust between Ready and me. I saddled him and I rode him in our open pastures. Slowly Ready learned to respect me and accept my leadership. Slowly I overcame my fear of him.

A horse is somewhat like a human. They have good days and they have bad days. When you get to the stable you never know which side of the bed your horse is going to wake up from.

Overnight Ready had an abrupt change in behavior. He pulled back on his lead rope, planted his feet in the ground and he refused to go into the arena. When I rode him in the open pasture he was agitated and non-compliant. He wouldn't stand still when I groomed him. He wouldn't let me clean his hooves and he nipped at me. I was confused and disheartened by Ready's sudden dejection of my leadership. His defiant behavior shot holes in my confidence.

I got motley opinions on what was wrong with him.

My riding instructor said, "He's a youngster. He's acting out."

My farrier said, "He's barn sour. He's buddy sour. He wants to get back to the barn to eat hay with his horse buddy."

My horse-enthusiast girlfriend exclaimed, "He's a left-brain extrovert. He gets bored easy. Ya need to raise your energy. Ya need to be fun and play games with him so he will see you as a good leader."

My vet advised, "A horse will act up if he is sick."

The owner of a horse tack store, told me, "He's not a pet. He's an athletic partner. Horses don't respond to petting and sweet-talk, in fact some horses regard it as pressure."

A Parelli instructor claimed, "He's been saddled and he's been ridden but he's never accepted the saddle. He needs to be desensitized."

Vera said, "He's lived all his life in a disciplined show horse environment. You gave him freedom and love. He gained confidence and he realized he has free will—and now he's expressing it."

Everyone's comments made sense, but it was disheartening to think I had to start over with Ready. I wanted to ride him. I wanted to play games with him. I wanted him to respect me, trust me, and enjoy my company. I agonized how to overcome my fear of Ready, avoid being injured by him, and get him to willingly obey my commands.

I had to regain Ready's respect and trust.

I was obsessed with having a meaningful relationship with Ready. I consumed more books on horse behavior and I watched my training videos. At night when I shut my eyes, I role-played, waving my savvy stick, I strategically moved Ready around the arena and I made him stay out of my bubble. I visualized how I would respond to his confusion or defiance. When I fumbled with his rope, or he abruptly stopped mid-circle, I told myself to exhale, relax, smile at him, and calmly try again.

I watched a video of a woman and her horse. Her horse refused to circle, or he would suddenly stop circling, or he would abruptly reverse his direction. The trainer in the video told the owner her energy was lukewarm; her techniques appeared "grey" to her horse.

"Horses respond to a person's energy," the trainer told the woman. "If there's not enough pressure your instructions will be vague, and the horse may not understand what he is supposed to do. He will see your leadership as being submissive, and he will assume the dominant role in your relationship."

A light switch clicked and the pieces came together. My commands sounded like, *pretty please,* instead of, *I'm the boss mare. Follow my lead. Do as I say. Get out of my space—or I will kick the crap out of you.*

I watched the video two more times. I knew what I had to do.

The next day I walked into Ready's paddock and I haltered him to a 22-foot lead rope. I had never circled Ready outside the small arena. His paddock was 60-feet wide and 200-feet deep. I knew this wide-open space would super-charge Ready's testosterone. I stood in the middle of the paddock, I backed Ready 10-feet away from me, I held the end of his rope in my left hand and I extended my savvy stick with my right hand and I pointed to send Ready out in a circle. Ready eyeballed me, stepped out to obey—and then he froze mid-step, faced me and stared at me in subtle defiance.

My heart expired!

I knew instantly I had to dominate Ready to gain his respect and trust.

My mind raced to review the training video.

When your horse deliberately stops or reverses the direction of his circle, hold his lead rope, walk backwards away from him, hit the ground with your whip three times behind him and send him out again.

Gulp!

I looked Ready solidly in the eyes. I grasped the rope. I pointed to the left. I stepped backwards and I slapped the ground behind him with my savvy stick. One. Two. Three.

Ready braced hard on his rope. His head jerked skyward, his nostrils flared and his muscular body seethed with indignation. His posture told me, *No way, Lady! You can't make me!*

My Woman Within squared her jaw and clenched her fists: Don't be a panty-waist. Don't back down! Don't let this guy outwit or outmaneuver you! Emulate the trainer in the video. Raise your energy. Be firm. Be fearless. Tell that big black castrated stallion, *I want Y-O-U—to go—in that—direction—NOW!* Don't let him dominate you—because if he wins, you will lose the respect and companionship of your horse.

I stood tall in my boots and I glared at Ready standing a mere 10-feet away. I grasped the end of his rope and I stepped slowly, boldly backwards. I pointed adamantly for him to go out in a circle and I hit the ground behind his rump with my whip hard, three times.

Ready lit out in a frenzied, angry gallop, circling me. I turned to watch him fearing he would side-swipe me. He circled me twice and then he bolted sideways, yanking me forward eight feet, and he faced off with me, his front legs stiff and his feet cemented in the ground, with me holding desperately to the end of his rope. His head was flung high in the air, his nostrils flared, and his eyes warning me. My heart thundered against my breast plate. I feared if I challenged him he would charge me.

Breathe. Breathe. Breathe.

My heart pounded wildly, my body quaked and my legs trembled, ready to collapse beneath me. My mind spun, scrambling for my next move.

Breathe. Breathe. Breathe.

I inhaled and exhaled long, deep breaths, waiting for my heart to stop pounding. I knew I had to clear my fear, and I knew I had to end Ready's session on a good note.

I feigned my composure, I led Ready back to the center of the paddock, and I pointed gingerly for him to circle me. He stepped out cautiously, circled me slowly, undecidedly, and then I brought him back to me and I put him in his stall.

The following day I haltered Ready and I walked him out to his paddock to reinforce the previous day's training. I wasn't sure what to expect. Would he bulldoze me into my grave? Or had I proven to him, for once and for all, I was the kick-ass, estrogen-crazed mare?

I backed Ready 10-feet away from me, I pointed to the right, I coolly raised my savvy stick and I held my breath. Ready looked at me, he hesitated, he stepped forward, he stopped and stared at me—and then he calmly walked off to circle me.

Whew!

After that Ready was a 1200-pound puppy. Standing with him in his stall, he nuzzled me and he lowered his head so I could easily halter him. He stood still so I could brush him and he allowed me to lift his feet to clean his hooves. He walked calmly beside me to and from his paddock. He ran to the paddock gate and he stuck his head over the fence to greet me. Inside his paddock he followed me and he turned when I turned, and he stopped when I stopped. Ready had learned to trust me. He looked to me for playtime, security and leadership. And although he was a spirited, powerful, and sometimes unpredictable horse, I knew if I remained confident, calm and predicable, he would be a loyal, respectful partner.

Horse lovers and experts say, for the most part, there is no such thing as a bad horse. A horse who displays bad behavior is reacting to his environment. If he tries to bite you, he may be in pain. If he bucks, his saddle may be too tight, or he may have a burr under his blanket. If he's disagreeable, he may have a pebble stuck between his teeth. If he rears or he attempts to flee he may be spooked.

A horse is a reflection of you; they give back what they get.

—Rick Gore

Horse experts claim you can learn a lot about yourself by spending time with a horse. Horses intuitively resist people who emit negative energy. If your horse is acting unfavorably to you, there is a distant reason. If you are ineffective in communicating what you want your horse to do, your horse will become confused and agitated. If you lack confidence, you will appear insecure, and your horse will disrespect you. If you are a perfectionist, you may apply too much pressure and your horse will resist you. If you have anger issues, or you are afraid of your horse, he will mistrust and fear you. In other words, if you're having a bad day—your horse will have a bad day too.

Don't ask the question if you don't want to hear the brutal truth.

Horse owners and trainers who experience behavioral difficulties with their horses are often motivated to examine their own behavior and attitudes.

I moaned to my trainer and my husband about Ready's defiant, rejecting behavior. Their comments caused me to reflect on my core personality.

"Slow down. You're going too fast. He's trying." Lucy said. "He's licking and chewing. Give him time to think about what you want him to do."

Her comment caused me to reflect on my behavior: I am a high-energy, extroverted, "driver" personality. I pushed myself and I pushed others to get things done.

Leon told me, "You expect too much. You want everything now. Look how much he's learned. He's only 5 years old. He's young. He needs time to learn."

Touché. I am a perfectionist. My mindset caused me to hyper-criticize and over-correct. My unrealistic expectations alienated my children, wreaked havoc in my relationships, and caused me to misjudge and undervalue my girlfriends.

A horse will teach you to exercise patience and understanding with your loved ones.

The more I learned about horses, the more I asked myself, What am I doing that triggers Ready's mistrusting, fearful nature?

Ready's unpredictable behavior would cause my heart to pound with apprehension. Driving to the barn to work with him, I prayed, *Dear Lord, please keep me safe with Ready. Please grant me confidence and intuition with him. Please help me to understand why he does what he does. Amen.*

That same morning I was upset with Leon for his mindless, inconsiderate behavior. I realized the parallel between my relationship with Ready and my relationship with my husband. I prayed, *Dear Lord, Leon is a good man. I know he doesn't intend to hurt me on purpose. Please help me to understand why he does what he does, and help me to forgive him. Amen.*

❦

Ready to Roll appeared in my life as if by magic. One day I was sucking down martinis and pinot grigio at Bricktops, and the next day I'm mucking stalls and picking straw out of my britches.

Being with Ready was more calming than ingesting a 10mg Xanax. Grooming Ready made me feel engaged, relaxed and productive. I brushed his massive body and I combed his mane and tail. I stroked his face and I laughed at him pawing the ground when he was impatient. When I was with Ready, I didn't think about drinking.

Ready to Roll was my 5 o'clock cocktail.

I learned a lot from Ready. I learned to be patient, reserve judgment, and remain calm when he was agitated or fearful. I learned to not take his mulish behavior personal, and I examined my attitudes and behavior. I allowed Ready to be a horse; to have good days and bad days. After all, isn't that the way we all want to be treated?

I overcame my fear of Ready. Training him gained me immense confidence. I taught him to respect my space. I walked boldly behind his hindquarters in his stall. I haltered him. I trailered him. I saddled him and I rode him. I stood firm in the face of his defiance. I thought if I can do this—*I can do anything!*

Ready and I are partners. He depends on me for safety, food and playtime. I depend on him to keep me real.

Thanks, Ready!

Epilogue: Reinvent Yourself

You don't have to be who you were yesterday.

You can achieve your goals and dreams—if you think about it continually, if you believe it passionately, if your actions relentlessly work toward your aspirations, and if you never give up—your hopes and dreams will one day materialize.

❦

I am the queen of reinvention. Through the years I have revamped my image, debugged my thinking, spit-shined my core identity, and refocused on a new life's direction. I changed jobs frequently for a new challenge, and hopefully more money, and with each new profession I enhanced my mind and my appearance. After each divorce I polished my rough edges. I spiffed up my wardrobe. I stepped up my exercise. I explored new wines. I exposed myself to new social settings, and I familiarized myself with hoity-toity restaurant menus. I was always looking for ways to build my confidence and improve my overall image.

I lost count of how many jobs I've had through the years. After high school I was anxious to earn a living and make my mark in the world. I was 19 when I got my first job as a secretary in the advertising department of a major grocery store chain. I adored my boss, he personified Don Draper of *Mad Men*. He was handsome, a robust drinker, heavy smoker, hard-nosed business man, gambling card player, Dean Martin devotee, and fervent golfer. He mentored me, teaching me how to layout grocery ads; years later I became an advertising manager of a small grocery store chain earning a woman's

1970's meager salary. When I couldn't shatter the glass ceiling, I went to work for a newspaper, hawking advertising space, a tough way to earn paltry commissions.

At age 34, I went back to college at night to study interior design, and I fast-talked my way into a sales position with an office furniture company selling Steelcase modular equipment. I worked long hours to master the intricate combinations of modular workstations. I produced my own floor plans so I could bypass the procrastinating, prima donna designers, get quotes to my customers pronto and close the deal. Within six months my commissions were sizable. As luck would have it, my narcissistic-Marxist boss didn't like my southern enunciation. He fired me a month before Christmas, telling me, I wasn't "Steelcase material." His derogatory comments cost him. He paid me my two week's severance pay, and I stayed at home with my small son, collecting three months of sizable commission earnings and unemployment checks. I found out several years later my boss was fired and he was delivering Steak-Out dinners.

After I was fired from my office furniture job I began tinkering with an arts and crafts hobby. My hobby turned into a home party business. At age 40, my home party business evolved into Miss Nancy's Tearoom and a small gift shop in quaint Olive Branch, Mississippi. I became Olive Branch's Merchants Association chairperson and Secretary of the Chamber of Commerce.

Age 42 rolled around, and I began seeing a counselor for my personal issues. I quit drinking for eighteen months, I thawed out, and my self-image went through a major transformation. I strived to be more informed and cultured. I brushed up on current events. I increased my vocabulary, and a girlfriend helped me iron out my Tennessee twang. I learned to say "breakfast" instead of "breaf-us," "idea" instead of "idear," "thing" instead of "thang," and "I'm getting ready to leave" instead of "I'm fixin to leave."

I sold my tearoom and gift shop and I began looking for a new career. Cellular phones were the new rage (the gray brick that weighed two pounds, had a half-hour of talk time and sold for $3,995.00). Cell phone salespeople made obscene commissions. I hounded the sales manager of a major cell phone carrier for a job for months. He finally hired me. The job was highly competitive and the sales quotas were brutal. I left that job a year later, and I went to work for a food broker selling institutional food lines to restaurants, hotels, hospitals and schools.

At age 45 I began a new career in skincare and cosmetics. I learned how to apply my makeup professionally. Skincare products erased years of wrinkles from my face. I discovered my best cosmetic and clothing colors. I eliminated unflattering clothes from my wardrobe and I gradually replenished my closet with more expensive designer lines. I budgeted for regular manicures and pedicures and I justified an occasional Botox. My job as a top ranked director was to train, motivate and help women realize their personal and business success. I found my passion for women's low self-esteem issues and I overcame my fear of public speaking.

Fifty-one crept up, and I landed the best career of my life as a trainer and consultant for a national cosmetic and skincare company, traveling the United States calling on 300 stores. My polished image helped me to land the job. Walking through the cafeteria of the Los Angles based company, as their newest regional consultant, someone remarked, *"Who is she? She'll be successful in this business!"*

My Woman Within rolled eyes and barked at me, *Good for you! Now get your teeth whitened!*

For roughly 30 years I had gazed in the bathroom mirror, applying my makeup and brushing my teeth, never noticing that my teeth were discolored from cigarettes and coffee. I was appalled when I realized my teeth were dingy and yellow. My dentist replaced my mouthful of silver fillings with sparkling white composite fillings and porcelain crowns, he repaired the childhood chip in my front tooth with veneer bonding, and I got bleaching trays for my teeth. For the first time in my life someone told me, "Your teeth are beautiful!"

At age 55 I began writing my first book, *Secrets of the Ultimate Husband Hunter*, a self-help book for single women who struggle with dating and relationship problems. My book was published in

2007. In theory there was nothing different about me, other than 288 pages of manuscript. But I felt different and so I acted different. In my mind I was no longer ho-hum Nancy from Podunk Tennessee, I was Nancy Nichols, a Houston-based, best-selling author. Because I thought like a best-selling author, I acted like a successful author, and because I acted like a successful author, people treated me like a celebrity.

I didn't have the money to hire a public relations manager to promote my book, so I posed as my own publicist. I booked my signings, TV and radio appearances and speaking events throughout the United States. I returned to Memphis and I immediately became a regular radio and TV talk show guest, and I began writing on my second book, *Never Date a Dead Animal.*

At age 62, I moved to Nashville and I launched a women's social and business networking group. I presented self-publishing classes at the local library and I mentored several authors, helping them publish their books. My second book was published. I signed up for Match.com. One and a half years later I married my fourth and final husband and I quit drinking. At age 65, I became a first-time horse owner, riding and training a 1200-pound equine.

It's never too late to begin again

—Joyce Meyer

How bad do you want it and what are you willing to do to get it?

Quitting smoking and quitting drinking were—*by far*—the two hardest things I've ever done. Drinking had been my lifelong psychological crutch. I had to reprogram my mindset and reconstruct my lifestyle to conquer my addiction. I had to envision myself sitting at dinner in a restaurant, or in a social setting, or a at business event, sipping on a club soda. I had to practice being in the moment, being poised and relaxed, conversing comfortably with people—instead of being wrought with angst, craving a glass of wine. When I met a girlfriend for a happy hour, I immediately ordered a grenadine club soda and an appetizer. My girlfriend looked at me in amazement and exclaimed, "*WHY?*" I suspected some of my girlfriends also had a drinking problem.

I gradually began to share my non-drinking status with my friends and family. They were accepting but extremely surprised. I cringed, *Could I profess my lifelong struggle with alcoholism to the world.*

Robin Williams committed suicide today. After a lifelong battle with depression and chemical dependency he hung himself with a belt in the bedroom of his California home. His untimely death saddened millions and moved several of my Facebook friends to publicly share their harsh realities. A male friend shared his lifetime struggle with depression and its associated medications. A woman friend shared her poignant fight with breast cancer. Another woman exposed her battle with the court system to protect her 6-year-old grandson from her daughter's pedophile-ex-husband.

I was moved by my Facebook friends who had the courage to strip naked in front of hundreds of friends and strangers, revealing their intimate struggles and heartbreak. I thought, *What good is a lifetime of misery, if I can't help others who also struggle with low self-worth and relationship difficulties?*

I have come to accept the fact that life is a never-ending series of ups and downs; our good times are eventually interrupted by events of difficulty and sorrow. The only way to maintain a balance of happiness, optimism and sanity is to adjust to and bravely endure our times of hardship, setbacks and heartbreak—knowing, and anticipating—that the next wave will again be a time of joy, stability and contentment.

It took me 4 years to write about the life-altering events that inspired *God, Please Fix Me!* I agonized and I struggled to finish my book. I finally sequestered myself to our home in Florida; alone and isolated for a month, I wrote long hours to finalize my manuscript. Four days after I returned home, I broke my left leg bailing off a runaway rescue horse. My leg was severely fractured and I sustained nerve damage to my left foot, leaving my foot numb and motionless. My surgeon stabilized my leg by inserting a titanium rod and five screws. After my surgery I was out of my mind for two weeks on oxycodone, followed by a month of intense pain, nausea and a mushy brain, and months of physical therapy. Five weeks after my accident, my husband had to assist me when I climbed the 15 steps to my upstairs office and computer. I completed my book's final edit while hobbling on a cane. Twelve weeks after I broke my leg, I released *God, Please Fix Me!*

**"If it were easy, everyone would be doing it,"
said, my son Roger.**

He's right! If it were easy, everyone would get three divorces, fall in love with and survive a sociopath, purge themselves of their dysfunctional behavior and self-absorbed agendas, quit drinking and smoking, train your first horse and break your leg, divulge your hurtful past and write three books, and rid themselves of a lifetime of regret and guilt.

My life had finally come full circle. I conquered my low self-worth demons. I forgave my past transgressions. I silenced my critical inner voice. I overcame my addictions. I shared my shame. I was a new person, inside and out.

I glanced up at the infinite blue sky, grinned smugly, and I murmured, *How d'ya like me now?*

Well done, daughter, Heaven replied. *Now let's work on your potty mouth!*

Source Notes

Chapter 1: Above All Things—Seek Wisdom

"Wisdom is supreme; therefore get wisdom. Though it cost all you have, get understanding." New International Version Bible, Prov. 4:7

"If any of you lacks… it will be given to you." New International Version Bible, Jas 1:5.

Chapter 2: Dear Lord, My Filter is Broken!

"We all view the world through individual filters… " Dr. Phil McGraw, *Life Strategies*, (Hyperion, 1999), p. 155.

"Your emotions are the slaves to your thoughts, and you are the slave to your emotions." Elizabeth Gilbert, *Eat, Pray, Love*, (Accessed April 12, 2015), https://www.goodreads.

"If you continue to view the world through a filter… dictate both your present and your future." Dr. Phil McGraw, *Life Strategies*, (Hyperion, 1999), p. 156.

Chapter 3: It's Supposed to Hurt

"revived continuously"… "part of our sense of self" … "pain-body"… "magnetic pull"… "falling in love"… "conquer and seduce"… "female love and attention that his pain-body craves." Eckard Tolle, *A New Earth*, (Penguin: Reprint edition, January 2008), pp. 178, 179.

"Pain bodies love intimate relationships… "provoke" and "push the buttons"… so it can "feed on the ensuing drama." Eckard Tolle, *A New Earth*, (Penguin: Reprint edition, January 2008), p. 148.

"It's hard to resist another person's pain-body… It instinctively knows your weakest… raw emotion looking for more emotion." Eckard Tolle, *A New Earth*, (Penguin: Reprint edition, January 2008), p. 148.

"People with heavy pain-bodies… their motivation to awaken becomes strong." Eckard Tolle, *A New Earth*, (Penguin: Reprint edition, January 2008), p. 143, 144.

Chapter 4: I Would Let Go If He Would Let Me

"If you choose the behavior... you choose the consequence of pain and suffering in your emotional life."—Dr. Phil, *Life Strategies*, (Hyperion, 1999), p. 68.

Chapter 6: How Long Will I Mourn?

"I used to think I was tied to a heartache; that was the heartbreak." Air Supply, *Even The Nights Are Better*, (Arista Records, Inc. © 2001).

"To give up the final hope may be the most difficult of all." Melba Colgrove, Ph.D., Harold H. Bloomfield, M.D., and Peter McWilliams, *How to Survive the Loss of a Love*, (Prelude Press, 1976) p. 58.

"Fear not, for I am with you; do not look around you in terror and be dismayed, for I am your God." Amplified Bible, Isa. 41:10.

"If we continue to dwell on our past disappointments we will block God's blessings in our lives today." Joel Osteen, *Your Best Life Now*, (FaithWords; Reprint edition, August, 2007), p. 180, 181.

"If we will quit mourning and get going... And it is better than we can imagine." Joel Osteen, *Your Best Life Now*, (FaithWords; Reprint edition, August, 2007), p. 180, 181.

"Your best days are not behind you. They're in front of you." Joel Osteen, *Become a Better You*, (Free Press, October 2007), p. 4.

"The process of healing and growth is not... the smooth progression many people assume." It's lightning bolt full of ups and downs... the healing process is under way." Melba Colgrove, Ph.D., Harold H. Bloomfield, M.D., and Peter McWilliams, *How to Survive the Loss of a Love*, (Prelude Press, 1976), p. 30.

Chapter 7: Forgiveness: The Final Emotion

"Baggage of old thought and emotion." Eckard Tolle, *A New Earth*, (Penguin: Reprint edition, January 2008), p. 66.

"Forgiving the person who hurt you is a choice... the farther you'll be from your destiny." Joyce Meyer, *You Can Begin Again*, (Faith Words, April 2014), p. 26, 27.

"Forgiveness is what you do for yourself, not for other people." Dr. Phil McGraw, "Making Peace With Your Past." (Accessed July 4, 2015), http://drphil.com/articles/article/328.

Part Two: Power Up

"For I know the plans I have for you… to give you hope and a future." New International Version Bible, Jer. 29:11.

Chapter 9: Logic: The Cornerstone of Sound Judgment

"Left Brain Function… uses logic… Right Brain Function… risk taking." Dan Eden, *Left Brain Right Brain,* http://viewzone2.com/bicamxx/.

Chapter 11: Can You Hold Your Ground with a Man

"Here's all you have to know about men and women… women are crazy is that men are stupid." George Carlin, *When Will Jesus Bring The Pork Chops?,* (Accessed April 12, 2015), https://www.goodreads.com.

Chapter 13: Intuition: A Woman's Supernatural Knowing

"Tracie Dean drove 300 miles… It was in my heart just to keep driving." Paraphrased, NBC News Atlanta, (January 27, 2006).

"Have the courage to follow your heart… Everything else is secondary." Steve Jobs, Stanford Commencement speech, (June 12, 2005).

"There is a wonderful phrase in psychology—'the power of thin slicing'… "rapid cognition"… "blink of an eye." Malcolm Gladwell, (Accessed April 12, 2015), http://gladwell.com/blink/blink-q-and-a-with-malcolm.

Information regarding: *"thin-slicing,"* Malcolm Gladwell, "Q & A with Malcolm I", http://www.gladwell.com/, (2003); Malcolm Gladwell, *Blink*, Back Bay Books; Little, Brown and Company, DVD (first published 2005).

"Do not forsake wisdom, and she will protect you; love her, and she will watch over you." New International Version Bible, Prov. 4:6.

Chapter 16: Change Your Thoughts; Alter Your Destiny

"How you feel about yourself… and whether or not you fulfill your destiny." Joel Osteen, *Your Best Life Now,* (FaithWords; Reprint edition, August, 2007), p. 56.

"The voice in your head is not who you are." Eckard Tolle, *A New Earth*, (Penguin: Reprint edition, January 2008), p. 147.

"The voice in our head will tell us sad, anxious, or angry stories... and we believe its distorted thoughts." Eckard Tolle, *A New Earth*, (Penguin: Reprint edition, January 2008), p. 147.

"You are not an accident... God prescribed every single detail of your body. He determined the natural talents... We were made to have meaning." Rick Warren, *The Purpose Driven Life*, (Zondervan, 2002), pp. 22, 23.

Chapter 17: Shut Up! Negative Self-Talk

"A belief is nothing more than a chronic pattern of thought.... to change our point of attraction." Ester and Jerry Hicks, *Money and the Law of Attraction*. (Accessed April 11, 2015), http://www.abraham-hicks.com/lawofattractionsource.

Chapter 20: Recipe for Trouble

"Nobody is good at everything, and no one is called to be everything." Rick Warren, *The Purpose Driven Life*, (Zondervan, 2002), p. 253.

"The ego lives through comparison. How you are seen by others turns into how you see yourself." Eckard Tolle, *A New Earth*, (Penguin: Reprint edition, January 2008), p. 45.

"Don't be envious of the runner in the lane next to you; just focus on finishing your race." Rick Warren, *The Purpose Driven Life*, (Zondervan, 2002), p. 253.

"God created us in a perfect image... He doesn't look down from heaven... Why can't you be more like Angelina Jolie." Rick Warren, *Oprah Lifeclasses*, (August 7, 2014).

Chapter 21: The Things That Don't Kill You, Make You Stronger

"Your most effective ministries will come out of your deepest hurts... and most reluctant to share." Rick Warren, *The Purpose Driven Life*, (Zondervan, 2002), p. 275.

"But you don't understand. I'm a whore... never been anything but an innocent... and beautiful woman." Les Misérables, Mandalay Entertainment, Columbia Pictures (1998 film adaptation of Victor Hugo's 1862 novel of the same name).

"It is estimated approximately one-third of abused and neglected children will eventually victimize their own children." U.S. Department of Health & Human Services, Administration for Children and Families; *Long-Term Consequences of Child Abuse and Neglect*, Author(s) Child Welfare Information Gateway (2008) https://www.childwelfare.gov.

"You are no longer defined by what you did... wonderful future awaits you." Joyce Meyer, *You Can Begin Again*, (Faith Words, April 2014), p. 31.

"We are healed to help others. We are blessed to be a blessing." Rick Warren, *The Purpose Driven Life*, (Zondervan, 2002), p. 229.

Chapter 22: Find Your Purpose. Find Your Authentic Self.

"Our authentic self... our real, true, genuine identity... hole in your soul." Dr. Phil McGraw, (paraphrased) *Self Matters*, (Simon & Schuster Source, 2001) p, 29, 30, 31.

"If you want to find your true purpose in life... connected to something far greater than your body/mind/ego." Dr. Wayne Dyer, *The Shift*, (Hay House, Audio CD, 2010).

"If we can share our story... shame can't survive." Brené Brown, *Daring Greatly*, (Accessed April 12, 2015), https://www.goodreads.com.

"I thank you heartily for your letter... With love in Christ, George Whitefield." English evangelist George Whitefield (1714-1770), (Daily Bread, August 18, 1992.)

"God loves to use imperfect, ordinary people... in spite of their weaknesses." Rick Warren, *The Purpose Driven Life*, (Zondervan, 2002), p. 273.

"God have given each of us the ability to do certain things well." New Century Version Bible, Jer. 1:5.

"Anytime you use your God-given abilities to help others, you are fulfilling your calling." Rick Warren, *The Purpose Driven Life*, (Zondervan, 2002), p. 229.

Chapter 23: Supernatural Assistance

Joel Osteen talks about living your "best life." Joel Osteen, *Your Best Life Now*, (FaithWords; Reprint edition, August, 2007), pp. vii-ix.

"This could be the day I see God's miracle." Joel Osteen, *Your Best Life Now*, (FaithWords; Reprint edition, August, 2007), p. 17.

"When I want to do good, I don't. And when I try not to do wrong, I do it anyway." New Living Translation Bible, Rom. 7:19.

Joyce Meyers testimony paraphrased from: Joyce Meyer Ministries, *Life Beyond Abuse* http://www.joycemeyer.org/articles; *"From Fenton to Fame and Fortune,"* Tom Hawksley, *St. Louis Dispatch Newspaper*, (Nov. 15 2003); Sternfield Thoughts, thttp://sternfieldthoughts.blogspot.com, (February, 28, 2013); *Abuse and the Miracle of Recovery*, Joyce Meyer, http://www.joycemeyer.org/articles; *Joyce Meyer Biography by Jack Zavada*, http://christianity.about.com/od/christiancelebrities/a/Joyce-Meyer.htm.

"God will help you, but you cast the deciding vote.... God to show up and work supernaturally in your life." Joel Osteen, *Your Best Life Now*, (FaithWords; Reprint edition, August, 2007), p. 74.

"Get into agreement with God, and He'll do more than you can ask or think." Joel Osteen, *Your Best Life Now*, (FaithWords; Reprint edition, August, 2007), p. 79.

Part Four: Supernatural Sobriety

"I don't like the word "alcoholic." I like to think of myself as an advanced drinker." Chelsea Handler, *My Horizontal Life: A Collection of One-Night Stands*. (Accessed April 12, 2015), https://www.goodreads.com.

Epilogue: Re-Invent Yourself

"It's never too late to begin again." Joyce Meyer, *You Can Begin Again*, (Faith Words, April 2014), p. 10.

About the Author

Nancy Nichols is an author, self-esteem leader and national motivational speaker. Her life's quest has been to understand the attitudes and behavior which create relationship harmony, business success and personal happiness. It was Nancy's lifetime of relationship failures and heartbreak which illuminated her insight into women's low self-esteem issues and inspired her writing career. As a women's advocate she imparts self-actualization and relationship understanding; her profound message empowers women with logical reasoning, intuitive decision-making and the power of positive thought. Her *God, Please Fix Me! Trilogy* concludes her 10-year writing journey. Her trilogy includes: *Secrets of the Ultimate Husband Hunter*, *Never Date a Dead Animal* and *God, Please Fix Me!*

To book Nancy Nichols for a TV or radio interview contact:
nancy@knowitallnancy.com

Nancy Nichols
Best-Selling Author, Self-Esteem Leader and Empowerment Speaker

"You can achieve your dreams—if you think about it continuously, if you believe it passionately, if your actions relentlessly work toward your goals, and if you never give up—your hopes and aspirations will one day materialize."

–Nancy Nichols

Nancy Nichols offers presentations for business men and women. As a keynote speaker she inspires the power of logical reasoning, positive thought and a "can-do" attitude. As a woman's advocate she empowers women with self-esteem building, relationship understanding and personal healing.

Nancy will tailor her presentation to the specific needs of your business, organization or women's group.

To book Nancy Nichols for a seminar, keynote speaker or group presentation
contact Nancy@knowitallnancy.com.

For more information about Nancy Nichols's presentations visit http://knowitallnancy.com/presentations.

Also by Nancy Nichols

A Trilogy of Personal Healing for Women

ISBN: 978-0-9795791-0-3

ISBN: 978-0-9795791-1-0

ISBN: 978-0-9795791-2-7

Trade Paperback, 5.5 x 8.5; Also Available in eBooks

Published by Epiphany Imprint; Email info@epiphanyimprint.com

Available everywhere books and eBooks are sold.

Available at www.knowitallnancy.com

To buy books in bulk contact info@epiphanyimprint.com